BOOK 2

A Moment in Time

Words of Encouragement for Parents

BOOK 2

A Moment in Time

Words of Encouragement for Parents

AMG PUBLISHERS

Carl Willis

A Moment in Time:
Words of Encouragement for Parents (Book 2)

Published by AMG Publishers, Inc.
6815 Shallowford Rd.
Chattanooga, Tennessee 37421

ISBN 13: 978-1-61715-541-3

First Printing—April 2020

Cover designed by Daryle Beam, Bright Boy Design, Chattanooga, TN.

Editing, interior design, and typesetting by Rick Steele Editorial Services (https://steeleeditorialservices.myportfolio.com).

Printed in the United States of America

To Christopher and Casey,

my children.

I am so proud to be called your Dad.

ACKNOWLEDGMENTS

There are far too many people who deserve to be acknowledged for inspiring me to begin writing these devotional thoughts back in 2016. But first and foremost is my precious bride of over three decades, Christine.

Secondly, I want to thank all my *Every Man A Warrior* (EMAW) colleagues (again, too many to name) for being there for me as I began and continued this journey. EMAW gave me the passion to start writing, which has not diminished. And these men were my literal sounding board as I shared many of these thoughts with them.

And finally, I want to thank all my family, who are the subject of many of these devotions. You are my delight and true loves. Thank You, Jesus, for blessing me with such awesome people in my life.

INTRODUCTION

This is the second book (Year Two) of a three-part series of *A Moment in Time* daily devotions. What started out as simply my efforts to be obedient to the Lord has resulted in the pagination of my thoughts and prayers throughout the Word.

Back in 2015, I began journaling my quiet times as part of a men's small group that was using the *Every Many A Warrior* study. This study gave me a renewed passion to study and memorize God's Word. In January 2016, at the urging of the Holy Spirit, I began the journey to write a short devotional blog for moms and dads in which I would cover every chapter of the Bible, all 1,189 of them! In total, these blog posts produced three years worth of daily devotionals.

Through a series of events, I was led to AMG Publishers, who has walked me in this process of publishing (something I never dreamed of) these blogs for families.

It is my prayer that you will read these as intended—to inspire you to see God working in each and every word of the Bible. We can't pick and choose which verses we want to live by. They all have purpose and application in our lives. Read, be encouraged and live it out!

JANUARY 1

CURSED TO CLEAN

Isaiah 1

BEST VERSE: 18

"Come now, and let us reason together," says the LORD, "Though your sins are as scarlet, they will be as white as snow; though they are red like crimson, they will be like wool."

Don't you just love this verse? When we turn to the Lord and confess our sins, He promises to purify us. They are changed from scarlet to white, from crimson to wool. What a picture! We don't deserve it, but because of the shed blood of Christ, we have been made clean. That should encourage you today.

TEACHING MOMENT

Have you ever finger-painted with your children? If you haven't, you should. There is just something about smearing paint on paper with your fingers. You may have seen an artist do this with whole hands on canvas. That feeling is awesome! You feel the paint on your skin and see the colors come alive on the paper or canvas.

But when you finish, you are left with all those colors of paint on your fingers. You have to clean them off with soap and water. I used to love to watch those colors disappear down the sink as I washed my hands. They mix together briefly, then just vanish.

How about getting with your kids and finger paint this week? Use red or black. Then talk about this verse as you are painting. As you clean up, describe how the Lord washes you clean too. And, just like the paint down the drain, the sin disappears. Scripture says the Lord remembers them no more. Wow!

I don't know about you, but I have a hard time forgetting my sins. I confess them, but still feel guilt. Let it go! Satan wants us to feel that way. The Lord doesn't. Remorse is a good thing, but guilt is not. They are different. Remorse helps us not repeat it. Guilt just keeps us down. Remember, as

Christians, we are white like snow. We are like white wool. Cleaned, washed, forgiven!

Redeemer and Lord, I know confession is good for my soul. Please forgive me. Cleanse me. Make my sin white as snow. Thank You for forgiveness!

JANUARY 2

WHAT IS LOVE?

Song of Solomon 8

BEST VERSE: 7

Many waters cannot quench love, nor will rivers overflow it; If a man were to give all the riches of his house for love, it would be utterly despised.

How would you define love? It's hard to put into words, but the words in today's verse come close. It's unquenchable. It overflows. It is costly. True? True! You love and love, and you love more. Your love for someone can cause your heart to overflow with passion and desire. And depending on what you are willing to give, it can cost you everything.

I love a lot of things. I love hunting and fishing. I love caramel cake. But my love for others goes way beyond. Even though I love stuff, the love I have for my wife and family is more costly. It is more fulfilling. It is more sacrificial.

TEACHING MOMENT

Do we have to teach our children to love? Yes! We are not born lovers. We are born sinners. Left untaught we will let our fleshly desires and wishes reign. But when we are taught what real love is, we can respond in kind.

The ultimate love, of course, is God's love. His love is endless and limitless. That's the kind of love we teach our children. We love Him because He first loved us. We help our children experience His love through His Word and through our prayer life. We exemplify God's love to them and show them the power His love has on us.

Who needs your love today? Who needs to be shown God's love today? How can you be the instrument of love to someone else? Allow the Lord to use you as His vessel. He can love anyone through you, if you will let Him.

Lord, You are the One who loves me beyond words. I want to love You with the same strength You love me. Help me teach others how to love You.

JANUARY 3

GRIEVING TO GRANTED

1 Chronicles 4

BEST VERSES: 9–10

Jabez was more honorable than his brothers, and his mother named him Jabez saying, "Because I bore him with pain." Now Jabez called on the God of Israel, saying, "Oh that You would bless me indeed and enlarge my border, and that Your hand might be with me, and that You would keep me from harm that it may not pain me!" And God granted him what he requested.

What a horrible name! Jabez! His mother named him Jabez! That means grieving or sorrowful. How would you like to be named Grief or Sorrow? All your life you would carry that name, and people would wonder why your parents named you that.

But look what happened. Jabez was more honorable than his brothers. He prayed for the Lord to bless him with land, provision and protection, and He did! The Lord must have seen something in Jabez worthy of blessing. He must have been an honorable man.

TEACHING MOMENT

We spend weeks, if not months, picking out our children's names. Many times, we use a family name, but not always. Sometimes we just pick names we like. I have known children who were named after foods their mom craved while she was pregnant. Seriously!

Our children, however, must make a name for themselves in the way they live. The most honorable and respected names mean nothing if they live in such a way to bring shame on them. My Dad would say a man's word is his bond. In other words, keep your word. If you say you will do something, do it and do it well.

But the most important name our children can carry with them is Jesus. Being named after Him (Christian) is the most respected name. Being known as His child is an honor. Even though the world may curse and spit at the name of Jesus and for what He stands for, we will wear that name proudly and try our best to "rename" as many as we can while we are here on this earth. We can share that name over and over, and it never loses its value. So, today share that name with someone. Help them to be seen as honorable in the site of God.

Father, I proudly carry Your name. I am thankful I am in Your family. Keep me from anything that may cause shame on the name of Christ.

JANUARY 4

DON'T FORGET

Nehemiah 9

BEST VERSE: 32A

Now therefore, our God, the great, the mighty, and the awesome God, who keeps covenant and lovingkindness, do not let all the hardship seem insignificant before You.

The ninth chapter of Nehemiah contains a story presented by some of the Levites who were standing before the people. They recited the history of Jehovah God with His people. They covered the entire story. But the purpose of this story isn't just a history lesson. It's a reminder that God is still with them.

The people hearing this story had returned from Babylonian exile to a city and nation that was unknown to them. They had the bloodline to be called Jews, but did they understand why? Most of them did not. They were Jews just because they were Jews. That is not enough.

TEACHING MOMENT

As believing parents, we have the responsibility to pass down to the next generation our heritage in Christ. They say the extinction of the church is only one generation away, unless we continue to share the good news. Our children need to understand where they come from. They need to know how and why we came to Christ.

Passing down our earthly heritage is fine. But passing down a spiritual lineage is so much better. I am thrilled to know that my grandchildren have all come to Christ. I am praying even now for their children to come to Christ. We parents must do that.

Are you passing down your spiritual heritage? Are you doing all the Lord wants you to do to make sure your children and grandchildren come to Christ and continue the legacy of faith? Spend some time around the table with your family, perhaps at an upcoming holiday, sharing your family's lineage in Christ.

The joy, O God, of knowing You as Father is overwhelming at times. Help me to refresh the memories of my family's journey of faith with my children and grandchildren. Show me how to instill in them the truths I have learned along the way.

JANUARY 5

HOW COULD I FORGET THAT?

Psalms 77–78

BEST VERSES: 77:11–12

I shall remember the deeds of the LORD; surely I will remember Your wonders of old. I will meditate on all Your work and muse on Your deeds.

We are so quick to forget all the Lord has done for us. To begin with He saved us. If He did nothing else, that's enough. But He doesn't stop there. He gives us the Holy Spirit to dwell in us to guide us daily. He gives us the church where we can fellowship with other believers. And I could go on and on.

We cry out to Him in times of trouble and forget Him as soon as it has passed. Asaph, the writer of this Psalm, realizes that. In fact, he recognizes that when he feels the Lord has changed, it's his fault, not God's. He is the one who has moved. He is the one who has forgotten.

TEACHING MOMENT

I guarantee you, your children have forgotten all you have done for them. Most children take for granted that mom and dad are going to be there. Most children, even the ones who are most grateful, tend to forget just how much they've been blessed. We should remind them, from time to time of the blessings God has given them.

I don't mean we need to make them feel guilty or try to shame them. I am saying that we truly need to help them remember and praise Him for His faithfulness. Lead by example, Mom and Dad. How about the last time your child was sick? Thank Him in front of your children for healing. How about finding the lost dog? Thank Him for that, too.

We aren't grateful most of the time. Have you stopped and thanked God for your blessings? Have you given Him praise for all He has done in your life? If not, do that right now. Thank Him. Praise Him! Glorify God! Let your children see you praising the Lord.

I will praise You, O Lord, for all You have done for me. You bless me when I don't even realize it. You are faithful even when I am not.

JANUARY 6

MORNING STAR

Isaiah 14

BEST VERSE: ISAIAH 14:12

How you have fallen from heaven, O star of the morning, son of the dawn! You have been cut down to the earth, You who have weakened the nations!

Consider today's devotion a history lesson. Now don't stop reading just because I said the words "history lesson." You need to understand this verse. Some commentators say the phrase "O star of the morning" is referring to Lucifer. Yet this interpretation conflicts later on when Christ is referred to as the Bright Morning Star. Let me quote Adam Clarke's commentary on this verse. "O how necessary it is to understand the literal meaning of Scripture, that preposterous comments may be prevented!"[1] That is so true.

The context of this verse is about Nebuchadnezzar, the king of Babylon. He saw himself as a god. He, in fact, suffered seven years because of that gross misconception. Sure, you could see how people might reference this verse to the devil, but you must stay true to Scripture and the context from which it is written. That applies to any verse you are quoting.

1. Adam Clarke, *Commentary on the Whole Bible* (Abridged Edition), (Iowa Falls, IA: World Bible Publishers, 1997).

TEACHING MOMENT

I bet you are thinking, How is Carl going to make application to my children in this verse. I am not! Surprise! But I am going to remind you to teach your children the Word in context. Don't take verses to fit your context. God's Word is rich enough to apply to any circumstance, but you must learn to apply it correctly.

If there was ever a lesson to teach your children, this is it. When they learn to search and apply God's Word to their everyday lives, they will find the true source of wisdom and knowledge. They won't hunt and peck. They will dig and study. They will seek earnestly to know the truth. That's the lesson for today.

How about you? Are you truly applying God's Word to your life? Do you pull verses out of context just to meet your needs? Take the time to do the digging. Look at why and where the verse was written. See how Isaiah meant today's verse to apply to us. It does. It always will.

Deliverer of all good things, thank You for giving us Your Word. Thank You for teaching me its truths. I want to know more. Help me share what I learn with others.

JANUARY 7

SORROWFUL

2 Corinthians 7

BEST VERSE: 10

For the sorrow that is according to the will of God produces a repentance without regret, leading to salvation, but the sorrow of the world produces death.

Why is it we think being sorrowful is a bad thing? We are always trying to "cheer up" those who are going through difficult times. God says very plainly here in this verse that sorrow which comes from God is good because it produces repentance. Feeling sorry or remorseful for a wrong we've done is a good thing. It drives us to repentance without regret.

Have you been sorrowful lately over your sins? Too many of our churches today are afraid to confront sin and bring believers to repentance—for fear of driving them off. Other churches want to accept anything just to keep up the membership. That is not of God. God demands repentance, and all of us need to repent. None of us have arrived.

TEACHING MOMENT

Your children need to understand that sorrow is not a bad thing, when it comes to God-produced sorrow. The Holy Spirit in them will convict them of sin, which can produce sorrow. That's okay! We do not need to stay there, but we must pass through it.

How can you tell your child is saved? Do they show remorse for a wrong done, not for getting caught? Do they truly feel bad and want to make it right? That is the Holy Spirit in them driving them to the cross. They may not use all the "churchy" language, but you will know when they repent.

As the old hymn asks, "How long has it been since you knelt at the cross and told Him your heart's hidden secrets?" We need to be on our knees so much more, bearing our souls in repentance. We need to be sorrowful for our wrongs. Don't allow the world to make you feel sorry for politically incorrect stupidity. That is world-produced sorrow that leads to a false repentance. As the verse says, false sorrow and false repentance lead to death.

Will you get on your knees right now and make things right with the Father? Will you thank those who confront you regarding your sin? Will you be obedient today as you hear the Holy Spirit speak your name?

Repent! Be sorrowful! And then accept the cleansing power of the Lamb.

I am sorry, Lord, for my sin. I am remorseful for the way I have turned from You. Thank You for sorrow that leads to repentance.

JANUARY 8

FOOLISHNESS

1 Corinthians 1

BEST VERSE: 18

For the word of the cross is foolishness to those who are perishing, but to us who are being saved it is the power of God

I have been accused of doing some foolish things in my life. And to be honest, I have done most of them. Some of them might have even been considered just plain stupid. Isn't it amazing the things we can get talked into?

But the wisest decision I ever made is one the world considers to be foolish. I remember when I came to Christ at 16 years of age. It was July 31, 1977, the summer before my senior year of high school. A lot of my friends thought my changes in behavior (which I won't go into) were foolish. Why would I stop doing all that "fun stuff" I had been doing the past several years?

TEACHING MOMENT

Do you want to be known as a wise parent? Then teaching your kids "the word of the cross" is the wisest thing you can do. Raising them according to God's principles may be considered foolish by some of your friends. So, the question begs to be answered. What is this "word of the cross"?

It is simply Christ crucified for the sins of the world. What! That's it! Yep! To the world that wants to make it difficult, that is just too foolish. How can one man die for all? Because He isn't just one man. He is the God-Man. Our faith teaches us that our God died for us. That just doesn't make sense to a "wise" world. But to us who have believed it is the "power of God."

Take time every day to point your kids to the cross, first for salvation and secondly for surrender. Every day! Seven days a week, fifty-two weeks a year, for as long as you have them. That may seem foolish to the world, but not to God. After all, that is all the really matters.

Lord, I know the world thinks I am foolish for following a God they cannot see. But they cannot see what they don't possess. And once You send Your Spirit to live in us, our eyes are opened to gaze upon You.

JANUARY 9

LOL

Job 8

BEST VERSE: 21

He will yet fill your mouth with laughter and your lips with shouting.

Don't you just love a good belly laugh? Some of the funniest videos online are of babies laughing. I still remember an old one of quadruplets all lying on the bed laughing. When one started, they all started. It was impossible to watch that and not smile.

I truly believe the Lord gives us laughter, not just for ourselves, but for others. He knows if we are joyful and full of laughter, we can bring a smile on the face of others. Bildad, the Shuhite, (who by the way was the shortest man in the Bible. Shoe height, get it? Made you smile, didn't I?) said these words to Job. Not much of what he said was any good, but these words are certainly true.

TEACHING MOMENT

It's not hard to teach our children to laugh. It comes naturally. But before long the childhood laughter ends due to the influence of the world. They begin to worry about stuff and get their feelings hurt. We have to be diligent to keep laughter ringing throughout our homes. They need to be reminded that laughter is good when it is pure.

What does that mean? I mean they need to know that we don't laugh at people. We laugh with people. We join in with them during those happy times and just bust our guts with laughter.

When is the last time you laughed until you cried? Don't remember? That's sad. You need to call up some old friends or go out to eat with some buddies and laugh. We need that. God knows that. Enjoy those laughing times. It is good for your soul! Does the Word call it medicine?

God of laughter, fill my heart with merriment today. Let the chuckles and grins brighten someone's day. Thank You for the gift of laughter.

JANUARY 10

THE LEADERS WE NEED

1 Chronicles 18

BEST VERSE: 14

So David reigned over all Israel; and he administered justice and righteousness for all his people.

EASY TO FOLLOW

Don't you just love this verse? If you read just the first part, it would sound like any other king of Israel. You have to read the second part.

It tells how he reigned—with justice and righteousness. Those two words change everything. Don't you think?

David administered justice. That means he did what was just for all. Those decisions probably were not easy. But if you are following the Lord, you will be just. Then it says he administered righteousness. Now, David wasn't righteous by himself. He relied on God to make him righteous, and through that righteousness flowed to the people.

TEACHING MOMENT

How do you teach your children about justice and righteousness? It is not easy. Only by allowing the Holy Spirit to reign in your life can you do that. And your children will only learn justice and righteousness through the saving power of Jesus.

Just does not mean fair. Just means according to God's justice. He will always be just and true. By allowing Him to reign, He can show your children true justice. And your children will only be made "right" through His righteousness. Anything else comes up short.

Are you "reigning in justice and righteousness"? Are you allowing the Holy Spirit to guide you in your everyday decisions? Remember, people are being influenced by you. Don't show them the flip side: injustice and unrighteousness. That would drive them further away from our Savior.

Lord God, You are beside me all the time. I know that. But help me as I seek to lead others in righteousness and justice. Let them see You and not me.

JANUARY 11

PRETTY FEET

Isaiah 52

BEST VERSE: 7

How lovely on the mountains are the feet of him who brings good news, who announces peace and brings good news of happiness, who announces salvation, and says to Zion, "Your God reigns!"

I don't know about you, but I have never seen very many pretty feet. Some are just downright ugly. My feet are kind of normal, I guess, but they still aren't pretty. My dad had wide, flat feet. He wore an 11 Triple E shoe. As he got older, he had some minor foot issues that made his feet hurt. My point is feet are just a part of the body that we just don't want to look at much. At least, I don't.

But this verse glamorizes feet. "How lovely . . . are the feet." Really? Now look at the verse. They are not recognized for how they look. The Lord is talking about what they do—bring good news. Now that makes anything look better. They announce peace and bring good news of happiness. They announce salvation and say, "Your God reigns." What a great message to deliver.

TEACHING MOMENT

We have a gaga ball pit at our church that our kids love. They will play for hours. But when they are in that pit playing, dirt is flying, and kids are getting dirty. Feet that aren't covered by shoes and socks get filthy. The kids don't care. They are having the time of their lives. The next time you wash your kid's feet (or have to remind them to wash them) talk about how they can use their feet to deliver the gospel message to someone. People cannot hear unless we go. Sure, we can deliver the message electronically, but there is still nothing like personally taking the message of the cross to someone.

Are your feet dirty from walking the path delivering the message to someone? Have you soiled your feet getting to some out-of the-way place to preach Jesus? Have you risked ruining a pair of shoes walking through water to bring the good news to someone who needs to hear it? Get your feet dirty! Get on the road! Step out in faith and allow the Lord to lead you as you walk the path He has for you!

Lord, my feet hurt sometimes. Unfortunately, it is not because I have been walking and delivering the gospel. Give me the desire to walk.

JANUARY 12

WITH A WHOLE HEART

1 Chronicles 29

BEST VERSE: 9

Then the people rejoiced because they had offered so willingly, for they made their offering to the Lord with a whole heart, and King David also rejoiced greatly.

David, Solomon and the leaders of Israel are celebrating. Why? Because they had just pledged to give generously to build the temple. Can you just picture the scene? They are all gathered. David announces the challenge gift he is giving and asks them to step up to the challenge. They do, and everyone rejoices.

Just recently at the church I serve, someone gave a $75,000 challenge gift and asked the rest of the body to match it. We experienced the same kind of excitement. People are stepping up to the challenge. This, too, is being done towards the completion of our church building.

TEACHING MOMENT

One of the most important things we can teach our children is how to give. Giving is liberating, exciting, and contagious. When you give your children money to put in the offering plate or to turn in for a mission offering, they get excited. Children love to give. Help them do that.

Most of our children here in America, at least in our church, are so blessed. They take much for granted. We are thankful for blessings from the Lord, but we must teach our children how to give generously to help those who are less fortunate. There are all kinds of ways to give, but putting those coins and bills in the plate can do so much for God's kingdom.

You are probably reading this and are thinking, This is NOT why I read your devotional, Carl. If I want to be put under guilt to give, I will just go to church. Well, don't blame me. The passage today was written by the Holy Spirit, not me. Take it up with the Lord. He obviously wanted this event recorded for us to read so we can be challenged to do kingdom work as well.

Why don't you take this opportunity to examine not just what you give, but why you give? I love the fact that the verse says "the people rejoiced," "they...offered...willingly," "with a whole heart." Can you say the same?

O, Giver of all things, give me a heart to give. Give me a generous heart. Show me the blessing I am to others, including my children, by giving how You want me to give.

WITH ONE HAND TIED BEHIND MY BACK

Isaiah 41

BEST VERSE: 10

Do not fear, for I am with you; do not anxiously look about you, for I am your God. I will strengthen you, surely I will help you, surely I will uphold you with My righteous right hand.

I just love how the Lord reassures me through this verse. Look at what he tells us not to do. First, He tells us not to fear. Then He says not to look anxiously about. In other words, "Trust Me." But He doesn't stop there. He says He will do three things:

- strengthen us
- help us
- uphold us.

I also think it's kind of neat that God tells us He will do this with one hand. That reminds me how we used to tease someone by saying, "I can beat you with one hand tied behind my back." God is powerful enough and strong enough that He only uses His right hand. Now maybe that's not what He meant, but it's a cool thought.

TEACHING MOMENT

When my kids were little (and that's been a while ago) they loved for me to pick them up and swing them or throw them in the air. They also loved to swing on my extended right arm. They would do that as long as I could extend my arm. Even though they were small, it didn't take long for my arm to get tired.

Do that with your kids, if they are still small. And when your arm wears out talk about God's right hand. It never gets tired. His right arm isn't made out of muscle and bone. His arm is all power and Spirit. He can hold us . . . well . . . forever, which He will. He will hold us for eternity. But He holds us now, too.

Are you allowing the Lord to hold you? Maybe you are too proud to be held. Pride says, I've got this, God. I don't want to be held. Put away the pride. Let God lift you up. He wants to. He wants to hold you with His righteous right hand.

Powerful God, I praise You that You are all strength and might. You can and will hold me forever. Remind me daily of your righteous right hand.

JANUARY 14

PRUNING

Isaiah 18

BEST VERSE: 5

For before the harvest, as soon as the bud blossoms and the flower becomes a ripening grape, then He will cut off the sprigs with pruning knives and remove and cut away the spreading branches.

I love tomatoes. Don't you? Most years I plant two or three plants and anxiously wait the appearance of the first blossoms which turn into little tomatoes. My dad taught me to keep the plants "suckered" in order to allow the fruit to grow bigger and get more of the nutrients. I do that, and every time I pull one of the little "sprigs" off, I think of him.

Pruning is a necessary part of fruit production. This also applies to our spiritual life. We have to prune away things in our lives that rob our time and energy. It is so easy to get bogged down with stuff that keep us from more time in the Word or in prayer. I am guilty of that myself and have to constantly be aware of those time robbers.

TEACHING MOMENT

If your child is passionate about a sport or a hobby, I bet they spend a lot of time either practicing or involved in that. Am I right? There is nothing wrong with that. But let me ask you a question. What is more important for their spiritual health, sports and hobbies or the Word? Now, I am not knocking sports and hobbies. I have plenty. But our primary mission as parents is to prepare our children spiritually.

If we spent a fraction of the time, energy, and money into building our children spiritually as we do in their sports and hobbies, we would be changing the world through our children. I truly believe that. If we put as much importance on the eternal things, our children would see that too.

What are you doing with the eternal? Will you join me today in re-evaluating your priorities? Will you do some pruning? I know it is not comfortable. I know it's not pleasant. But it is worth it.

Master, You command me to prune myself so I can produce more fruit for others. Help me see the unnecessary or dead growth that is preventing that. Then give me the determination to take action and cut those things away.

JANUARY 15

THE MIND OF CHRIST

1 Corinthians 2

BEST VERSE: 16B

But we have the mind of Christ.

Just think about it. We have the mind of Christ. Once we ask Christ into our lives, the Holy Spirit indwells us. And with the Holy Spirit comes the mind of Christ. How is that possible? Because the Holy Spirit and Christ are one with the Father. So, not only do you have the mind of Christ, you also have the mind of the Father and the Holy Spirit.

If that is true (and it is) how should we be thinking? What would Christ be thinking about? Certainly not paying that bill or buying a new boat. Not to presume, but Christ's mind was always on pleasing the Father. Doing His will was all that mattered. Shouldn't that be all we think about also?

TEACHING MOMENT

The next time you sit down to dinner with your kids, tell them you want them to NOT think about something. Tell them, "Kids, I do not want you to think about ice cream." What do you think their little brains start thinking about? Ice Cream. We can focus our brains on things so quickly.

Now tell them to think about God or Jesus. Ask them what comes to mind. Just let them explain how they see God. Get them to talk about Jesus. It is just as easy to think godly things as it is worldly things (not that I think ice cream is worldly. I believe it is heavenly). The point is to teach our kids that they can actually control what they think about.

What are you thinking about right now? Heavenly or worldly things? I pray you will train your brain to be in sync with Christ's mind. Let Him have control of your thought patterns. If that happens, He will also control your tongue, eyes, legs, and arms. Give your full attention to pleasing Him.

Father, Your mind is beyond comprehension. I am promised the mind of Christ. Help me to "tap into" His way of thinking every day, all day.

JANUARY 16

MARRYING WELL

1 Kings 11

BEST VERSES: 1–2

Now King Solomon loved many foreign women along with the daughter of Pharaoh: Moabite, Ammonite, Edomite, Sidonian, and Hittite women, from the nations concerning which the LORD had said to the sons of Israel, "You shall not associate with them, nor shall they associate with you, for they will surely turn your heart away after their gods." Solomon held fast to these in love.

How many of us pray that our children marry well? I might guess—ALL! Who would want their children to marry unbelievers? Who would want their son or daughter to be "unequally yoked"? We want our children to find mates who share their love for Jesus and are committed to raise their future children (your grandchildren) to love Jesus.

God had the same desire for His children. He warned them NOT to intermarry with the pagans of the land. But here we see Solomon, the wisest man alive, fall into the trap of marrying pagan women. I have to guess these were probably beautiful women. Why else would the king of Israel marry them? He could have married any woman in Israel, but he chose pagan women. Why? What drove Solomon to disobey the Lord in this way?

I have often wondered why, if Solomon was so wise, he would want all those wives and concubines. The answer is really simple. He wanted his own way. I am the same way. You are the same way. And guess what? Your children are the same way.

My guess is also that these women were nice, pagan women. Solomon wouldn't have married a mean or vicious woman. But their unbelief and their ties to pagan gods disqualified them as legitimate, God-approved spouses for anyone who believed and worshiped Him as Jehovah, the true God.

TEACHING MOMENT

The same is true for your children, but they must make their own decisions regarding their mates. They also, like Solomon, must live with the consequences. Solomon's choices of wives and concubines led him away from the one true God and eventually cost his son, Rehoboam, the kingdom.

We must point our children toward God's choice for them. That doesn't mean we arrange their marriage, but that we lay the biblical foundation that will guide them as they seek God's will for their future. Pray hard!

You are the ultimate match maker, God. I am not asking for that, but I am asking that you send godly individuals you have for my children into their lives. Let them honor You first!

JANUARY 17

SNAKE BIT

Acts 28

BEST VERSE: 3

But when Paul had gathered a bundle of sticks and laid them on the fire, a viper came out because of the heat and fastened itself on his hand.

What luck Paul had! He had just survived a shipwreck and now, while trying to build a fire to stay warm with the rest of his crew, he gets snake bit. That had to hurt, don't you think? And then, to top it off, the islanders start shouting that he must be a murderer because he got bit.

Some days, everything seems to go wrong, doesn't it? Everything you do or say just comes up short. But Paul isn't worried about the shipwreck or the snakebite. He calmly goes about his business, and nothing happens to him. He knows his God is with him and has a mission for him to complete. I have said it before, "We are all immortal until God takes us home." By that I mean, our days are numbered by God Himself.

TEACHING MOMENT

Have you explained life and death to your children? There comes an age when it is appropriate to tell them about that. Just telling them that someone has "gone away" is not helpful. If that person who has passed away is a believer, they need to know that we, as believers, will see them again one day. That's a promise from the Father.

Snakebites, shipwrecks, automobile accidents, or any other accident will not take us from this world until the Lord is good and ready to take us home. But when He does, we can rest in the fact that it is our time.

Wow! This devotion seems . . . well . . . morbid, doesn't it? It is not meant to be. I just believe we need to be reminded that God loves us and has a home for us. That is why it is so important for us to do everything within our power to lead our children to Christ. Eternity is a long time!

I am so thankful, Lord, that this earth is NOT my home. You are preparing a place for me to dwell. Give me the wisdom to talk to my children about this when the time is right. I know You will tell me what to say and when to say it.

JANUARY 18

HEAVENLY REVELATIONS

Job 20

BEST VERSE: 27A

The heavens will reveal his iniquity.

One day, no matter what we do, all we have done will be revealed. The difference between believers and unbelievers, though, will be that all the believer's iniquities are covered under the blood. When they are revealed, Jesus stands and says, Excuse me, Father, but I took care of that. Boy, I am so grateful.

On the other hand, all those who are not in Christ will be judged, and those unforgiven iniquities will bring ultimate judgment upon them. God knows and sees everything. There is no hiding from Him, now or later.

TEACHING MOMENT

Your children may think you have eyes in the back of your head right now. You know what I mean. Parents just know when their child has been up to no good. Moms are the best at it. They can tell when their children are lying. As good as you may think you are at that, God is sooooooo much better. He knows all, including the very thoughts your children have.

The key to teaching this truth to our children is found in their relationship with Christ. As they surrender to Him, there is no fear in that truth. We teach them that in Christ we are truly free of the fear of judgment. Their sins were judged and paid for by Christ on that cross. Nothing can undo that.

Are you struggling with the truth of your forgiveness? Satan wants to rob you of the joy of your salvation. He wants you to think you are not worthy. You are a child of the King, if you are believer in His Son. Claim it. Believe it. Live it.

Mighty Judge, thank You for cleansing me of my guilt and shame. I will live in the freedom of Christ. I will live a life devoid of Satan's toothless accusations—because of Jesus.

JANUARY 19

JOB REVISION

1 Chronicles 23

BEST VERSE: 26
Also, the Levites will no longer need to carry the tabernacle and all its utensils for its service.

How many times have you had a job with a job description, and that job description changes? New duties are added. Others are taken away. Revisions are made in your duties. Sometimes those come with more compensation or less compensation. Regardless, those who are your authorities are the ones who have the power to make those changes.

Here we see David making preparations for the temple, which his son, Solomon, is going to build. He knows that once the temple is completed, the Levites will need to have new jobs. There will no longer be a tabernacle to carry. The temple will replace it. So, David gives new assignments. He revises their job descriptions. There is no record of a rebellion or a call for a union vote. They accepted their new duties from their earthly king because they knew the Lord had appointed him.

TEACHING MOMENT

Children need to be taught to submit to all authorities. Anyone who is over them (parents, teachers, coaches, police, etc) should be respected and adhered to. Now, it is important to note that your children may not always agree with those authorities. That is a moot point. They must submit unless, of course, that authority is telling them to do something illegal or immoral.

We see too much anti-authority attitudes today. Young people, children included, are rebelling against any kind of authority. I have found one to be true in those I have encountered who have that attitude. They are also at odds with God. If you are surrendered to God, you will surrender to your earthly authorities also.

Are you surrendered? I mean, are you surrendered to God in ALL things? We don't get to pick and choose our surrendered items. The old hymn reads, "I surrender all; I surrender all; All to Thee, my precious Savior, I surrender all." So, I ask you again, have you?

I bow before You today, O mighty and holy God. Forgive me of my rebellious attitude. Give me the heart of surrender. I give you EVERYTHING. Take it and use it how You want.

JANUARY 20

GOOD RIDDANCE

2 Chronicles 21

BEST VERSE: 20

He was thirty-two years old when he became king, and he reigned in Jerusalem eight years; and he departed with no one's regret, and they buried him in the city of David, but not in the tombs of the kings.

Jehoram was not a good king. He wasn't even a good man. The moment he became king at age 32, he killed all his brothers. His father, Jehoshaphat, had been such a good king, but Jehoram wanted nothing of that. He wanted everything for himself.

The phrase in this verse "with no one's regret" is sad. It means no one was sad to see him die. They were glad he was gone. There was nothing pleasant about Jehoram, so there was nothing to miss. Have you ever been to a funeral like that? It's sad.

TEACHING MOMENT

Our children should be taught to live their lives in such devotion to the Lord that people will truly miss them when they are gone. That may seem kind of strange to say, but think about it. We are either going to be missed when we are gone or not. I would hate to know when I die that no one would even notice. I know I am not indispensable, but I do want people to know I'm gone. Ha!

So, how do we "leave our mark" on this world? Simple, we show our children how to impact others. We share the gospel so that others become His children too. We love others so they will love others. We lend a hand to others so they, in turn, will lend a hand to others. That will leave a mark on this world so that when we are gone people will say, "We are going to miss him."

How are you "marking" the world? Jehoram left a mark, but it wasn't a good one. What do you want written on your gravestone? Have you thought about that? What will your family say at your funeral? What will the memories of you be about? Those are the marks you leave.

Father, please let me leave Your mark on this world. Allow me to share the Word with others so that You can stamp your image on them. That would be all I need to be remembered for, for being the one to lead them to You.

JANUARY 21

DON'T YOU LOVE PARADES?

Psalms 99–100

BEST VERSE: 100:4

Enter His gates with thanksgiving and His courts with praise. Give thanks to Him, bless His name.

When I read this so familiar verse from Psalms 100, I get a picture in my head of a parade. I can see the saints marching down Beulah Avenue and turning right on Glory Highway. They are singing and praising God. They are waving banners with His names like Jehovah Jireh and Jehovah Rapha.

Don't you want to live in that spirit every day? Don't you want to be in a constant attitude of praise instead of worrying and fretting about the everyday challenges in your life? You may be thinking, *That's not possible, Carl! I can't do that.* You are exactly right! You can't! But He can!

TEACHING MOMENT

Most children are quick to get in a party atmosphere. Why? Because they aren't burdened with life yet. They are free to celebrate and sing. They are excited when they see the opportunity to dance and praise. So how can you learn from your children? How can you develop or regain that carefree spirit?

Surrender! Give it up! Let Jesus have the concerns of today. I know that is easier said than done. I am the son of a chief worrier. My mom worried about not having something to worry about. But, I know I have to give it all to Him on a daily basis. Shoot, I have to do it on a minute-by-minute basis.

Will you join with me and your children in thanksgiving and praise today? Will you join the parade marching to Glory? Will you clap your hands and lift your voice to praise the Almighty King of the Universe? Will you acknowledge today that you are incapable of praise unless you first bow down and give it all to Him? He is worthy of our praise! Let's get our praise on!

I praise Your name, most Holy God. I lift the name of Jesus higher. I magnify Your name!

JANUARY 22

BETTER TRUST THE ONE YOU KNOW

1 Kings 13

BEST VERSE: 19

So he went back with him, and ate bread in his house and drank water.

Do you know this whole story found in this chapter? A "man of God" had come to Jeroboam, the King of the ten Northern tribes, and rebuked him because of the altar he had built. God had told him to deliver the message and return home by another route. God also told him not to eat or drink anything while there. But another old prophet convinces him to come to his home and eat and drink with him. He said God had told him to tell the "man of God" it was okay. It wasn't. He was killed by a lion when he left!

Hmmm! One was a ly-ing, and there was also a li-on. Get it? Sorry, couldn't resist.

TEACHING MOMENT

Our children have to know that people will try to trick them. Some will actually tell them God said it was okay to do things that you, their parents, have taught them is wrong. Others will tell them that God's Word doesn't have all the answers when you have taught them it does. There is only one truth—God's truth. And the source of that truth is His Word.

We are so quick to teach them about "Stranger Danger." We warn them not to trust people they don't know. We warn them about choosing their friends carefully. But do we teach them to trust what the Lord says regardless of what others may say? Do we tell them to stick to their core values and convictions?

The "man of God" didn't do anything horrible. He simply ate and drank something. It wasn't what he did. It was that he did it. He disobeyed. That was the bottom line. If God says to do or not do something, you have to believe there is a reason for it. Trust Him! Teach your children to trust Him. Better yet, look for ways to show your children that you are trusting Him in a circumstance. That will teach them!

Lord, I want to do what You say when You say it. Help me to teach my children that too. I want them to want to follow You and trust You.

JANUARY 23

CHECK IT OUT

Acts 17

BEST VERSE: 11

Now these were more noble-minded than those in Thessalonica, for they received the word with great eagerness, examining the Scriptures daily to see whether these things were so.

Paul had the gift of agitation. Just follow his missionary journeys. Everywhere he went, with few exceptions, his visit ended with him getting run out of town. He had a way of inciting people with his words. But here, in Berea, the people responded differently. They were students of the Scriptures, so they checked out Paul's words and found them to be true.

Are you a Thessalonian or a Berean? Do you get agitated and upset when something someone says convicts you? Do you think, How dare they judge me? Paul didn't mind upsetting people if it meant they might be convicted and turn to the Lord. His goal was not to make friends. He wanted to make disciples. Don't misunderstand me. We don't want to insult people, but we do want them to see their sins and confess them to Christ.

TEACHING MOMENT

You need to be careful with your children to not constantly point out their sins. It is not your job to force confessions out of them. No amount of nagging and scolding is going to bring them to repentance. You need to present the truth to them and show them how their choices don't measure up to God's Word. You are always to point back to the Word, not what you think is best.

Give them verses to read that deal with the issues they are facing. Show them through your life that it is God's Word that guides you. As appropriate, share stories with them of your own struggles and how God's Word directed you.

As you go through your day meditate on these words and see how you compare: "examining the Scriptures daily." There is no other way to ensure you will make good choices. Do not rely on any other source. Trust the Word!

Father, Your Scriptures are God-breathed. Help me to remember that Your Word teaches, convicts, corrects, and trains in righteousness. May I examine the Scriptures so that I will be ready to lead my child.

JANUARY 24

LETTER WRITING

2 Corinthians 3

BEST VERSES: 2–3

You are our letter, written in our hearts, known and read by all men; being manifested that you are a letter of Christ, cared for by us, written not with ink but with the Spirit of the living God, not on tablets of stone but on tablets of human hearts.

People don't write letters anymore, or at least very few people do. Emails, texts, and tweets seem to rule the day. We are still communicating, but with shorter conversations. But don't you get excited when you get an actual letter from someone you know and love? There is just something about holding that handwritten letter and studying every word.

Paul is telling us in these two verses that as we invest in the lives of others in Christ, we are writing letters "on tablets of human hearts" that will be read by others. We are penning the very love of Christ on them that others will see and want to read.

TEACHING MOMENT

We, as parents, do the same with our children. We invest in their lives when they are young and pour our love and devotion into them. We teach them all we know about life and help them develop into fine young men and women when they leave home. Others who meet them will see and hear not only them, but us too.

What better way to reach a lost and dying world than to send our children out as "missionaries" of the love of Christ. I am not saying they should all be actual missionaries, but any believer who carries the name "Christian" is one. We can do that letter writing on their heart as we teach them about Christ and how to walk with Him.

Of course, the actual writing is done by the Holy Spirit, but He uses us to prepare the paper. It's hard to write on a surface that is not prepared. Won't you prepare, as best you can, the surface of your children's hearts to hear and receive the love of Christ so that they can be that letter of love to the world?

I am thankful, O God, that You have written my name in Your book. The day I asked Your Son into my heart, my name was penned for eternity. At the same time, His name was engraved on my heart.

JANUARY 25

HARD-HEADED

Isaiah 48

BEST VERSE: 4

Because I know that you are obstinate, and your neck is an iron sinew and your forehead bronze.

I know some hard-headed people, myself excluded, of course. Yeah, whatever! Have you ever been accused of being hard-headed? The Lord is calling the people of Israel that right here in this verse. They were obstinate, stiff-necked and hard-headed. Wow! Talking about calling names—the Lord does that here.

The Lord is about to lead them into exile for their hard-headedness. Look at these two verses later in the chapter. "If only you had paid attention to My commandments! Then your well-being would have been like a river, And your righteousness like the waves of the sea. Your descendants would have been like the sand, and your offspring like its grains; their name would never be cut off or destroyed from My presence." He wanted to bless them, but they just refused to listen.

TEACHING MOMENT

Do you have a hard-headed child? Maybe they are strong-willed. Most of the time those children can grow up to be strong leaders who aren't afraid to make the tough decisions. They can be self-confident and sure of themselves. Don't you want them to be that way? But we have to steer them in the right way to make those decisions. Strong-willed children can pose a challenge. They can be obstinate, stiff-necked, and hard-headed, just like Israel. We have to hold them accountable for their actions. We bless them for the right ones and discipline them for the wrong ones. Don't be afraid to do that.

Whenever possible, let those strong-willed kids make their own decisions. Explain to them the possible outcomes of their decisions. They have to live with them. Even if outcomes are not the ones you want for them, if they are not life threatening, give them room to make wrong decisions. Yep, I said that. That is hard. We want to avoid those uncomfortable situations. But we have to let them make their decisions or they will never learn how to do that. It is much better for those decisions to be made while they have you to direct them.

Trust the Lord that He loves your children much more than you do. He wants what is best. Point them in His direction and let Him have His perfect will done in their lives. Only He can make them compliant, flexible, and clear-headed.

As strange as it may seem, Lord, I thank You for strong-willed children. For I know once they receive You, they will be rock-solid in You.

BUT I WANT IT

Song of Solomon 7

BEST VERSE: 10

I am my beloved's, and his desire is for me.

How many times have you REALLY wanted something, but you knew you couldn't have it? Maybe it's that new car or house. Perhaps it's a new dress, ladies. Men, it might just be that bass boat or gun. Whatever it is, just how bad do you want it? Does your mind constantly go there? Is it all you can think about?

God's desire is for us. His mind is always on us. He longs for our fellowship. He wants to bless us. He gets pleasure in our obedience and in our prayers. The Word says our prayers are a fragrant aroma in His nostrils. He desires us! But do we desire Him?

TEACHING MOMENT

Every year little children start making out their wish lists for Christmas. They will make that list and describe exactly what they want. They may even tell you where to find it. They may text it, email it, or write it out. But I guarantee you, they will let you know.

What a perfect time to talk about desires. Read this verse and remind them that as much as they desire those things for Christmas, God's desire for them is so much bigger. Even if they were promised every toy on the list, their desire to receive them would pale in comparison to His desire to just spend time with them.

Do you believe God desires you? Do you desire Him? Do you change your schedule to make time for Him? Or do you give Him the leftover minutes of the day? Do you think of Him first thing in the morning and the last thing at night? Is your mind fixed on Him? He is fixed on you. You are His desire. Make Him yours.

My Beloved, my desire is for you. I long to be with You and hear Your words. I want to be with You more than anything. Draw me close.

JANUARY 27

WITH ALL MY HEART

2 Chronicles 31

BEST VERSE: 21

Every work which he began in the service of the house of God in law and in commandment, seeking his God, he did with all his heart and prospered.

Have you ever told someone, "I love you with all my heart"? Did you mean it? I will have to say I have said that at times when I really did not mean it. In fact, I have said it to people in the past whom I haven't seen in years. Isn't it funny how we think we love someone or something so much and how quick that love fades?

Hezekiah, however, loved his Lord with all his heart. It must have been true because Scripture tells us that. And we know that all Scripture is true, right? Right! Look at the result of that love. He prospered. Because he was committed to obeying and loving his God, God prospered him. Who doesn't want that?

TEACHING MOMENT

The next time your children tell you they love you with all their heart, read them this story. Then explain what loving someone with all their heart means. That kind of love moves from the emotional to the mental. It is a choice to love. Even when your emotions are fading, you choose to love. You give yourself to them wholeheartedly.

Your children are going to give their hearts away many times as they grow up. They are probably going to have their hearts broken by someone along the way. Bring them back to this passage. The only sure love is God's love. The only constant love is through Him. That love will never end.

How do you love? Do you love with all your heart? What are you holding back today? Give it up to Him. Let Him take all that excess stuff in your life that is holding you back. He can show you what real love is if you will let Him. Love Him!

Lover of my soul, I do love you. Help me to love you as Hezekiah did—with all my heart. Show me how to love others as You do.

A GOOD THIEF

2 Chronicles 22

BEST VERSE: 11A

But Jehoshabeath the king's daughter took Joash the son of Ahaziah, and stole him from among the king's sons who were being put to death, and placed him and his nurse in the bedroom.

Stealing is wrong. Don't believe anything else. But here, in this verse, we find a good thief. What did Jehoshabeath steal? Joash, the eventual child king. Joash's grandmother was killing all her rivals for the throne after her son died. She wanted it for her own, and actually had it for a while. But Jehoshabeath did the right thing and hid Joash to save his life.

Have you ever had to protect someone? Did protecting them put you in danger? I'll never forget protecting my little sister when I was in the second grade. She was in the first grade. A school bully was picking on her during recess, and I saw it. I stood up to that bully, who everyone was scared of, and defended my sister. Sometimes, we have to stand up for what's right, no matter the consequences.

TEACHING MOMENT

I am not telling you to teach your children to steal or fight. I am saying your children should be taught to be bold and stand up for the right thing. What's the right thing? Whatever God's Word says. We should defend the innocent. We should stand for life. We should stand for our beliefs and values.

Your children are going to be challenged by this world. They will be called intolerant and biased for taking a stand for the things of God. Let them. Teach them to take pride in that. Doing what's right feels good. It pleases the Father. We don't know what happened to Jehoshabeath on this earth, but I bet God rewarded her for her actions.

Do your actions please the Father? Are you doing the things you are doing to satisfy yourself, someone else, or God? That's the bottom-line question. Nothing you do should be about pleasing anyone but Him. Then He can bless you for pleasing Him.

Lord, thank You for giving me the wisdom to do what's right. You give me the words to follow each day in Your Word. Help me be bold and courageous in the face of opposition.

JANUARY 29

JUST TOUCH IT

ESTHER 5

BEST VERSE: 2

When the king saw Esther the queen standing in the court, she obtained favor in his sight; and the king extended to Esther the golden scepter which was in his hand. So Esther came near and touched the top of the scepter.

Can't you just picture this scene in your mind? Dressed in her royal gown, Queen Esther approaches the inner court of the king. She knows this action is risky. She hasn't seen the king in a month, and there is no telling what kind of mood he will be experiencing. She could be dead in minutes.

It doesn't say, but I believe Esther probably sent a prayer up to the Lord. "Oh God, please don't let him kill me. Please let him extend the golden scepter." She approaches, and sure enough, the king smiles and extends the scepter. Esther reaches out and touches the scepter, accepting his offer of grace.

TEACHING MOMENT

When was the last time you extended your child grace rather than law? Many parents are so focused on keeping the rules that they forget the importance of teaching grace to their children. Sure, we need to be consistent and hold our children accountable. But there are times when giving grace teaches so much more.

This is a wonderful passage to use to teach that to your children. Stories like this in Scripture paint a picture in such a way that the image is burned into their little brains. You could even use a prop as you read this to them. Let them reach out and touch a golden scepter. More importantly, let them experience grace when you could give punishment.

Do you remember the last time God gave you grace instead of law? Boy, I do. It was, well, today. All I deserve is death, but He gives me life. All I deserve is eternal punishment, but He gives me eternal reward. Why? It's not because of anything I have done. It's all because of Jesus. Don't forget that.

Father, as I approach Your throne room each day, I thank You that Jesus is right beside You. He is the golden scepter which You extended to me on the day of my salvation, and He is the same one that is extended to me today.

JANUARY 30

SWEET NOTHINGS

Song of Solomon 4

BEST VERSE: 2

Your teeth are like a flock of newly shorn ewes which have come up from their washing, all of which bear twins, and not one among them has lost her young.

Okay, have you ever whispered sweet nothings to someone special? You know what I mean. You tell that special someone how precious they are and how beautiful they are. You compliment them over and over. Usually, you say those things to someone you really care about, and you don't exaggerate too much, or they will think you are making fun.

Well, I can't help but laugh when I read this verse. The groom is complimenting his bride on her teeth. He compares them to sheep that have been washed (they are white). He goes on to say, "And you have all of them. You don't have any missing teeth." Perhaps that was a compliment back in those days, but I would dare say that would not be appreciated much today.

TEACHING MOMENT

How do you apply this verse to your children? How will they respond? Paying compliments should be truthful. Paying compliments should come from your heart. Flattery may sound like a good idea in order to get something. But flattery for flattery's sake will always be found out.

Teach your children to only give compliments if they mean them. You don't want your child to be known as someone who tries to grease the palm of every one they meet just to get what they want. Truthfulness is always the best way to go.

Examine your compliments. When you compliment someone, ask yourself why? What is your reason behind complimenting that person? Compliment, but mean it. Better yet, bless them in the name of Jesus. You can't get much better than that.

I am so sorry, Father, for speaking the wrong words at times. Forgive me for saying what I know the other person wants to hear, even if it is not true. Let my words always speak truth.

JANUARY 31

SLOW BURNER

Nahum 1

BEST VERSE: 3

The LORD is slow to anger and great in power, and the LORD will by no means leave the guilty unpunished. In whirlwind and storm is His way, and clouds are the dust beneath His feet.

Aren't you glad our God is slow to anger? If He responded quickly to my every mess up, I would be a smoldering ember. But instead He is patient and kind. That does not diminish His power or His character of truth, as the verse says. We can rest assured that He will punish those who are against Him. He has no choice. He demands holiness.

But thanks be to God, He has sent the Rescuer, His own Son Jesus Christ. He showed us how to respond in the face of persecution. He showed us how to deal with those who would want to harm us. Jesus could have "zapped" all His enemies. He could have literally stepped down off the cross. But He was forgiving, instead.

TEACHING MOMENT

Children must learn this skill. They must learn to respond to those who hurl insults at them. They must learn how to allow the Lord to deal with those who would want to harm them. There really is no other way. The Lord is the One with the power, not us. He will use us, but only in a way that brings glory to Him.

The next time your child comes home with the report that little Jimmy at school is picking on him, use this verse to teach him. He may never see Jimmy dealt with regarding His behavior. That's okay. God will handle it when He is ready to handle it. Help them pray for Jimmy. Teach them to be Jesus to him.

Now, this sounds easy, right? Well, it's not. It's impossible. You can't do it. But you don't have to. He will do it through you. Nahum was prophesying about God's power and His ability to do what was right at the right time. He is still that same God.

O God, give me the ability today to not lash out at those who speak evil against me. Help me instead to pray for their salvation. Teach me to trust You as You deal with those who speak evil against those who follow You.

IT'S NOT US!

Acts 3

BEST VERSE: 12

But when Peter saw this, he replied to the people, "Men of Israel, why are you amazed at this, or why do you gaze at us, as if by our own power or piety we had made him walk?"

Can you believe Peter's response? Too many today want the attention and crave the accolades. Too many would claim the power. Not Peter! Remember, he had just been filled with the Spirit. This was the Spirit talking through him. He was just the vessel being used.

Just like Peter, we have the power within us to accomplish incredible things. Our problem is we don't believe it. Some of you are thinking, Not me, Carl. I could never heal someone. With that thought you can't. Now, I am not saying you should just start trying to heal people with no guidance or direction from the Lord. That is definitely not what I am saying. But we can do anything the Lord asks us to do through His power.

TEACHING MOMENT

Our children should be taught to depend on the power of God to accomplish great things. Of course, in order for them to be able to do that, they have to have the Holy Spirit living in them. But once they have asked Christ in their lives, they need to learn to depend on Him and not themselves.

What could your children accomplish if they did that? God may lead them to do incredible things for Him. Nurture your child to depend on Him, not you. Turn them over to Him. Let them go! That's hard, I know. But they weren't yours to begin with. They have always belonged to Him.

Are you allowing the Spirit to work through you? Are you willing to be used to do whatever He asks? He may ask you to pray for healing over someone. He may ask you to witness to someone and lead them to Christ. Now that is power!

Lord, thank You for allowing me to be used. I am nothing. I am not worthy. But You have chosen me to be used by You to accomplish great things.

YOU SHALL CALL HIS NAME

Isaiah 7

BEST VERSE: 14

Therefore the Lord Himself will give you a sign: Behold, a virgin will be with child and bear a son, and she will call His name Immanuel.

Naming a child is such an important thing. Of course, today the gender reveal party has taken the nation by storm, and now it seems the name of the baby pales in importance to revealing the gender. But here in Isaiah, the Lord gave the name - Immanuel—God with us. What a perfect verse for this season of the year.

God is with us—every day of the year. Why is it we seem to only use this name of Jesus at Christmas. We don't hear Immanuel mentioned much the rest of the year. Ironically, we act like the world most of the year. We don't live as if God is with us. We don't treat others like God is with us. We don't talk like God is with us.

TEACHING MOMENT

Our children need to know that God is with us. They need to be able to feel secure that no matter what may come into their lives—God is with them. As believers in Jesus Christ as their personal Savior, there will never be a time when God is not with them. He indwells them through His Holy Spirit. They cannot escape His presence.

This is so important for them to understand as they leave home. When your son or daughter head out your door on their own (okay, grab the tissues), you can rest assured that God is with them. They may make some decisions that are not very godly, but God is still with them. They may go some places you wouldn't go, but God is still with them. Immanuel is in them. They can't run away from Him.

Do you get the theme for today? God is with us. Even if it is not Christmas season, remember to tell your family every day that God is with them. Remind them that His holy presence is among them. Do this year round! Then Christmas will become even more special and have more meaning.

Thank You Lord, for sending Immanuel to live, not only on earth, but also in me. His presence in my life through the power of the Holy Spirit gives me the strength to live each new day.

FEBRUARY 3

A NEW DIRECTION

Acts 10

BEST VERSE: 3

About the ninth hour of the day he clearly saw in a vision an angel of God who had just come in and said to him, "Cornelius!"

This verse may seem to be just a verse about another angel appearance, but don't believe that. This verse marks the opening of the "Gospel to the Gentiles." If the Lord had not sent an angel to Cornelius to instruct him to send for Peter, it would have been years, maybe even generations, before the gospel was shared with the Gentile world. Peter, the lead disciple at that time, realized the Lord had given the believers a new direction.

I love Cornelius' response. He was humbled at the appearance of the angel and Peter. He was a powerful, important leader in the Roman army, but he recognized true power and bowed in its presence with a servant's heart. I have to believe after Peter left that the Lord used Cornelius to spread the good news of Jesus to his soldiers and neighbors.

TEACHING MOMENT

Our children must learn that God can use anyone who is surrendered to Him. Perhaps the Lord is preparing your child right now under your leadership to be the next Billy Graham. Now that's scary, isn't it? That's a lot of responsibility, but perhaps God may be asking you to allow Him to mold your child into a spiritual leader for the world.

So, if God is asking you this, how is that working? What are you doing to accomplish that task? I bet Peter didn't think he would be asked to go to a Roman commander's house to share the gospel. But he was, and he did. You need to find ways every day to pour the truth into your son or daughter. You do not know what God has planned for them. You are shaping them for the future. You are shaping them to be world shapers. God may use them to reach that last soul before Jesus returns. Teach! Mold! Build!

Father, give me a servant's heart to spread the good news to those you put in my path today. May I never squander the time I have to teach, mold, and build my children up in Jesus!

FEBRUARY 4

WAGES

Romans 6

BEST VERSE: 23

For the wages of sin is death, but the free gift of God is eternal life in Christ Jesus our Lord.

"Wages" and "free" don't often occur in the same sentence, do they? This is one of the most quoted verses in Scripture. It's part of the "Romans Road" which you use to share the gospel with someone. But think about the words. Wages are something you receive for work you have done. We all, at some point in our lives, have probably complained about our wages. But none of us who are still living have received death as our wages.

Now contrast that with the free gift of God. Eternal life! No wage on earth is eternal. It is all fleeting. The more you get, the more you normally spend. But this gift is eternal. It never loses its value and never ceases to exist. What a deal! But this free gift does cost you. It costs you everything! You must surrender your all to Him.

TEACHING MOMENT

Do you give your children allowance for chores they do around the house? I hope you don't just give them an allowance for breathing. That doesn't really teach them anything. If you give them allowance for chores, then this verse is a great verse to use. Just as their allowance is payment (wages) for chores, death is the payment for an unsurrendered life, a life not given over to Christ, a life full of unconfessed and unforgiven sin.

Contrast this with your child's birthday gift (which I am sure you spoil them with). They get that gift simply for being born into your family. Eternal life is our "birthday gift" for being born into God's family. But this gift, unlike the breakable toy you gave your child, never wears out. That eternal life is waiting for us whether we live to be 20 or 120. It's value never diminishes and when we finally claim it at death, it is just beginning. Wow!

Are you ready? Have you claimed your free gift of God? Do you know someone who hasn't? Why not share with them today? Check out the "Share Your Faith" app for your smartphone. It is an easy way to guide someone to their eternal life in Christ.

Father, I choose the free gift over death. I know I can do nothing to deserve this gift. I only have to receive it.

FEBRUARY 5

NO ROOM TO COMPLAIN

2 Corinthians 11

BEST VERSES: 23-27

Are they servants of Christ?—I speak as if insane—I more so; in far more labors, in far more imprisonments, beaten times without number, often in danger of death. Five times I received from the Jews thirty-nine lashes. Three times I was beaten with rods, once I was stoned, three times I was shipwrecked, a night and a day I have spent in the deep. I have been on frequent journeys, in dangers from rivers, dangers from robbers, dangers from my countrymen, dangers from the Gentiles, dangers in the city, dangers in the wilderness, dangers on the sea, dangers among false brethren; I have been in labor and hardship, through many sleepless nights, in hunger and thirst, often without food, in cold and exposure.

Have you ever known a complainer? I mean someone who constantly whines about how bad they have it? You mistakenly greet them with, "Hey, how are you?" Then you spend the next thirty minutes listening to their every little ailment and life challenge. Don't get me wrong! We should be concerned for others and truly care for them. But many of us just complain too easily.

Look at Paul's life after his conversion. Talk about having a bad day! He was constantly harassed and threatened. Even when he was pursuing the Lord's will in his life, he faced challenges. I need to learn to keep my mouth shut when I compare my "sufferings" with Paul's.

TEACHING MOMENT

Do your kids complain? I bet they do sometimes. They can't find their favorite toys or tv shows. They don't like what you have prepared for dinner. They don't want to go to Grandma's house. What whiners! But these are opportunities to talk to them about how blessed they are. Read them this passage. Tell them a story you may know about a missionary friend who struggles to just wash clothes in clean water. Being grateful is something that we have to teach our kids. We don't want them to take things for granted, and we want them to know from whom these blessings come. Amen? Let it start with you.

Lord, when I begin to complain or whine, remind me how blessed I am. Any sufferings I have to endure are a gift from You to make me more like You.

FEBRUARY 6

HIS STRENGTH

Psalms 59–60

BEST VERSE: 59:9

Because of his strength I will watch for You, For God is my stronghold.

I was visiting a daycare program recently and had the opportunity to spend some time on the playground with a classroom of 3-year-olds. They will wear you out! One little boy kept showing me his muscles after each turn on the monkey bars. He would push up his little sleeves and point his bent elbow toward me. Then he wanted to see my muscles. When I exposed my bulging bicep (sarcasm intended here) he would say, "Wow!" He was impressed with my adult-sized muscle. It takes little to impress some people.

Isn't it great to know that we do not have to see bulging muscles to know God's strength? The word "his" is translated as "his," "my," and "your" depending on the version you are reading. The idea is still the same. David knows God's strength is the only strength that can sustain him and protect him. He needed God's strength to protect the children of Israel.

TEACHING MOMENT

So, let me ask you a question. Whose strength are you relying on to protect your children? Do you look in the mirror each morning, dads, and say, "Bring it on! I am too strong for anyone"? Of course, you don't. At least I hope you don't. Instead you need to start each day on your knees asking the Lord to protect and defend you and your family. Because only He is capable.

The next time your child walks up to you and shows you their muscles, remind them that God Almighty is watching over them and wants to protect them. But the only way He can is if they allow Him to be their Savior and Lord. God has no covenant with what is not His. No relationship, no protection. But the second we are His, all the angels of heaven are ready to fight for us. Hallelujah! "Our God is so big, so strong, and so mighty. There's nothing that He cannot do."

When I stop to think of your enormity, God, I can get overwhelmed. Your strength cannot be measured. Your power is unfathomable. So why do I worry about anything? Thank You for being there always.

FEBRUARY 7

NAME DROPPER

Romans 16

BEST VERSES: 1, 3, 5–15, 21–23

I commend to you our sister Phoebe, . . . Greet Prisca and Aquila, . . . Greet Epaenetus, my beloved . . . Greet Mary . . . Greet Andronicus and Junias, . . . Greet Ampliatus, . . . Greet Urbanus, . . . and Stachys . . . Greet Apelles, . . . Greet those who are of the household of Aristobulus. Greet Herodion, my kinsman. Greet those of the household of Narcissus, . . . Greet Tryphaena and Tryphosa, . . . Greet Persis . . . , Greet Rufus, . . . Greet Asyncritus, Phlegon, Hermes, Patrobas, Hermas . . . , Greet Philologus and Julia, Nereus and his sister, and Olympas, . . . Timothy . . . Lucius and Jason and Sosipater, . . . Tertius, . . . Gaius, . . . Erastus, . . . and Quartus, the brother.

Paul mentions thirty-five people in this chapter, not counting Jesus. Most of these names appear nowhere else in Scripture—only here in Romans 16. I bet these people had no idea their names would be recorded for eternity. But here they are in Romans, one of Paul's many letters which the Holy Spirit inspired him to write.

Now this "name dropping" does not compare to those other incidents you may have encountered. You know what I mean. Some people have to mention they know someone or have met someone to bring attention to themselves. No, Paul is mentioning these names to give them honor in their service to Jesus.

TEACHING MOMENT

Our children need to know their name is important to God. He knows them by name. He even knows their middle names. He knows everything about them. And, although their names won't be listed in a book of the Bible, if they are a believer, it is written in the Lamb's Book of Life. That is where it really matters.

Our children need to know that, although they may think their service to the King isn't important, He is noticing. He is pleased with their sacrifice. He is blessed by their obedience. It does not matter if anyone else on earth knows what they did, God does. That is all that matters.

How about you? Are you down in the dumps because no one has "patted you on the back" lately? Why are you serving? Why are you doing what you are doing? It is NOT for men's applause. It is to please your Father in heaven. Let Him be pleased. That is all that matters.

Lord, I know You know my name. You value my name as one of Your beloved. But thank You for giving me Your name!

FEBRUARY 8

THE FACE OF AN ANGEL

Acts 6

BEST VERSE: 15

And fixing their gaze on him, all who were sitting in the Council saw his face like the face of an angel.

I will have to admit—no one has ever said that about me. Ha! Well, maybe my mom did when I was little, but not lately. But haven't you said that at least once in your lifetime about someone, probably your own little one?

I mean, come on, when that little face turns to you and starts that little cherub face thing, you just melt. You wonder how you could ever love anything anymore.

Here is Stephen, whom they are about to stone, and they "all" saw his face like the face of an angel. But that did not matter to them. They didn't like what he as saying about Jesus, and when he refused to stop preaching about Him, they stoned him.

When you hear someone preaching the Word, do you think they have a face of an angel? Do you see the Spirit of God flowing in them? Do you see the face of Jesus as they proclaim the message of deliverance? You should, because those who rely on the Spirit to teach through them are literally the mouthpiece of God. They are only sharing what the Lord has given them.

TEACHING MOMENT

Recently we had our children's musical at our church. As I watched the children singing and speaking, I had this same view of them. They truly looked angelic. Now, I know these kids, so I know most of them are not angelic, but that night in that environment as they proclaimed the gospel in song, they took on the faces of angels.

Won't you put on that face today? Won't you encourage your children to put on that face? Putting on the face requires that we take off our old flesh face and then let the Spirit shine through. After all, the Spirit is so much lovelier to look at.

God, Your face is all I want to see. But I want others to see You reflected in my very countenance. I want them drawn to You by the simple words I say.

FEBRUARY 9

OUR GOD IS TOO BIG

2 Chronicles 2

BEST VERSE: 6

But who is able to build a house for Him, for the heavens and the highest heavens cannot contain Him? So who am I, that I should build a house for Him, except to burn incense before Him?

Solomon, at the very beginning of his reign as king, recognized just how big his God was. He had been instructed by his father David to build a temple for worship. Solomon knew the "house" he was going to build could not contain God. It would simply be a place to which the people could come to burn incense and offer sacrifices to their God.

If only Solomon had remembered that all his life. We know how he strayed to other gods and was wooed away to worship them by some of his concubines and wives. He seemed to forget just how big his God was.

I wonder what he thought of the temple in those latter years when his heart strayed.

TEACHING MOMENT

When you take your little son or daughter to church on Sunday, ask them if they know why they go. As you drive past other churches on the way, ask them why people go there. Ask them who they are going to worship. And then ask them how God can be in all those churches at the same time. Their answers may surprise you.

Children need to understand that God is not bound to a building today. He loves to see us worship Him in our church. That is important, but He doesn't live there. The church is NOT God's house, as so many people call it. We are! As believers, He dwells within us through His Holy Spirit. So, wherever we go becomes His dwelling place.

Now keep that in mind the next time you are tempted to visit some place you shouldn't go. Keep that in mind the next time you treat your body as your own. Our God is too big to live in us, but He chooses to because of our faith in His Son. Don't forget that.

I am Your temple here on earth, Father. I know that. Remind me to treat my body that way. I am thankful You dwell within me.

FEBRUARY 10

TOUGH CONSEQUENCES

1 Kings 20

BEST VERSE: 36

Then he said to him, "Because you have not listened to the voice of the Lord, behold, as soon as you have departed from me, a lion will kill you." And as soon as he had departed from him a lion found him and killed him.

All this guy had to do was strike the prophet. That's it. Just hit him. The request didn't make any sense. Perhaps he was afraid to hit the prophet. But back in those days if a prophet was known as a true prophet of God and he told you to do something, you had better pretty much do what he said.

As a result of not doing the Lord's bidding, he was killed by a lion. That's harsh. Boy, if that had been my consequence for not obeying the Lord, I would have been lion food a long time ago. I am so thankful for mercy and grace. Aren't you?

TEACHING MOMENT

The next time your little ones disobey, you threaten them with a lion attack. Just kidding, of course! Seriously, your children need to know that when they disobey your rules (which, by the way, should always mirror God's Word), they are really disobeying God. They don't have to be concerned about lions, but God is not pleased.

Can you think of the most recent time when your children have disobeyed? Now ask yourself this question. When was the last time you disobeyed God? Before you are too hard on your child, you need to correct your own behavior. You are still a child of the King.

We parents think that just because we are the adults we don't have "to mind." Oh yeah, we do. Admit it. But we are to be obedient children of the Lord so our children will follow our example.

Father, I am Your child, and I apologize for my disobedience. Forgive me, Father, for "bowing up" at You all the time. Teach me to model obedience to You so others will follow You also.

FEBRUARY 11

DIFFICULT QUESTIONS

1 Kings 10

BEST VERSE: 1

Now when the queen of Sheba heard about the fame of Solomon concerning the name of the Lord, she came to test him with difficult questions.

Don't you want to know what the queen of Sheba asked Solomon? I do. But it is not revealed to us. It just says the questions were difficult. Could they have been math questions? That would have been hard. Or could they have been questions about Jehovah? We just don't know.

Have you ever been asked difficult questions? I have. I have been through a couple of depositions for court cases. Often the attorneys will ask difficult questions or will word the questions in such a way that you are almost forced to answer in a way you don't want to. What do you do? You simply tell the truth.

TEACHING MOMENT

But the best way to answer difficult questions is to rely on the knowledge of the Lord, the Truth. Jesus told us He would give us the words to say. The Word also says that the Spirit would groan for us when we don't have words to say. Your children need to know that the Lord will speak for them and through them if they will just rely on Him.

Now this doesn't mean He will give them the answers to test questions for which they haven't studied. But I do believe He will help them recall answers they have studied. Your children are going to be asked difficult questions. Perhaps a lost friend at school will question their faith. Teach them to trust in Jesus to answer through them to help lead their friend to Christ.

What answers are you searching for right now? What questions are you trying to ask of the Lord? What questions are you trying to answer for someone else? Go to God. He is the ultimate source. He was Solomon's source.

O God, I know You have the answer to every question that has ever or will ever be asked. Show me the right answer. Help me rely on You and teach others to do the same.

FEBRUARY 12

ALL JOBS ARE IMPORTANT

Nehemiah 11

BEST VERSE: 19

Also the gatekeepers, Akkub, Talmon and their brethren who kept watch at the gates, were 172.

When you read Nehemiah 10–11 you see a list of people and responsibilities. These were the movers and shakers of the rebuilt Jerusalem. These are the ones who would re-establish order and society in a place that had suffered so much neglect.

Then you read verse 19 of chapter 11. Two names are mentioned—Akkub and Talmon. They and their "brethren" had the job of gatekeepers. They didn't serve in the temple. They didn't rule anyone. They may have thought they had less prestigious jobs. But their jobs were critical to the safety and order of the city. Gatekeepers were probably some of the toughest dudes around.

TEACHING MOMENT

Your children will probably get selected for tasks they think are too small for them. It could happen at home or at school or even when they grow up and get jobs. As parents, we are to teach our children the importance of every role assigned.

Explain to them how important it is for us to have people who pick up our trash. We may think that job is beneath us, but just go a week without your household garbage being picked up, and you will think that guy is the best thing you ever saw the next week. We all have our jobs to do. And this is so applicable to the kingdom of God as well. There are no big "I's" and little "you's" in the kingdom.

Are you feeling sorry for yourself right now because of the straw you drew? You feel you are above your present position. You think you are doing a job meant for someone else. Well, you be faithful in the little things. God is watching and will bless your loyalty and servant heart.

Thank You, Lord, for giving me every job you have ever given me. Some were better than others, but all helped shape me into who I am today. Let me be an example to others as I serve where You have planted me.

FEBRUARY 13

HOW SMART ARE YOU?

Job 35

BEST VERSE: 11

Who teaches us more than the beasts of the earth and makes us wiser than the birds of the heavens?

You have probably seen, or at least heard of, the TV show *Are You Smarter Than A Fifth Grader*? It is pretty amazing how little adults know in comparison to the average grade school child. Most of us have forgotten all the stuff we learned back then, especially dates and events in history.

But this verse in Job today reminds us that God has gifted us wisdom. He has given us intellect to make us smarter than the other created things. Scientists will tell you how "smart" certain animals are, but I don't see animals studying about humans in schools. We are truly God's greatest creation, created in His image.

TEACHING MOMENT

This is an easy lesson to teach your kids. How many of you help your child with math or science? Aren't you constantly assisting them with projects or vocabulary tests? Of course, you are. While you are doing that, share this verse. Remind them that as mundane and boring learning may seem, God has given us the ability to learn and grow mentally. We have the ability above all God's creations to think and reflect on things.

Your children need to learn that God has gifted them with the ability to learn, but the most important thing to learn will not be found in a textbook. It is only found in The book. God's Word is the sole source of wisdom for us. It contains all the answers to all of life's hardest questions. There is no test too difficult that the Bible cannot give the answer.

So, why aren't you digging deeper into it daily? You say, "Well, Carl, I just don't have the time." Or "I have too much other stuff that demands my attention." Really? Don't neglect the opportunity you have to learn from His Word. It is the only book you can read over and over again and learn something new each time.

O God, help me to memorize Your Word. Stretch my mind to the limit. Help me learn it and then live it.

FEBRUARY 14

WATCHING AND WAITING

Acts 25

BEST VERSE: 11

If, then, I am a wrongdoer and have committed anything worthy of death, I do not refuse to die; but if none of those things is true of which these men accuse me, no one can hand me over to them. I appeal to Caesar.

This may seem like a strange verse to pick for a devotional thought. What can you possibly get out of a verse like this? Paul is sounding defiant and almost obnoxious in the face of Festus. But I have to point you back to Acts 23:11 for you to understand why I picked this verse.

"But on the night immediately following, the Lord stood at his side and said, 'Take courage; for as you have solemnly witnessed to My cause at Jerusalem, so you must witness at Rome also.' "

Paul saw an opening as he stood before Festus to carry out the orders Jesus had spoken to him earlier. He was obviously just waiting for some sign this was about to happen. He was ready to go to Rome. Here was his chance.

TEACHING MOMENT

Do you look for opportunities each day to pour a new truth into the lives of your children? Or are you so busy with the daily schedule that you fly right past the chance? Do you realize at the end of your long, hard day that you missed it? May I encourage you today to take the time to pause and pour?

You only have your children for a short while. I know you don't see that now, but you will. I wish I could go back and re-parent my son and daughter. I would definitely do things differently. But I can't. I have two great kids and now four beautiful grandchildren, but I can't redo any parenting in my kids' lives.

Don't miss your chance to change your kid's life for eternity. Don't miss that truth-telling moment. The Lord has told us (my paraphrase), "Take courage; if you missed that opening I gave you yesterday, I will give you another tomorrow. Don't miss it."

Father, forgive me for missed opportunities. I know I can't redo those missed ones, but I can be more aware of the upcoming ones. Open my eyes to recognize those moments.

FEBRUARY 15

GOD THUNDER

Job 37

BEST VERSE: 5

God thunders with His voice wondrously, doing great things which we cannot comprehend.

I grew up in South Georgia where thunderstorms are pretty common. I am amazed when I meet someone who has never experienced one. Thunderstorms can be oddly invigorating or terribly frightening, depending on where you are standing when the lightning strikes. When you are safe inside a good building, you can enjoy the lightning bolts as they dash across the sky and then wait with anticipation for the boom that follows.

Elihu is speaking here and rightly compares God's voice to that thunder. God truly is behind the storms in our lives. I am not saying He causes them, but, as a believer, I must believe that He allows them. But if God allows the thunder and lightning in our lives, He will protect us. He is that strong shelter defending us from the storm.

TEACHING MOMENT

Do your children like storms? Most children don't. They come running for mom or dad when the thunder starts. What a perfect time to read this verse and talk about God's thunder! Tell them that thunder can be scary, but they can trust Him. Tell them that God will never allow anything to touch them that He hasn't already touched Himself.

Now, we don't purposely run into thunderstorms. It is smart to seek shelter. In the same way we teach our children that they should always go to the Father. They should never choose to run into a storm. But if they face one (and they will), they should run to His shelter.

Are you in a storm? Have you faced those lightning bolts and thunder that you were sure were going to tear you apart? Look to Him. Listen to His voice in the storm. He will guard you and protect you. You are His. He loves you with an everlasting love.

God of the storms, calm my heart when lightning strikes. Hold me close and reassure me of Your presence. Let me hear Your voice whisper my name.

MARCHING IN GREATNESS

Isaiah 63

BEST VERSE: 1

Who is this who comes from Edom, with garments of glowing colors from Bozrah, this One who is majestic in His apparel, marching in the greatness of His strength? "It is I who speak in righteousness, mighty to save."

I am a visual person. When I read a verse like this one, my mind starts picturing it. I can just see the Lord, dressed majestically and marching down the road. I can just see the armies of heaven all around. I can just see His might and strength being exhibited to all around.

Now, remember this: the Lord doesn't need an army to defend Him. He can speak just one word, and the enemy is defeated. I truly believe He has the hosts of heaven for our benefit. It is easier for us to believe in His strength and might when we read about that than to imagine a one God army. That's okay. He understands. But it doesn't change the fact that He is the Mighty One.

TEACHING MOMENT

The next time you and your children watch a parade, talk about this verse. You may see a drum major leading a band down the street. Point out the drum major's clothes, how they are different than the rest of the band. Talk about how he or she is the one leading and in charge. Point out how that shows their authority.

But then compare it to God's authority and might. Explain to them, the best you can, how God has the strength to just speak and defend us. He is always majestic, but He will come down for us at the mere mention of His name. He is always holy, but He is also the ruthless defender of the innocent, of His children.

Are you relying on your Great Defender today? Look at Him. Look at His regality. Look at His majesty. Be in awe of Him. But know also that He is your God. He wants to be called by you. He stands at the ready to hear and show His power in your life.

O holy and majestic God, I stand in awe that You would love me. I find it hard to believe that You know me personally and will come to me when I call. I love You, and will serve You.

FEBRUARY 17

TOO BIG FOR HIS BRITCHES

2 Kings 14

BEST VERSE: 9B

The thorn bush which was in Lebanon sent to the cedar which was in Lebanon, saying, "Give your daughter to my son in marriage."

Amaziah, King of Judah, had just defeated Edom and was feeling very powerful and arrogant. So, he challenged Jehoash, King of Israel. Remember, Israel was ten tribes and Judah was one. Jehoash tried to avoid the battle, but Amaziah was insistent. The result—defeat for Judah.

Arrogance and pride will make you a little too big for your britches. Boasting and showing off never leads to good. While here on earth Jesus still had the power of all the heavens at His fingertips, but He never called them down when challenged. Instead, He humbled Himself to the point of death.

TEACHING MOMENT

Children will naturally want to brag on stuff. They may even brag about you (and you must admit you like that). But we have to teach them humility and the right kind of pride. Unfortunately, humility has to be learned firsthand. You can't give them a lesson on it. They have to experience it themselves.

You can model humility for them, and you should, but for them to truly understand it, they have to experience it. I am convinced, however, that once they experience true humility in the name of Jesus, they will know the joy that comes with it.

Are you bowing in humility today? Or are you proud and boastful of who you are? We are nothing outside of Christ. Our only boast-worthy thing is Him. We stand before Him humble and abased. But in Him we boast!

Lord Jesus, You are the perfect example of humility for me to follow. I see Your strength in Your humble life and Your willingness to lay it all down for others. Help me live like You today.

STICKTOITIVENESS

2 Chronicles 8

BEST VERSE: 16

Thus all the work of Solomon was carried out from the day of the foundation of the house of the Lord, and until it was finished. So the house of the LORD was completed.

The temple wasn't a quick project. It took years to complete. Solomon was involved from the foundation up and even oversaw the manufacture of the utensils and all the furnishings. He was determined to stick with it to the end to make sure this temple truly was worthy of Jehovah God.

Isn't it sad, that after all this work on the building that Solomon eventually turned his back on God and began to worship other gods that his wives introduced to him? He was led astray from his own faith. If only his determination regarding building the temple had carried over into his faith.

TEACHING MOMENT

This is a great example to teach our kids. Their faith walk doesn't begin and end at salvation. It is a lifelong process. They must stick with it to the end. God will give them the strength and determination to remain loyal to Him, if they ask. But they can't just check off "the box of faith" and then go on and live as they wish.

As parents, our job is to guide them in this walk. I was asked recently by some parents about the believability of their six-year-old son's salvation. They have questioned and questioned him to make sure his salvation is true. My advice was to believe with him that it is and do all they can to disciple him in his walk. Only God knows for sure the reality of anyone's salvation. Help them "stick with it."

Are you "sticking with it"? Do you have the determination to remain loyal and true to the Lord? What is stopping you from seeing your faith through to the end? The Lord will allow things in our lives to test us in order to make us more like Him. These tests will allow our faith to get stronger. Trust Him in those times.

Father, give me the sticktoitiveness I need to remain loyal and true. Help me to pass on this to my children so they too will see it through.

FEBRUARY 19

GIVING

2 Kings 12

BEST VERSE: 9

But Jehoiada the priest took a chest and bored a hole in its lid and put it beside the altar, on the right side as one comes into the house of the LORD; and the priests who guarded the threshold put in it all the money which was brought into the house of the Lord.

Don't you love to give to others? Don't you love to see the smile on their faces when they receive the gift? Don't you love it especially when they know how much you enjoy giving to them?

It's the same way with the Lord. He loves to receive from us. He doesn't need anything we have to give, but He loves to see us giving to Him out of a loving and gracious heart. You know our gifts to Him, whatever they are and whatever the amount, please Him.

The people had not been giving as they should have to restore the temple. The king went to the priests and basically said, "Enough of this! Let's get this done!" So, they brought out a chest to collect the gifts. It took a visible object beside the altar to stir the people to give.

TEACHING MOMENT

How do we as parents encourage our kids to give? How do we stir their hearts to give to the Lord? Some kids are just natural givers while others squeeze Lincoln until he squeals, as my daddy use to say. How do we show our kids the joy of giving?

Well, they watch us. Now, I'm not just talking about money. We can give in all kinds of ways. Some can give money. Others give time. Still others give of their skills and talents. Find a way for your kids to give to the Lord. And when they do, celebrate that with them. Praise them for their faithfulness. Find ways to bless them so they will be encouraged to give even more.

Perhaps you can make a box for your house where the kids can put money for missions or the homeless. Make it visible! Set a goal! Let them see how the money is used once they collect it. You will be setting them on a lifetime journey of giving that can continue for generations.

Lord, You allow me to give. You allow me to be part of Your work. That is a joy and privilege. Help me show that to others.

FEBRUARY 20

INSULATED, NOT ISOLATED

2 Corinthians 6

BEST VERSE: 14

Do not be bound together with unbelievers; for what partnership have righteousness and lawlessness, or what fellowship has light with darkness?

There is nothing wrong with having nonbelievers as friends. That is not what this verse is saying. We must reach out to the lost and lead them toward our Savior. What Paul is saying is we should not partner with them or work with them on anything that goes against our values as believers. The words "bound together" are really one Greek word (*heterozugeō*) that means unequally yoked. Do you get the picture? That is pretty plain!

TEACHING MOMENT

So how do we teach our children this principle without them thinking we are supposed to stay to ourselves and avoid all contact with the world? Simple, we show them. Unfortunately, we believers are sometimes so involved in our churches that we do not even think about looking around for unbelievers to influence for the gospel.

We are protected by the Holy Spirit, and as long as we stay true to Christ in our beliefs, there is nothing an unbeliever can say or do that can lead us astray. We are insulated by the protective hands of the Father. But we cannot isolate ourselves in our little Christian world and watch as the rest of the world dies in their sins.

Your sons or daughters may make friends at school or on a ball team who are not believers. That is great! Use those friendships to show them how to love those families in Christ. Use those friendships to invite those children to your home where they will be exposed to godly principles and values.

In essence, you are shaping your children to be more and more like Christ by reaching out to those who need the Physician the most. We have the cure for the lost. It's Jesus! Don't keep it to yourself. But as you reach out, make sure you are staying close and true to Him. He will protect you and lead you.

Father, put me in the midst of sinners to be a light. Keep me safe from their influence, but let me influence them to be salt and light.

FEBRUARY 21

JUDGMENT DAY

Isaiah 24

BEST VERSES: 21–22

So it will happen in that day, that the Lord will punish the host of heaven on high, and the kings of the earth on earth. They will be gathered together like prisoners in the dungeon, and will be confined in prison; and after many days they will be punished.

These verses are most likely referring to the judgment that was going to fall on the kings, rulers, and leaders of that time. God was not going to look the other way when those he had placed in authority had abandoned Him. But we can also refer to these verses in reference to the end of times. Now, I am not reading into the verses or taking them out of context. I am just comparing this situation to what will happen later.

God will judge us all. It won't matter what position you held or what your excuse is. God will reward the righteous and punish the wicked. You can bank on that. It is just so critical to understand, though, that we who walk with Christ, have nothing to fear. Sure, we will have our good works judged before God, but our ultimate judgment has been paid for, in advance, by Christ.

TEACHING MOMENT

Our children fear judgment from us, don't they? Oh, I remember hearing those dreadful words from my mom, "Just wait until your father gets home." Man, those were dreaded words. I would watch the clock, knowing that he would be home around 3:05 pm every day. I could hear his truck coming and start to panic.

However, I don't "dread" facing my heavenly Father. I know my debt has been paid. It is so important that we stress that with our own children. If they are "paid up" through Jesus, they have no fear of judgment. They should welcome the day to see their Father in heaven.

Are you welcoming or dreading that day? Are you walking each day with Christ as if it could be your last? Are you following Him in order to obey Him? The Lord God wants you to listen and obey. He wants to bless you.

Father God, thank You for rescuing me from eternal punishment. Thank You for sparing me the "rod" of discipline. You are a faithful God who has promised to welcome me into Your kingdom, fully forgiven through Christ's blood.

FEBRUARY 22

LEGAL REPRESENTATION

Isaiah 33

BEST VERSE: 22

For the Lord is our judge, the Lord is our lawgiver, the Lord is our king; He will save us"

Have you ever had to go before a judge? Have you ever needed a lawyer? I have only had to retain legal counsel a couple of times in my life. Neither time was it my choice. It was a matter of necessity to protect my legal rights in an unpleasant situation. But having an experienced person who knew the legal system was important.

The Lord is our legal system. He knows our guilt but declares us innocent. Not because of anything we have or have not done, but because of His Son's act of taking our guilt and punishment on Himself. As believers, Jesus is advocating for us daily. Shoot, in my case, He is probably advocating every second. But I can rest in the fact that my final verdict reads "Forgiven through the blood of the Lamb."

TEACHING MOMENT

When is the last time you have caught your child red-handed? There was no doubt about their guilt in the commission of a sin. Perhaps they lied to you about something. Perhaps little Blake hauled off and hit little Ryan right in front of you. Perhaps Susie stole something from her brother Caleb. Whatever, you know they are guilty. Here is an opportunity for you to portray forgiveness. They need to know that justice must be served, but this time, you are going to pay the price for them. You want to illustrate very clearly that Jesus has done the same for them for eternity.

Now, you can't do that every time (and there will be more times), or they will begin to think they can "get away" with anything. But what a perfect chance to teach them grace and mercy. There may still be consequences for their actions, but the punishment is removed. Wow! That is what we all have in our judge, lawyer, and king.

Have you forgiven yourself? Have you allowed the Lord to remove the guilt you are feeling for past sins? Don't wallow in the mud. Let the fresh, clean waters of forgiveness wash over you today. Walk in newness. Enjoy the grace and mercy bestowed on you today. That is what our Lord has done for you. Hallelujah!

God, You are a just and holy God! You demand holiness from us, too. I am holy, not because of anything I have done, but because of Your Son. Praise His name.

FEBRUARY 23

IN-LAWS

1 Chronicles 2

BEST VERSE: 17

Abigail bore Amasa, and the father of Amasa was Jether the Ishmaelite.

Isn't it interesting how families form? When you marry into a family, you get a whole other family, warts and all. When your siblings marry, you gain brothers or sisters-in-law. Their choice becomes your family.

The Abigail here in this verse is the sister of David, the king of Israel. Now, we don't know when exactly she married her husband. We don't know if she was older or younger than David. But we do know she married Jether, the Ishmaelite. We just can't choose our siblings' spouse, can we?

TEACHING MOMENT

When it comes time for your son or daughter to marry, I know you pray they will marry someone who loves the Lord and will raise your future grandchildren to honor and love Him. That is why it is so important for you to begin early teaching your children about marriage. What? Carl, you are crazy? Indulge me for a moment.

As you model your marriage as a Christ-centered marriage in which you honor and respect their father or mother, they will see that. You are driving down pegs in their mind as to what a spouse and marriage should look like. You can help direct them as they begin to date by teaching the godly qualities to look for in a mate. In-laws can't be chosen, but you can steer your children's choices.

Back to your in-laws. I bet you have at least one who isn't a believer. Perhaps the Lord led them into your life for just the reason to lead them to the Lord. God has a way of having our paths cross with others for such a reason. Pray how you can reach an in-law for Christ.

Father, thank You for all the family You have given me, in-laws or "outlaws." Help me see opportunities to share Jesus with those who don't know You. I pray today for their salvation.

FEBRUARY 24

SOUNDS FAMILIAR

Isaiah 4

BEST VERSE: 5

Then the Lord will create over the whole area of Mount Zion and over her assemblies a cloud by day, even smoke, and the brightness of a flaming fire by night; for over all the glory will be a canopy.

When I read this verse my mind flashed back to the Exodus of the Hebrew people from Egypt. Do you remember? God led them in the wilderness by a cloud by day and a pillar of fire by night. He protected them from Pharaoh by that pillar of fire all night. You see, the cloud and fire mentioned here in Isaiah are referring to God's presence. Don't you want God's presence in your life?

We may not see a cloud or pillar of fire guiding us, but we can rest assured that God is present with us. How do I know? Because He lives within me through the presence of the Holy Spirit. How do I know that? Because He promised. How do I know that's true? Because He has never broken a promise.

TEACHING MOMENT

Teaching children about the presence of God is no easy task. They want to see something. Try this. Have them stay in one room of the house and you go to another so they cannot see you. Then have them call out to you. Answer them, "Can you see me?" When they say no then ask them, "Then how do you know I am still here?" They will probably laugh and say, "Cause I hear you Daddy." Then say, "How do you know it's Daddy?" They will undoubtedly say, "Cause I know your voice."

Then come back into the room and tell them that's exactly how I know God is here. He speaks to me and I know His voice because of the Holy Spirit in my life. I don't have to see Him to know He's there.

Do you want to know God is there? Then talk to Him. Hear His voice. Feel His presence through the Spirit of God in you. If you are not a believer, I know I just lost you. You can't relate. But I promise if you know Jesus as Your personal Savior, you can hear God if you listen closely.

Father, remind me today of Your presence in my life. Let me hear Your voice as You direct me today.

FEBRUARY 25

WORDS TO LIVE BY

2 Chronicles 20

BEST VERSE: 15C

Do not fear or be dismayed because of this great multitude, for the battle is not yours but God's.

I love this story about Jehoshaphat. A great army is coming down to destroy Judah. So, what does Jehoshaphat do? He turns to God. He calls all Judah to prayer, and God answers. He gives these words to Jahaziel who prophesied to the group.

Look what God said. 1) Do not fear; 2) do not be dismayed; 3) do not fight, and 4) watch God fight. Wow! Those are really good words to live by. We need to turn our battles over to God. He will handle our enemies. What happened to Judah? Nothing. The army which had come to destroy Judah turned on itself and destroyed itself. Our enemies will, in the end, do the same.

TEACHING MOMENT

Your children will face enemies. They may not be a huge army with swords and arrows, but they will feel just as deadly to them. Read them this story. If they, like Jehoshaphat, will turn to the Lord and allow Him to fight for them, their enemies will be defeated. How? I don't know, but He promised He would defeat them.

As a parent, we can show our kids how to rest in God when we face enemies. Once again, they are watching to see how we respond to life situations. Lead them in praying for their enemies. What? Pray for them? Yep, that's what Jesus would do. Remember, Jesus died for them too.

I bet you can name one or two "enemies" you could pray for today. Why not add them to your prayer list with your children? In fact, make sure your children know that these people are not your friends, but they still need prayer, and you have been commanded to pray for them. That will send a clear message to your children.

O Father, you know those who would want to destroy me. I ask You to lead them to salvation. I ask You to bring peace to their hearts. I ask You to give me Your love for them.

BRING THEM BACK

2 Chronicles 19

BEST VERSE: 4

So Jehoshaphat lived in Jerusalem and went out again among the people from Beersheba to the hill country of Ephraim and brought them back to the Lord, the God of their fathers.

What a beautiful picture of love and concern for his people. Jehoshaphat, the king of Judah, is the one who went out to his people to bring them back to the Lord. He was challenged by Jehu, the seer, to seek the Lord. And he did just that.

We have the same challenge today from our Lord. We should be going out to the people to bring them back to the Lord. Our hearts should be broken for the lost around us. If we don't go out to them, they are destined for an eternal destruction. Doesn't that break your heart?

TEACHING MOMENT

Children naturally want to tell people good news. They can hardly keep it a secret. When your little son or daughter comes to Christ, they will want to tell others about it. Teach them how.

We are witnesses through our words, our deeds, our changed lives and our hunger for His Word. Teach your children how to tell their story of salvation to others. Teach them to point others to Jesus by the things they do for Him.

Are you a witness? Are you reaching out to bring others into the fold? We all have a responsibility to do so. It is not just the pastor's job or the missionary's responsibility. Every believer is a minister of the gospel. Take your story to the lost world and tell others about the life-changing power of the Messiah.

Father, I am grateful for the way You have changed me through Your Son. Show me how to spread the news. Give me the boldness and courage to share my story.

JUST DO IT

2 Kings 5

BEST VERSE: 13

Then his servants came near and spoke to him and said, 'My father, had the prophet told you to do some great thing, would you not have done it? How much more then, when he says to you, "Wash, and be clean?"

Probably one of the most frustrating things on earth is putting together a child's toy on Christmas Eve. Am I right? I remember putting together a Power Wheel Jeep for my son one year. We didn't have anywhere to hide it before Christmas, so I had to wait until the night before to put it all together. There must have been a thousand parts. (Okay, I am exaggerating maybe just a little.)

But I just followed the instructions, and at the end of the night it was ready. The next day when my son saw that Jeep and started driving it around, joy filled my heart. He literally drove the wheels off that toy.

TEACHING MOMENT

Naaman just needed to follow the instructions given by Elisha. He was expecting some great moment from the prophet to cure his leprosy, but Elisha told him to go wash in the Jordan seven times. How absurd, right? But when he relented and did it, he was healed.

Our children need to be taught to follow instructions, no matter how silly they may seem. You see, it's not about the rules. It's about obedience. The Lord wants us to follow Him, wherever He leads. Our children will find that by following the rules, by obeying, they will receive the blessings of their parents, but also the blessings of God.

As you read this story of Elisha to your children (and there are many great stories about him) point out the part about following the instructions. Encourage them to be obedient also. Remind them that the only commandment which contains a promise is the one that says for us honor our parents.

Are you following God's instructions for your life? Sometimes what He tells us to do makes no sense. Remember He sees the big picture. He knows your life ten years from now. He sees you in eternity. Trust Him to direct today.

O Father, I know You know all things. Help me trust You with each day as I trust You with my eternity.

FEBRUARY 28

A HOLY INTERRUPTION

2 Chronicles 5

BEST VERSES: 13–14

In unison when the trumpeters and the singers were to make themselves heard with one voice to praise and to glorify the Lord, and when they lifted up their voice accompanied by trumpets and cymbals and instruments of music, and when they praised the Lord saying, "He indeed is good for His lovingkindness is everlasting," then the house, the house of the Lord, was filled with a cloud, so that the priests could not stand to minister because of the cloud, for the glory of the Lord filled the house of God.

God just butts right in, doesn't He? Solomon had built the temple, moved in all the stuff, and began the worship service. Notice the order of how this happens. It says, "when . . . with one voice to praise and to glorify the Lord, and when they lifted up their voice . . . and when they praised the Lord." When praise went up, glory came down.

God's glory was shown to be so powerful the priests could not stand to minister! Have you ever experienced the power of the Spirit like that? I have once. I was in a worship service at a Pastors' conference in Kenya. The praise and worship portion of the service was going on, and, all of a sudden, I could just feel the power of the presence of the Spirit. It felt as if a cloud had entered the room. You could almost reach out and touch it.

TEACHING MOMENT

So, what is the principle to teach our kids from this verse? If they want the presence of God in their lives, they need to praise Him. Praise Him at all times, not just at church. Praise Him when things are bad (glory falls). Praise Him in the good times (glory falls). Praise Him in nature (glory falls). Praise Him whenever (glory falls).

Now what do I mean when I say "glory falls"? I don't expect they will see a cloud like they did in the temple (but they may). But they will sense the very presence of the Holy One in their midst, if they are sincere and pure in their praise. It's not for show. It's surrender.

Are you surrendering your praise to Him today? Are you expecting His glory to envelop you? I am. Every morning as I read His Word and lift His name in praise and as I pray and meditate, I expect His glory to fill me. That requires me to be "confessed up" and ready to receive it. Are you?

Father, we praise You today. We ask that you fill this very room with the majesty of Your glory.

MARCH 1

CHAINED

2 Corinthians 2

BEST VERSE: 14

But thanks be to God, who always leads us in triumph in Christ, and manifests through us the sweet aroma of the knowledge of Him in every place.

I can still hear Ron Dunn, an evangelist I knew, preach "Chained to His Chariot." He used this text to share how we have been made slaves to Christ through our surrender of our will to His. Just as the Roman generals would chain their defeated foes to their chariots and lead them into the city upon their return home, we are chained to the "chariot" of Christ, willingly and obediently following Him.

My problem is I keep pulling at the chains. I want to go my own way. I want to be identified with Christ, but I also want to be the one leading the chariot. Have you ever felt that way? Come on, be honest. We all do from time to time.

TEACHING MOMENT

Obedience and surrender of our will to the Father is a sweet thing, if we will just offer it. It gives us such freedom because everything becomes the responsibility of the Master. He directs our every step. We simply do as He asks. We are not mind-numbed robots, but we are eager to serve and please Him.

Parents, this is exactly why we teach our children obedience. We are preparing them to be obedient to the Father. We are teaching them to be obedient to a future employer. We are simply teaching them submission. A child that won't submit to the authority of their parents is a child destined to struggle in all other relationships in the future. I truly believe that.

So, are you helping your child by letting them have their way? Are you really preparing them for a successful future by allowing them to dictate what and when they do things you have asked them to do? I believe in giving children choices, but there also needs to be some boundaries which they cannot cross.

I don't know about you, but I need to get back behind that chariot, readjust my chains and simply follow my Master. Why? Because I know He will only lead me where He is going!

Where You lead me, I will follow; Where You lead me, I will follow; Where You lead me, I will follow; I'll go with You, with You all the way!

MARCH 2

DON'T GET FLEAS

1 Corinthians 5

BEST VERSES: 9–11

I wrote you in my letter not to associate with immoral people; I did not at all mean with the immoral people of this world, or with the covetous and swindlers, or with idolaters, for then you would have to go out of the world. But actually, I wrote to you not to associate with any so-called brother if he is an immoral person, or covetous, or an idolater, or a reviler, or a drunkard, or a swindler—not even to eat with such a one.

You have probably heard the expression "If you lie with dogs you are going to get fleas." Well, that's kind of what Paul is saying here. He is warning us not to associate with "so-called" brothers or sisters. We have to live in the world; thus, we have to be around unbelievers. But we do not have to hang out with those who pretend to be believers. That is warned against.

Do you know those people? I hope and pray you aren't one of them yourselves. That would not be good for you or the Body of Christ. We should live in a way that we are above reproach and only bring honor to our Lord. I, for one, have been that other brother in the past. Thankfully, the Lord convicted me and has brought me to a place of repentance.

TEACHING MOMENT

This is one truth that our children need to learn. They must be careful when choosing friends, especially those who say they are believers. Today many say they believe, but in reality, they just have the appearance of being believers. It is easier in some places to say you are a believer just to get people off your back. That is not what is expected by us. We must be true to our Lord.

When your children come home and tell you that "so and so" is doing things that you know would bring dishonor to the Lord, counsel your children wisely. They will learn the skill of friend-making from you.

Are you "hanging out" with "unbelieving believers"? You too need to be careful. You don't want fleas, do you? Don't let other "believers" bring you down. Don't let their impure thoughts and actions influence you. Don't let their judgmental attitudes corrupt your walk.

God, I want to be "flea free." Direct me to those believers who can walk with me in this life. They will be my true friends.

MARCH 3

THE REBELLIOUS CHILD

1 Kings 1

BEST VERSE: 5A

Now Adonijah the son of Haggith exalted himself, saying, "I will be king."

From all we know about King David, he was a loving and patient father. In fact, in verse 6 it says David "had never crossed him at any time by asking, 'Why have you done so?'" Adonijah had been loved as a son and never crossed by his father. But he still rebelled.

Sometimes, kids just make bad decisions. Notice I didn't say they are bad children. They just make bad decisions. Why? Because of that ugly sin nature we are all born with. We parents can love and nurture and provide all the right things, but sometimes that sin nature just wins out. Outside the power of the Holy Spirit in their lives, sin wins.

TEACHING MOMENT

Have your little children rebelled against you? Have you felt the sting of resentment from them? Have they questioned your authority as a parent? If not, count your blessings. But don't get all haughty and arrogant and think you have this parenting thing down. We have to stay on our knees, begging God for wisdom to parent every day.

You may know a parent who is beating themselves up for "letting" their child go wild. They may feel it is all their fault when they have tried to do everything right. You need to come alongside them and encourage them. Other parents may have allowed their children too much rope which led to rebellion. But the root cause is not the DNA. The root cause is sin. Every time!

Are you being a rebellious child right now? Are you questioning God's authority in your life? Are you shoving the conviction of the Holy Spirit back down so you can have your way? Stop! Yield! Repent! Return! Let God have your will and make it His own.

Heavenly Father, I come to You today begging for forgiveness. I repent of my rebellious attitude. Let others see my repentance and be drawn to do the same.

MARCH 4

IT'S NOT EXTERNAL

1 Corinthians 7

BEST VERSE: 19

Circumcision is nothing, and uncircumcision is nothing, but what matters is the keeping of the commandments of God.

So many religions focus on the external, what you have to do to be holy. You have to do this or do that. You have to look this way and not eat this food. Paul, who knew all about law-keeping, makes it clear that it is not about what we can or can't do.

Don't forget the fact that this is Paul, the former Pharisee, speaking here. He was a law-abiding Jew before he came face to face with the Lord on the Damascus road. Paul was confident in his abilities to keep the law and wanted to force everyone else to do the same. Christ showed him different and then sent him to preach to the very people he had despised.

TEACHING MOMENT

I bet you have rules for your children to follow. Am I right? Most of us have house rules. There is nothing wrong with rules. However, don't forget that rules are designed to teach, not control. If your children grow up thinking that rules are their dictator, they will rebel. If they understand that rules are meant to teach them to be obedient to authority (parents, teachers, bosses, etc.), they will appreciate the boundaries they have.

Today, all over the world, we see two extremes. On the one hand, young people are rebelling against any kind of authority. They do not want to be told how to do anything. They think they should be able to do whatever whenever with whomever they wish. On the other hand, we have a radical following of Islam that demands obedience or death. Neither is the answer.

Mom and Dad, be firm with your children as you enforce rules, but teach them why there are rules. Your children need to know the why behind the what or it doesn't matter how many rules you have.

Speaking of rules, how many did you break today? Driving over the speed limit, taking that pen from work, or telling that little "white lie" are all examples of how we stretch things. We must be the model for our children in keeping the rules that are set before us, not to be legalistic, but to be obedient.

Law Giver, I know You demand obedience. I want to obey out of love, not fear. I will obey You today. I will allow You to teach me through obeying You.

MARCH 5

BRAVERY REQUIRES TRUST

1 Chronicles 5

BEST VERSE: 20

They were helped against them, and the Hagrites and all who were with them were given into their hand; for they cried out to God in the battle, and He answered their prayers because they trusted in Him.

First Chronicles is full of genealogies, which could seem to be a bit boring. But hold on. You need to read them slowly and see what hidden gems are in those lists. Today for instance, in the genealogy of Reuben, Gad, and Manasseh, this little gem pops out.

These tribes were called valiant warriors, yet they cried out to God when they were in battle. That may appear to show weakness! NO! They knew in whom their strength laid. They knew only the Lord could deliver them and help them conquer the Promised Land. Sadly, just a few generations later, they desert the Lord for foreign gods.

TEACHING MOMENT

We need to teach our children to cry out to God. They need to know in whom to trust. They must rely on Him to fight their battles. But this is one of those lessons that you can't live for them. You can model it for them, but they have to do this for themselves.

You may be asking yourself, What battles do my children really have? Oh, believe me, they have battles of which you are not aware. Temptations galore are out there. Pressure from peers is tremendous. All those battles will be lost unless the Lord fights for them. Show them through prayer and supplication how to trust the Lord.

So, are you crying out and trusting yourself? Are you allowing the Lord to be your shield? Will you trust Him to fight your battles? Put down your sword today. Listen closely to the Great Warrior. Let Him swing His mighty sword in your defense.

O Father God, help me to lay down my own battle gear and pick up Yours. Show me how to trust You, even in the midst of the storms. I claim victory in Your name because it is You who are doing the fighting for me. Hallelujah!

MARCH 6

JUST A GIRL

1 Chronicles 6

BEST VERSE: 3A

The children of Amram were Aaron, Moses and Miriam.

If you read through 1 Chronicles 6, it is a long list of the sons of Levi. It lists and lists and lists all the sons, grandsons, great grandsons, and so on. The list literally goes on and on. But there is only one daughter listed—Miriam, the sister of Moses.

Why do you think she is the only girl listed? She was certainly not the only daughter in that long line of children. Miriam was special because of a number of things. She was the one who put Moses in the river as a baby. She was the one who spoke to Pharaoh's daughter and got her mother as the wet nurse. She was the one who held up the nation of Israel for several days when she was struck with leprosy for making fun of Moses' Cushite wife.

TEACHING MOMENT

This verse is an important one to show your daughters. In a world dominated by men, Miriam stood out and was remembered. Your daughters can stand out too. They can be remembered for standing for God. They can be known as virtuous women who love Jesus. They can be known as great daughters, sisters, mothers or grandmothers.

I am not ignoring what they can do outside the home. But that all starts inside the home. Whatever they grow up to be, it won't matter unless they are known for how they live with family. Teach your daughters to be holy, pure, and modest. Teach them to love others as Christ would. That's much more important than being remembered for their career successes.

Moms, this verse is for you today. How do you want to be remembered? When you come to the end of your days, how do you want your family to remember you? Make those memories now. Be the moms, sisters, daughters, and grandmothers they will hold dear in their hearts long after you are gone.

Lord, thank You for my mother. Thank You for the memories she gave me. Thank You for her loving heart and selfless attitude toward her children.

MARCH 7

NO MATTER WHAT

Job 1

BEST VERSE: 21

He said, "Naked I came from my mother's womb, and naked I shall return there. The LORD gave and the Lord has taken away. Blessed be the name of the LORD."

Don't you just love Job? I mean, come on, he has just lost everything—flocks, crops, children—and he blesses the Lord. Could you say that?

Could you bless the Lord if you lost everything? Could you be like Job? Yes, you could, but only if you abandon any pretense of ownership in your life and recognize God as owner and proprietor of possessions and all that is dear to you.

Do you realize that your clothes aren't your clothes? Do you realize your house is not your house? And do you realize your children are not your children? Nothing in this world truly belongs to us. They are gifts from God. If we hold them with our hands open, if and when they are taken from us, we can willingly let them go.

TEACHING MOMENT

But how in the world do we teach our children such a concept? When we take away a favorite toy as a consequence for bad behavior you would have thought we had cut off a finger. Our kids get way too attached to stuff, don't they? Today every child believes they have a right to a cell phone or tablet computer. We do not help them by indulging them.

Now there is nothing wrong with having stuff. We just have to hold it loosely. One of the best ways I know to show our kids how unimportant things are is to get them involved with a mission opportunity where they can see others who don't have what they have. They can learn that you don't need stuff to be happy. Have them take one of their favorite toys and give it away. Don't force that, just encourage it.

We have been blessed with so much. But when all you have is Jesus, you discover He is all you need!

I am so thankful for the way You have blessed me, Lord. Teach me to give to others and bless them too. But more importantly, help me teach my children to do the same.

MARCH 8

JUST ONE

2 Kings 19

BEST VERSE: 35

Then it happened that night that the angel of the LORD went out and struck 185,000 in the camp of the Assyrians; and when men rose early in the morning, behold, all of them were dead.

God's power is amazing. In this passage today, Sennacherib, king of Assyria, is threatening to destroy Jerusalem. Worse yet, he is mocking the God of Israel. Isaiah tells Hezekiah not to worry. God is going to fight for him. So, God sends one angel (I believe this "angel of the Lord" is Jesus) to destroy Sennacherib's army. 185,000 were killed in one night. Wow!

So, let me ask you a question. Why do you think that same God can't defend you against your enemies? He still has "the angel of the Lord" to send to fight for you. He still has the same power He had back then. He can snap His fingers and bring any enemy we face to their knees.

TEACHING MOMENT

This is a wonderful story to share with your children when they are scared. The people in Jerusalem were scared. This was a great army that was threatening them. But their wise king reached out to the Lord, and the Lord came to their defense.

Our children need to know that the Lord is that close. He has His ear bent toward earth for them also. He longs to be involved in their daily lives, but they must let Him in. When they are scared, teach them to call on His name. When they cry out in the night, go to them and immediately call on the Lord to give them peace.

Are you scared right now about something? What are you facing that sends chills up your spine? Lay it down. Lay it at the feet of Jesus. That "angel of the Lord" loves you and will defend you. He will rescue your heart from fear. Allow Him to soothe your spirit and give you rest.

O precious Lord and Savior, thank you for being my defender. Thank you for coming to my aid in the midst of uncertain times.

MARCH 9

WHO IS THIS SAVIOR?

Isaiah 19

BEST VERSES: 20–21

It will become a sign and a witness to the Lord of hosts in the land of Egypt; for they will cry to the Lord because of oppressors, and He will send them a Savior and a Champion, and He will deliver them. Thus the Lord will make Himself known to Egypt, and the Egyptians will know the LORD in that day. They will even worship with sacrifice and offering, and will make a vow to the LORD and perform it.

This verse has been hotly debated. Did it refer to Alexander the Great or another human "deliverer" who came in and rescued the people? Or, as other scholars think, did it refer to Jesus Christ who would come and rescue all Gentiles? No one can be absolutely sure, at least not until we get to Glory. Right?

We do know that Jesus came to deliver all mankind. He is the only Savior worthy of recognition and praise. He is the only one who has conquered death. He is the only one who can truly save people. No one else ever could or ever will. He is the only one.

TEACHING MOMENT

How is this taught to our children? By showing them His saving power. By showing them how He has delivered you. By showing them His works in and through you and others of faith. Little children need to see actual evidence of Christ working. And there is plenty of evidence. Just look around at your own family and in your own church.

How awesome would it be to invite someone who has such a "deliverance" story to dinner one night so they can tell your children personally how God intervened in their lives? Our children need to rub shoulders with these people. They need to see and hear them tell all about the adventures they have had in Christ.

Then you can help your children begin making a journal of all the things God does or has done in your family. Call it a blessing box and put in a slip of paper listing the blessing each time it occurs. At the end of the year, open the box and reflect on the works of your Savior.

Father, You are the Savior of the world. Whether You are the one referred to in our text today doesn't matter. You are still delivering mankind today. Thank You for all You do!

KEY HOLDER

Isaiah 22

BEST VERSE: 22

Then I will set the key of the house of David on his shoulder, When he opens no one will shut, When he shuts no one will open.

OPEN AND SHUT CASE

Someone has to be in charge. The prophecy concerning Eliakim is an interesting one. Not much is known about him, but he must have been a trustworthy man. To have the key to the house of David was quite an honor. Eliakim alone controlled who came and went.

Aren't you glad that no one restricts our access to the Father? As a believer, we have full access to come to His throne each and every time we need to. No one locks the door on us. We just come, and He receives us.

TEACHING MOMENT

Do you allow your children to lock their bedroom door to keep you out? Stop it! Remember, it's your home. You have the right to access any part of that house anytime. That doesn't mean you don't respect their privacy. Knock before you enter their room. But under no circumstances should they refuse you entry.

You are probably asking, What does this have to do with the verse, Carl? I'm glad you asked. Teach your child that, just like their room is available to you anytime, God's throne room is available to them anytime. God grants complete freedom to us to come and "see" Him. While they may not like us having that freedom to enter their room, God is not like that. He wants us to come in. In fact, He would prefer we just stay right there with Him.

When is the last time you visited God's house? I don't mean church. I mean the place where He dwells. His door is open and never closed. Go to Him now. There's no need to knock. He's expecting you.

I am so thankful that Your door is open and never locked. I want to come and visit often. I want to be at home where You dwell.

A SAFE PLACE

2 Chronicles11

BEST VERSES: 5–6A

Rehoboam lived in Jerusalem and built cities for defense in Judah. Thus he built Bethlehem.

Rehoboam probably had no idea when he fortified Bethlehem as a city of defense in Judah that one day the Messiah would be born there. I think it is only fitting that Jesus would be born in a safe place. After all, He is the safe place. He is the designated Savior of the world. Who better to be from a safe place?

Now, there were a lot of years between Rehoboam and the birth of Christ. I don't know all that happened to the city of Bethlehem in that time, but one thing I do know: it remained the safest place in the world for Jesus to be born. God the Father chose a place to bring an infant into the world that would allow Him to be born safely. He does the same for us. He gives us a safe place.

TEACHING MOMENT

What kind of safe place do your children have? They have you to protect them. They have parents who will do anything to keep them safe, right? But as diligent as you are, you cannot protect their hearts and souls. That is God's job. That is why you must lead them to Him as early as you can.

I get so puzzled by parents who will make their kids go to school, ball-games, and family events, but will let them make their own choice about attending church. Well, they need to make her own mind up about religion. Hogwash! If you allowed them to make their minds up about school, do you think they would go? We cannot make them accept Christ, but we must have them in the environment where He is taught. That's their ultimate safe place—their Bethlehem.

How safe are you today? Are you relying on Him to keep you safe, or are you making it on your own with attitudes that communicate, God, I've got this. That kind of attitude will lead you into very unsafe territory. Turn to the Child of Bethlehem, the fortified city.

God, thank You for sending Your Son to be my safe place. I know I can rest in Him. He will guard my soul and heart.

MARCH 12

UNJUST AND UNCLEAN

Job 25

BEST VERSE: 4

How then can a man be just with God? Or how can he be clean who is born of woman?

The shortest man in the Bible is talking to Job here. This is Bildad the Shuhite (shoe height, get it? You will later, :-). Bildad is telling Job, "There is no man who is just before God, including you!" Oh, what Bildad doesn't know! He assumes Job's guilt. He assumes Job had sinned some terrible sin or sins. But he doesn't know the real story.

Also, Bildad does not know about the coming Messiah. Jesus makes everyone righteous who accepts Him as Savior. We are not made just because of anything we do. It is all because of Him. We are seen as clean because of His shed blood. He makes us just and clean.

TEACHING MOMENT

The next time your son or daughter comes in from a long day of playing outside and is dirty and filthy, this verse should be shared with them as you are cleaning them up. Just like our physical bodies, our spiritual "bodies" are dirty and filthy before Christ. But when we ask Him into our lives and accept Him as our Savior and Lord, we are washed clean. What a perfect visual for your kids.

Kids understand concrete things. Make it visible to them. Let them see the verse come alive. It can mean so much more. Years later, when they are bathing their own children, this verse will come back to them. Unjust to just. Unclean to Clean. The miracles continue.

Do you need a good scrubbing? Have you asked the Lord to make you just and clean? Now is the time. Perhaps you are a believer, but you have been living a life not pleasing to the father. You have gotten sin stained, sins that are already forgiven but are unconfessed. Take those to Him now.

Lord of all, You are the only One who can make me just. Only You can cleanse me. I praise You for the power of Jesus' blood to make this possible in my life.

MARCH 13

BLESSED BY GOD

1 Chronicles 26

BEST VERSES: 4–5

Obed-edom had sons: Shemaiah the firstborn, Jehozabad the second, Joah the third, Sacar the fourth, Nethanel the fifth, Ammiel the sixth, Issachar the seventh and Peullethai the eighth; God had indeed blessed him.

If you just read these verses you may think, Big deal! He had eight sons. Why does that mean God blessed him? Well, you have to go back a little further in the story. Obed-edom was the man who kept the ark after the incident when David was moving it the first time and the cart tilted and Uzziah put his hand out to stop the ark from falling and was killed on the spot. Remember? He welcomed the ark into his home after that.

But then Obed-edom followed the ark to Jerusalem when it was moved the second time by David (this time the proper way by hand). He could have stayed in his home, but he wanted to be near the presence of the Lord. Can you imagine having the ark in your home? How could he not follow it?

TEACHING MOMENT

We don't have an ark to follow today. As followers of Christ, we have something even better. We have the presence of God in our lives through the Holy Spirit. And it will never leave us. That is the message for your children. God blessed Obed-edom for his obedience and faith. God will bless us for the same reason.

It is so exciting to know that no matter where we go, He is with us. Your children need to understand that and believe that. No matter how they are feeling, He is there. No matter what is happening around them, He is there. We just have to acknowledge His presence and rest in it.

Are you aware of His presence today? Do you feel Him working in and through you? He will, if you will let Him. Even though He is there, He will not force Himself on you. He will not turn you into some sort of spiritual robot. But when you yield, He works miracles.

Father, thank You for Your presence in my life today. Help me to yield to Your leading. Let me encourage others along the way.

MARCH 14

FINAL WORDS

Acts 7

BEST VERSE: 60

Then falling on his knees, he cried out with a loud voice, "Lord, do not hold this sin against them!" Having said this, he fell asleep.

If someone was trying to kill you, would these be your last words? I would hope they would be mine, but I am not so sure. Persecution is real! It is happening all over the world right now. Believers are losing their lives just for loving Jesus and telling others about Him. Can we be like Stephen and make those our final words?

TEACHING MOMENT

It's one thing for we adults to claim we can do that, but what about our children? How in the world do we teach them this kind of faith? How do we teach our children that this life is not worth living unless we are willing to lay it down for Jesus? That seems an impossible concept. Let me explain.

Our children aren't ours to begin with. God has blessed some of us with our own precious children. We sacrifice for them. We bandage their knees when they are skinned. We take them to the doctor when they are sick. We spend a lot of money to feed, clothe and educate them. But they aren't ours. And as with everything we are given by God, we hold them it loosely in our hands should He ever ask for them it.

That's the concept! We teach our children that everything we have belongs to Him, even our very lives. So, if and when He asks for our lives, we willingly hand them over. That might mean when we are called upon to lay down our lives for the cause of Christ, we do just that, knowing that being absent from this body means being present with the Lord.

I am sure this devotional thought won't be on your top ten list. But listen Moms and Dads! Hold your children loosely. They don't belong to you! They are His! You are just the stewards of them for a short time. Invest in them and prepare them for Him!

God, I know my children were given to me by You to raise and teach to honor Him. They are Yours, not mine. Thank You, Father, for the privilege of being a part of Your plan for their lives.

MARCH 15

CAN YOU HEAR ME NOW?

Psalms 65–66

BEST VERSE: 66:1

Shout joyfully to God, all the earth.

In the last several years of my dad's life he got extremely hard of hearing. This was caused by forty-five years in a textile mill where the machinery was loud, and they didn't wear ear protection for most of those years. He did break down and get hearing aids, but he would do the funniest things. He was a man of habits. His nightly routine, after dinner, was to sit down at the kitchen table and take out his hearing aids, get his shower and then watch television—WITHOUT HIS HEARING AIDS! Yep! The volume would be on like 70! You literally could feel the volume, so you had to shout to be heard. That's funny now, but not then.

Think how loud our shouts would be if every believer all over the world could shout at the exact same moment to the Lord! I bet you would be able to feel the shouts to God. Wouldn't that be incredible? I don't know how you could arrange such an event, but it would be cool to try.

TEACHING MOMENT

Do you ever tell your children to stop yelling? Do they ever get too loud in the house? Of course, they do. Children can get loud when they are playing or arguing or just being kids.

Wouldn't this be a great verse to share with them the next time you have to call them down for being too loud? Compare their shouts with what

David said here. He said to "shout joyfully to God." You could explain what it means to shout joyfully compared to their shouts.

How would you shout joyfully? What words would you use? How about "Praise You God, my Savior and Lord!" Or "To You I give all honor, and glory and power!" Or how about "You are the Mighty One and my Defender!" It's not so important the words you use as the heart behind the words. Shout joyfully today! Get your family together and shout to Him today. He is listening and will be well pleased!

My heart shouts to You, O God, my Redeemer and Lord. Let my voice lift the rafters as I praise Your name.

MARCH 16

MAKE NO DOUBT

Job 15

BEST VERSES: 34–35

For the company of the godless is barren, and fire consumes the tents of the corrupt. They conceive mischief and bring forth iniquity, and their mind prepares deception.

Eliphaz is at it again. In chapter 15 he is confronting Job's words and accusing him. These verses above, meant to turn Job from his sin, speak truth. Eliphaz assumes Job is in sin and needs to repent. So, we can read these words and hold them to heart if they apply.

The company of the godless is barren! There is no doubt about that. Fire will consume the corrupt one day. These evil people think of mischief and iniquity, and their minds are always deceitful. Evil is Evil! Don't forget that.

TEACHING MOMENT

Our world will teach our children the exact opposite of God's Word. The world will tell them all that "evil" they read about in Sunday School isn't really all that bad. Heck, you don't even have to believe God made you a boy, if you feel like a girl. EVIL!

Our job as parents is simple. We speak truth into our children every day. We point them to the One True God who is the only right one. His goodness can fill them. His love can penetrate them. And when it does, He will reveal to them what evil is.

Have you drunk the Kool-Aid of society? Are you believing the deceit of the evil one? Are you compromising your convictions to fit in? Return to the truth. Call evil what it is—evil. There is no other name.

Thank You, Father, that I can rely on You to always tell me the truth. You are Truth. You know no other way. Help me to always see things with Your eyes.

MARCH 17

IS THERE AN ECHO?

1 Chronicles 22

BEST VERSE: 13B

Be strong and courageous, do not fear nor be dismayed.

Have you ever been somewhere like a cave, large room, or mountain valley where you could yell something and hear the echo? It's pretty cool, especially if you hear your words repeated two or three times before it fades away.

In this passage David is giving his son, Solomon, a charge regarding building the temple for which David had gathered all necessary items and materials. And in the midst of that charge, he repeats the words God told Moses as he prepared to send the people into the Promised Land. Moses shared the same words with Joshua as Moses prepared him to lead the people. And now we hear that echo again in 1 Chronicles.

TEACHING MOMENT

Will you echo those words to your children? Be strong and courageous, do not fear, nor be dismayed. Those are great words for your children. No matter what they face in life, they can rest in the knowledge the Lord God is there.

When your children see you being strong and not weak, being courageous and not cowardly, trusting and not fearing and confident and not dismayed, they will learn to do the same. Do that! Be that!

But perhaps today you are thinking, Carl, I just have too much stuff in my life. It does not matter. God has issued this charge to us today. Those words spoken to Moses, Joshua, and Solomon apply to us just as strongly.

Father, help me be strong, courageous, fearless, and not dismayed. I want to rely on You for everything I need. Let me be that role model for others.

MARCH 18

CONTINUALLY?

Acts 13

BEST VERSE: 52

And the disciples were continually filled with joy and with the Holy Spirit.

I love this verse, but it is a bit puzzling. Paul and Barnabas had been sharing the gospel, and the crowds were building. The Jews get jealous and ran them out of town. This verse follows that. Why were they filled with joy and the Holy Spirit? Paul and Barnabas had been forced out of the district, not just the town.

I believe Paul and Barnabas gave these new disciples some marching orders when they left. "Hey guys, we have to go. But this is your home. You are the ones God is going to use to see these people changed. You have to continue preaching the Good News of Jesus to them." Now those words are not in the Bible, but I believe this is why they responded in the way it says in verse 52: continually filled!

TEACHING MOMENT

We have the privilege to teach our children what it means to be continually filled. Do they see that in you? Or do they just see you put on your "spiritual mask" on Sundays? Do they even hear you mention God's Word or Jesus the other six days? Are you continually filled with joy and the Holy Spirit?

I am not saying you have to walk around with a permanent grin on your face with your hands lifted up. But I am talking about having the shekinah glory all over you. We can shine for Jesus even when we are having a bad day. Our kids need to see that. They need to see us living out our faith when everything is falling apart. They need to hear us speak truth when all around there is uncertainty.

Are you "continually" doing those things? Will you commit today to surrender? Will you let Jesus live out His desires in your life today? He will—if you let Him.

I want to be continually filled with joy and the Holy Spirit just like the disciples were. When I surrender my will to Your Word and Your way, I will automatically be filled with joy.

MARCH 19

WHERE IS YOUR HEART?

Isaiah 29

BEST VERSE: 13

Then the Lord said, "Because this people draw near with their words And honor Me with their lip service, But they remove their hearts far from Me."

Oh man! The Lord will not tolerate lip service. Do you know what that is? It's like when people praise and shout to the Lord on Sunday but live like the devil the rest of the week. Their lips say one thing, but their hearts are somewhere else. They don't even have to "live like the devil." They can just ignore God the rest of the week.

Listen, God doesn't care about your words of praise if your heart isn't praising Him! Our attention should be God-focused at all times, not just while we are at church. Our priority must be "Him first." Nothing else is as important.

TEACHING MOMENT

Don't let your children fall into this trap. Hold them accountable. Don't let them play pretend with God. That's cute when they are little and playing dress up. That's cute when they are walking around in your adult shoes and wearing your jewelry. It isn't cute when they are pretending spiritual things.

I have seen too many children pretend to be such Christ followers around other believers, when they are disrespectful to their parents and other adults. That is giving lip service. Confront those attitudes. If you don't, they will grow up thinking they can get by with this all their lives.

Maybe you are playing pretend with God. Maybe you are acting one way in public and another way at home. God demands honesty. He will not tolerate you making a mockery of His name and your relationship with Him. It is too holy.

O Lord, I am so guilty of not being honest with You so many times. I want to give You my all at all times. Forgive me of my lip service. Help me teach others to give You all.

MARCH 20

ORDER

1 Corinthians 11

BEST VERSE: 3

But I would have you know, that the head of every man is Christ; and the head of the woman is the man; and the head of Christ is God.

I will probably get cards and letters (or, in this day and age, lots of emails) by posting this devotional thought. That's okay. I didn't say it—God did. Okay, on with the thought.

God has given us specific guidelines on how a home should be established. The man is the leader, and the woman is his partner. Notice I didn't say his slave, servant, or subservient mate. But God does establish the fact that the man should be the leader in the home just as the man is to follow Christ. Christ is his leader, and the man is his wife's leader.

Unfortunately, we men have given up our leadership role, or worse, we have polluted it and made it something totally wrong. We have to re-establish proper roles in our Christian homes if we truly want to see God bless them. I am calling out all the men to step up to their God-given responsibilities. I am calling out all women to be obedient to the role God has given you.

I attended a wedding last night with my wife and our three grandchildren. The wedding vows they said included the duties of the husband and the wife to each other. I was praying that our grandchildren were listening and not just watching. At their young ages it is so important to learn these roles.

TEACHING MOMENT

Moms and Dads, in your roles as husband and wife, live out God's principles of marriage. Live out the order God has established for the home. Let your children see it in you. Let them see Jesus in the very order of your home.

I am forever thankful for the roles You have given us, God. From the dawn of creation to the very moment You have given us duties to perform. Help me teach my children these roles from Your Word and not from the world.

MARCH 21

I CAN'T SEE

Job 17

BEST VERSE: 7A

My eye has also grown dim because of grief.

Job's days aren't getting better. He says he is grieving so much his eyes are getting weak. Have you ever wept so much your eyes swelled up? I have. I remember one time I cried so hard, and my eyes swelled so big that someone thought I had been punched.

Grief is a horrible thing and a wonderful thing. Grieving, in and of itself, is not a bad thing. Grieving allows us to vent emotions over the loss of something or someone. These emotions need to come out for us to remain healthy. But too much grief, unresolved grief, will lead to depression and worse. Give your grief over to the Lord, which Job has not done yet in chapter 17.

TEACHING MOMENT

Have you seen your child grieve yet? It's a horrible sight for a parent. It's a helpless feeling to see them hurting and crying. There is literally nothing we can do to stop it. All we can do is pray with them and for them and hold them. If you haven't experienced this yet, you probably will sooner or later.

How do we teach "proper" grieving? How do we teach godly grief? Only by modeling it to them and taking them to the Word. Kids learn by example. If they see us holding on to our own grief, they won't learn to let go of their grief. If they see us using grief as an excuse for behavior, they will learn to do the same. Like I said earlier, grief can be healthy if handled correctly. But it must be given to Jesus. He understands your grief.

Are you grieving right now over something in your life? Do you have unresolved grief? Hand it over to the Master. He gave you that heart, and He knows how to ease the pain. Trust Him with your emotions.

Heart Maker, take my emotions and turn them Godward. Take my hurt and grief and turn them into joy. Help me be the kind of example of godly grief to which others can turn.

MARCH 22

STUPID

Psalms 91–92

BEST VERSES: 92:6–7

A senseless man has no knowledge, nor does a stupid man understand this: That when the wicked sprouted up like grass and all who did iniquity flourished, it was only that they might be destroyed forevermore.

I know what you are thinking. We don't use the word "stupid" in our house! Well, I agree, but here it is in God's Word. The Hebrew word for "stupid" in this verse can be translated as fool or stupid man. So, if God uses the word in His Word, I guess it is a legitimate word. Right?

But the word itself is not the psalmist's point. The point is what follows. Verse 7 says the fool or stupid man does not understand that although the wicked seem to be getting away with everything, they will be punished. Have you ever felt that way? It seems the wicked just keep getting richer while you struggle to make ends meet.

TEACHING MOMENT

I bet your kids come home sometimes complaining about a neighbor kid who is mean and gets all the cool toys. They don't ever get punished by their parents. Your kids don't understand that. That is the time to pull out this verse. Explain to them that one day those people will suffer a much harsher punishment. But your children will grasp the importance of obedience and humility.

It's hard for little boys and girls to see that, I agree. It's hard for teens to grasp it. But as we continue to pour the Word of God into their hearts and minds, they will begin to get the bigger picture. You see, the fools or stupid only see what's in front of them. The wise see the eternal, and that is the important thing.

How are you doing, Mom and Dad? Are you so focused on now that you don't see ahead? Are you so worried about your children now that you are not preparing them for eternity? Forget your worries of today. Turn them over to the Lord.

I will focus on the eternal value of things today. I will look at everyone I encounter through Your eyes. Lord, give me the wisdom and understanding I need.

MARCH 23

JUST WHEN THINGS WERE GOING SO GOOD

2 Chronicles 32

BEST VERSE: 1

After these acts of faithfulness Sennacherib king of Assyria came and invaded Judah and besieged the fortified cities, and thought to break into them for himself.

This may seem a strange verse for a devotion, but it struck me hard. Hezekiah had been a good king. He had restored worship in the Temple, destroyed the idols in the land and was providing for the priests. He had done so many wonderful things and God seemed to be blessing the nation. Everything was rosey!

But this verse says, "After these acts of faithfulness." You would expect it to continue "and God blessed Hezekiah and Judah with many wonderful things." Nope! It goes on to say that Assyria invades. "What? All this good stuff we are doing and now God is abandoning us?" Those were probably the thoughts of the people and maybe even Hezekiah.

Why does God allow trials in our life just when things are going so well? There is no easy answer, but one thing is for sure: He only wants what is best for us. God never allows things to come into our lives to tear us down. He is always about making us more like Him—even if it means allowing a severe trial.

TEACHING MOMENT

Our children need to learn from us that trials are expected. Trials are not bad, just difficult. God wants us to trust Him. Our children need to see us trusting Him even when things seem to be going all wrong. Even when we can't see the solution, we know the problem solver. Even when all hope SEEMS lost, He is faithful.

Hezekiah was faced with an overwhelming enemy force, yet he trusted Jehovah. Hezekiah never had to lift a finger in defense of his country. God did the fighting for him. Won't we let God fight for us? With one word He can wipe out the enemy. Trust Him to come to you when you cry out. Wait for Him to yield the sword of battle. Bow before Him so your children can learn to bow too. Let them see the mighty deliverance of their Father.

I am thankful, Lord, for the abundant days You give. But I also know when hard times come You are still there. You are faithful to me in all times.

MARCH 24

IMPORTANT WORDS

Isaiah 16

BEST VERSE: 5

A throne will even be established in lovingkindness, and a judge will sit on it in faithfulness in the tent of David; moreover, he will seek justice and be prompt in righteousness.

Isaiah is telling the nation that the throne of their king will be reestablished. You have to recall that they had undergone judgment from God through which He had used pagan nations to punish them. But now the time has come for their own king to be seated on the throne again.

What struck me in this verse, though, is the descriptive words of the throne. It will be a throne of lovingkindness, faithfulness, justice and righteousness. Who does that sound like to you? That's right, Jesus. He is all those things, and He sits on His throne forever.

TEACHING MOMENT

Do you like role playing? Sometimes, with kids, it helps them learn a concept. This would be a fun verse to roleplay. Set up a chair in the house somewhere and make a crown for son to wear. Give him a scepter (a spatula makes a great one, lol). And now here comes the fun part. Have his siblings or friends be the subjects. Let him rule over them and make some "proclamations."

Now, don't give him any instructions on the type of laws. Just let him "reign." After he gets through, read this verse and compare how he reigned and how the king in this verse reigned. I bet you will find a vast difference.

We do the same, don't we? We may not sit on a throne, but we think we do. Do we "reign" over our households with lovingkindness? Do we show our family that we are faithful to them? How about justice and righteousness? We can learn a lot from this throne. How will you reign today?

Father, I am not worthy to lead, but You have chosen me to do just that. Help me lead with these qualities today.

MARCH 25

HIS SHEEP

Psalms 79–80

BEST VERSE: 79:13

So we Your people and the sheep of Your pasture will give thanks to You forever; to all generations we will tell of Your praise.

I am not sure how I feel about being called His sheep. After all, sheep aren't the smartest critters. But then again, neither am I. I need a shepherd. I need someone to lead me beside still waters. I need someone to take me to the grazing fields. I need someone to watch over me and protect me from my enemies. I guess I am a sheep.

And my job as a sheep is to give thanks to Him forever and tell all generations about His praise. Sheep talk to sheep, right? So, I have to talk to other people. I have to tell others about how great my shepherd is. I will tell them how much He loves me. I can praise Him and thank Him so that the other generations see and hear me.

TEACHING MOMENT

Get your children to make a list of all the things they are thankful for. Let it be their list. When they are done, tape it to the mirror in the bathroom or their bedroom. Let it be a daily reminder of God's faithfulness. Teach them to share these "blessings" with others, too.

Have them make a list of people they want to share Jesus with. This could be family, friends, or someone they just met. Help them figure out how to do that. Better yet, let them watch YOU share with someone on your list. Yes, you need a list, too. You need to be sharing so they will see how it's done.

Aren't you excited to tell someone good news you have received? Then why wouldn't you tell them about the greatest news? Tell them about Jesus. Tell them about His greatness. Tell them how much He loves them and wants them to be part of His flock of sheep.

Lord, place people in my path today with whom I can share about You. Let me be Your mouthpiece. Give me the words You want me to share.

MARCH 26

IF YOU'RE HAPPY AND YOU KNOW IT

Psalms 97–98

BEST VERSE: 97:12

Be glad in the LORD, you righteous ones, and give thanks to His holy name.

How many times have you seen someone you know who is a believer with the biggest scowl on their face? You want to say, "Tell your face you are saved." Now, I know no one can smile all the time, but goodness gracious alive, some Christians never look happy.

Look at the verse for today. "Be glad in the Lord, you righteous ones, . . ." What part of that verse implies frowns or sad faces? Nothing! We should let the world know of the joy in our hearts. Not to do so robs them of the blessing we can be to them when they ask, "Why are you smiling?"

TEACHING MOMENT

Smiling isn't an instinctive thing so don't just assume your children will know how. That may sound strange. But children will learn to mimic you in your facial expressions. Why not show them smiles rather than frowns? Don't fake it though. They will see through that sooner or later. Let the joy of Jesus show on your face to them.

There is nothing much worse than for your child to see you suddenly change expressions when the phone rings or someone crosses your path. They will probably think, "Why wasn't Mom smiling with me? Why did Daddy get all happy around them and not me?" Smiles are contagious. Spread them.

Watch your expressions today. Try to consciously smile more. People will probably ask you why you are smiling so much. What a great opportunity to tell them how much Christ loves you. That is why you smile. That is why you have such joy in your heart.

Thank You Lord for the smile You have put in my heart. Help me to spread that joy as much as I can with my smile. Let my smile speak without words.

MARCH 27

HOLY KISS

2 Corinthians 13

BEST VERSE: 12

Greet one another with a holy kiss.

Our world has so polluted affection that even reading this verse gives us pause. What would happen if next Sunday someone greeted you at the church door with a kiss? You would be repelled. You would be shocked. You would be horrified.

But Paul says this is how we should greet our brothers and sisters in Christ. It does say "holy" which means it can be nothing but sanctified and special. There is nothing wrong with a holy kiss. It is done to express our true expression of love and closeness. Unfortunately, we have made a kiss something unholy.

TEACHING MOMENT

Don't you love your children's kisses? I remember when our children were just babies and toddlers. They loved to shower (literally sometimes with their baby drool) us with kisses. They would slobber all over our cheeks. As parents we loved that. But now, in the age we are living, we warn our children to not show much affection for others for fear of being misinterpreted. I guarantee you Jesus would be greeting us with a kiss.

So how do you follow this instruction from Paul and not offend someone? The same way we do anything else as believers. We walk in oneness with each other and never do anything to offend. You know who would receive this as it is intended and who would not. The Holy Spirit guides you. Your children have to learn to let the Holy Spirit guide them in this and every other aspect of their walk.

Now, let me be clear. I am not telling you to kiss everyone you meet next week at church. I am telling you, however, to love them and honor them. And, by all means, greet them with the love of Jesus.

Father God, I want to feel Your kisses on my face each day. Allow me to spread Your love with affection and sincerity each day.

MARCH 28

WHERE DOES YOUR STRENGTH COME FROM?

Acts 9

BEST VERSES: 19, 22

And he took food and was strengthened. But Saul kept increasing in strength and confounding the Jews who lived at Damascus by proving that this Jesus is the Christ.

Paul has just been saved after meeting Christ on the road to Damascus. He had been blind for three days until Ananias came, and the scales fell from his eyes. These two verses both use the word "strengthened" or "strength," but interestingly enough, they are two different words for "strength" or "strengthen" in the Greek. Verse 19 uses the Greek word *ischus*, which deals more with physical strength or health. Verse 22 uses *dunamoo*, which relates more to the power to perform.

Okay, I probably just lost you. No, listen! Verse 19 focused on getting Paul physically healthy after his encounter with Christ, and verse 22 shows the empowering of God in his life to face the Jews. God was the source of healing and empowering. He was at work in all aspects of Paul's conversion, physically and spiritually.

TEACHING MOMENT

Our children need to know that God has His special touch for each aspect of our lives. When we are physically weak or sick, God can reach down and heal. When we are spiritually weak or weary, God can give us the power to rise up. He wants to work in every part of our life, but we have to allow Him to do that.

Paul was made blind for a purpose. Remember, he was a learned man and may have just jumped on his own agenda. God made him rely on others to even get to Damascus after being struck blind. He made him rely on Ananias for healing. He made him rely on Him to have the power to confront the Jews.

Our children have to learn to completely rely on God. It doesn't matter what they are facing, the only strength that matters is His, not theirs. Won't you model that also? Won't you show them that you too rely on God for the strength to carry on?

Giver of life, I know You are the Sustainer. I know I am totally dependent on You for my existence. I want to depend on You for each and every thing I do and say.

MARCH 29

BIRTH NAMES

Isaiah 9

BEST VERSE: 6

For a child will be born to us, a son will be given to us; and the government will rest on His shoulders; and His name will be called Wonderful Counselor, Mighty God, Eternal Father, Prince of Peace.

My dear, sweet mother was born in the South and had a beautiful southern drawl. You know what I mean? But one part of her southern drawl had her put a "r" on the end of a lot of words that just didn't have it. For instance, instead of saying "window," she would say "windor."

So, when we named our first child, we named him with a name that ended with an "r," Christopher. We were going to name him Joshua, but we didn't want to hear Joshuar all his life. I sure miss my momma. I would give anything to hear her say that now.

TEACHING MOMENT

Jesus was named long before He came to earth. He was given many names, as we see in our verse today. And He lived up to every one of them. How about your children? Did you name them what you did for a reason or just because you liked the name? Let me encourage you, if you haven't, to research the meaning of their name. And when you have the meaning, make sure your kids know it.

Now, a name doesn't determine one's destiny. Only God can determine that. But our children should be taught to carry their names proudly. Their names and their reputations mean something. When they are referred to by others, their names should stand for integrity, honesty, trustworthiness, and loyalty. We should all have that kind of reputation as believers. We carry His name as Christians—CHRIST-ians.

Are you carrying His name proudly? Are you fulfilling the meaning of His name? Whatever you do or wherever you go, make sure you live up to the standards Christ set. We are to be holy and set apart. That doesn't mean isolated from others, but it does mean we are different and should act different.

Lord, help me bear the name of Christ proudly and unashamedly. Let me be known by others as one who stands for Christ at all times. Let others see Jesus in me.

JUST ONE DAY

Psalms 83–84

BEST VERSE: 84:10A

For a day in Your courts is better than a thousand outside.

Don't you just love this verse? Can you imagine standing in the court of God? Many people fear that. I don't. Why? Because I am welcomed. I am an heir to His kingdom. He extends His scepter towards me in a gesture of acceptance. I had rather spend seconds with Him than eons without Him.

Being in God's court means You can see Him rule and reign. Being in God's court means You can observe His mercy and grace. Being in God's court means You can see the multitudes who are bowing before Him. Nothing will compare with being in His court.

TEACHING MOMENT

Take your child to court. Now, I don't mean to get him straightened out. Let them observe a court room. Most kids have never seen that, so this verse doesn't make sense to them. If possible, let them meet a judge. Explain to them what the judge does. He dispenses justice. That's his job.

Let them walk up to the judge's bench. While sitting up there you can see the whole courtroom. Nothing is hidden from your view. That's how it is with God. He rules from above and can see all eternity. His rule is just and fair. He rules equally.

Where are you in the courtroom? Are you trembling before our holy Judge? I hope not. I pray you are there just in awe of His presence. I pray you walk in without trepidation or fear, knowing that Jesus is your defense. The accuser may come, but his arguments against you fall short. If that isn't you, make it so today.

Judge of all, I stand before You innocent because of Jesus. My case has been dismissed. I praise You for the mercy and grace You extended me.

UNKNOWN POTENTIAL

ESTHER 2

BEST VERSE: 7

He was bringing up Hadassah, that is Esther, his uncle's daughter, for she had no father or mother. Now the young lady was beautiful of form and face, and when her father and her mother died, Mordecai took her as his own daughter.

Every time I look at a room of children, I wonder what will become of them. I wonder how many of them will become doctors or lawyers or preachers. How many will marry and have children? Will one of them grow up and find a cure for a horrible disease? You just never know the potential that lies in the room.

Mordecai adopted his first cousin, Hadassah (Esther), because her parents were dead. He had no idea when he did that she would eventually be chosen as the queen to Ahasuerus. He had no idea that a threat to kill all the Jews would be imposed. He had no idea Esther would be used by God to rescue His people. You see, you just never know.

TEACHING MOMENT

Your children have such hidden potential. I know sometimes you wonder if you are going to survive their child rearing. You will, and you will be amazed how they will turn out. But the secret to child raising has nothing to do with you. It's all up to the Lord. You have to allow Him to have them. Turn them over to Him and allow Him to teach them.

Your little Johnny may grow up and be a great evangelist. Susie may be a missionary to an unreached tribal group. Whatever they turn out to be, and however God chooses to use them, you need to prepare them for service. I am sure Mordecai raised Esther in such a way that she was worthy to be chosen as queen. Just do your part.

Did you know God wants to use you every day? He does. But He can't unless you are willing to be used. God doesn't force us. He desires us to surrender to His Will. Let Him use you today to shape the lives of your children and others toward service to Him.

Father God, I want to be used today. I want to see my children used by You. Show me how to prepare them for when You call them to active duty.

THAT'S DISCRIMINATION!

Nehemiah 7

BEST VERSES: 64–65

These searched among their ancestral registration, but it could not be located; therefore, they were considered unclean and excluded from the priesthood. The governor said to them that they should not eat from the most holy things until a priest arose with Urim and Thummim.

If you read these verses without knowing the reason you would think Nehemiah was being prejudiced or discriminatory. In today's society he would probably be sued by these individuals, and they would win a million dollars. That's now and not then.

God had delegated one tribe to serve as priests—the Levites. It was imperative that only men from the lineage of Levi serve in that capacity, and that they serve exactly how God prescribed. Until these men could prove their lineage they could not be allowed to serve in the temple. The reason the people of Israel and Judah had been sent into exile in the first place was their disobedience to God's order. Nehemiah wasn't going to repeat that.

TEACHING MOMENT

Our children must learn that there are certain guidelines which God sets for us. And they must follow these guidelines if they want to be obedient to Him. Today everything is gray. There is no black and white. The "line in the sand" keeps getting moved. The world will tell them "right" is relative. No! It's not.

As we parent our children, they are going to feel we are being unfair when we enforce our rules and God's Word. That's okay. Structure and order are important. Disorder is not of the Lord. Now, the Lord isn't OCD, but He does have lines drawn to keep us safe. Listen to Him.

Are you standing on the edge of the line right now pushing the limits? Are you seeing just how far you can go without falling? Back up. Take another look at the order of God's Word and thank Him for it. All His commands are for your protection.

O Heavenly Father, I know sometimes I complain about having to follow Your rules. But I want to thank You today for keeping me in line. Thank You for giving us all order in our lives.

APRIL 2

SHOUT!

Psalms 95–96

BEST VERSES: 95:1–2

O come, let us sing for joy to the Lord, let us shout joyfully to the rock of our salvation. Let us come before His presence with thanksgiving, let us shout joyfully to Him with psalms.

Loud people can really be obnoxious, can't they? Some people just have to make sure everyone hears them. They are loud, but for the wrong reasons.

I love that the psalmist says here to "shout joyfully." We are to sing for joy, come before Him with thanksgiving and shout joyfully! Doesn't that sound fun? Doesn't that sound like a celebration. He is worthy of our praise.

TEACHING MOMENT

Now here's a skill that won't be hard to teach to our kids. Being loud is just part of being a kid. We will, however, have to teach them how to do it with joy. Our joy needs to be directed at God, our Father and Redeemer.

The next time you are having family time in the Word, make a list of great things about God. Write down several. And then . . . shout them to the Lord. I promise your kids will like this and ask to do it again soon. Sing praises to Him. March into your den or living room with thanksgiving. Act out these verses.

Are you marching in thankfulness today? Are you singing praises? Are you shouting joyfully or just shouting? Take a minute and evaluate your own quiet times. These are times when you can also "act out" these verses. Have a private celebration. Enjoy your God.

Father, You are worthy of all praise. You are worthy of our shouts of joy. You are worthy of our thanksgiving.

COME ON IN

Romans 5

BEST VERSES: 1–2

Therefore, having been justified by faith, we have peace with God through our Lord Jesus Christ, through whom also we have obtained our introduction by faith into this grace in which we stand; and we exult in hope of the glory of God.

I love this passage. The word "introduction" in verse 2 is the main point to me. The word actually means "access, admission." Let me try to give you an example.

I left home pretty much at age 17 to go off to college. I came home from time to time and even still had my own house key. But there came a point when I gave that key back to my dad. But I knew my dad and mom kept a key to their house hidden outside. I knew where it was. Do you know what that meant? It meant I could go home anytime, take that key, open the door and walk right in. Why? Because that was still my home. I was always welcome. I could go in and get some good ole sweet tea from the fridge (it was always there) and even grab some food. It was home.

TEACHING MOMENT

We need to teach our children that the Father is always welcoming them home. Once they receive Jesus as their personal Lord and Savior, they too have a key to His house. That key is Jesus. That key gives us access to all the riches of heaven. We will never be homeless if we have Jesus in our lives.

No matter where your family lives or how many times you move, your heavenly home is always in the same spot and is always open for you. But let me ask you these questions. What are you bringing home? Who are you bringing home? Are you sure you are going home? That's your homework for today. Talk to your children about your heavenly home. I know they would love to hear all about it.

Jesus, You dwell in home sweet home! My home is heaven. I long to see it. I long to live with You, but let me leave here having left a lasting imprint of You on others.

NOW WHAT DO I DO?

1 Kings 14

BEST VERSE: 12

Now you, arise, go to your house. When your feet enter the city the child will die.

You need to read the entire chapter of 1 Kings 14 to get the full story. Short version—Jeroboam had disobeyed God, and God could not stand for that. In this verse, Ahijah the prophet is telling the wife of Jeroboam that their son is going to die.

What would you have done? I think I would have stayed gone so he could live. After all, Ahijah says, "When your feet enter the city..." I would have been thinking if I stayed out of the city he could live. We know nothing about this mother, but she must have believed Ahijah's words were from God and would come true.

TEACHING MOMENT

Our children need to be taught that God's Word is God's Word. Nothing we can do can change that fact. When it says "obey your parents," it means obey your parents. When it says "do not lie," it means do not lie. What He says He means.

But listen to me parents. We model that when we tell them something. We can't waffle on our words either. We are to be a model for them to follow. If we are never following through, they will begin to think that no one will, even God. We model God's Word with our actions.

What has the Lord told you lately? Have you heard Him in your prayer life? Have your heard Him speak through His Word. Then you had better "take it to the bank." His Word will come through. Trust His Word. Trust Him!

Oh Lord my God, help me hear when you speak. Help me to listen to Your directions and commands. And help me lead others to trust You too.

TRUST NO ONE

Isaiah 31

BEST VERSE: 1

Woe to those who go down to Egypt for help and rely on horses, and trust in chariots because they are many and in horsemen because they are very strong, but they do not look to the Holy One of Israel, nor seek the LORD!

There was a television series on in the 90's called *The X-Files*. I am a bit of a sci-fi geek, so I really loved this show. Fox Mulder and Dana Scully were the main characters who tried to solve cases involving extraterrestrials (you know, ETs). Fox's main motto was "Trust No One." The problem with that, however, is no one's got your back.

We don't have to worry about that as believers. God has our back. We can completely and totally trust Him. It doesn't matter what we are facing, He is there. When we are at our lowest, He's there. When we are fighting depression, He's there. When we are jubilant, He's there. Isaiah was trying to tell the people to not trust in other nations to defend them. Trust Jehovah God.

TEACHING MOMENT

Trust is something that is very hard to teach our children. Heck, it's hard to teach anyone. I have heard it said that trust is the glue that holds relationships together. You trust your children until they break that trust. You forgive them and start building that trust again. The best way you can teach trust is by being trustworthy.

How do you do that? One way is by keeping your promises. When you say you are going to take them to the park, take them. When you tell your daughter you will be at her piano recital, be there. When you tell your son you will take him fishing, take him. This will teach them to trust you and help them learn to trust others as well.

But we must be constantly pointing them and others to trust in our Savior. You will let them down. God will never do that. You will disappoint others. God never disappoints. Won't you trust Him today? Won't you let Him prove Himself faithful? He is not scared of being trusted. He is complete trust.

O God, You are the faithful One. I know I can place my complete trust in You. Show me ways to teach my children what that means so they will trust You with their lives.

APRIL 6

HYPOCRISY

2 Chronicles 23

BEST VERSE: 13C

Then Athaliah tore her clothes and said, "Treason! Treason!"

When Athaliah's son, Ahaziah, was killed, she decided to usurp the throne herself. So, she killed all the royal family of Judah. This is the woman who had committed treason herself by hollering, "Treason! Treason!" That is, as the saying goes, the pot calling the kettle black. She was the ultimate example of hypocrisy. It is like someone striking a match and burning a house down while yelling, "Fire! Fire!"

But do you know what I thought of when I read this? We are the same. We don't kill people, but we point at their sins and scream, "Sinner! Sinner!" All the while, we are just as guilty of our own sin. When is the last time you have "judged" someone for their sin? Remember, when you point your finger at others there are three fingers pointing right back at you.

TEACHING MOMENT

I bet your little Johnny or Susie have come home talking about someone at school or church. All kids do that. As the parent, you need to nip that quickly. Playing judge is not only wrong, it's not fair. As I mentioned above, we all have issues. Some are just more visible than others.

But do your children hear you judging others? Do they watch you putting people down for their "faults"? They will model what they see in you. If you want them to treat others like Jesus, guess what? You have to do the same.

Will you today be extra cautious of judging others? Make a point to see their strengths rather than their weaknesses. Find a way to build them up and not tear them down. You will feel much better about them and yourself at the end of the day.

Father, I am thankful that You see me with eternal eyes. Help me see Jesus in others and not their failures. Give me the words today to encourage someone.

APRIL 7

FIRST AND LAST

Isaiah 44

BEST VERSE: 6

Thus says the LORD, the King of Israel and his Redeemer, the LORD of hosts: "I am the first and I am the last, and there is no God besides Me."

We find it hard to understand this. If you are the first person in a line, you can't be the last person. Let me explain it this way. If you are elected as president of a brand-new club, you would be the first president. Then, if that club disbands while you are president, you would be the last president. You would be the first and last.

That is a feeble attempt to use an earthly example to explain a heavenly concept. But God was the first in anything. Nothing existed before Him, and nothing will exist after Him. He is the last. Remember, time is eternal to God. He sees all of eternity in one glimpse.

TEACHING MOMENT

So, what does that mean for you and your children? It means God has been and will always be there. He is the only true God. When He says, "I will be there," He means it. He is not going anywhere. Your child may have had people leave them. That is not who God is. He is there—period.

Children need security. There is no greater security than knowing that God is always by our side. Even when we can't see Him working, we know He is there. Just knowing that gives us peace.

Do you have that peace? Do you rest knowing that God is the first and last? Beloved, rest! Rest knowing that He will never fail or forsake you. Rest knowing that Jesus is interceding on your behalf before the Eternal One. He is there.

O God, You are the first and last. You are always. You are eternal. You are the only true God, and I praise You.

EAT LIKE A BIRD

1 KINGS 17

BEST VERSE: 6
The ravens brought him bread and meat in the morning and bread and meat in the evening, and he would drink from the brook.

Let me tell you no one has ever accused me of eating like a bird. I love to eat. I am not extremely picky, so when my wife and I are trying to decide where to go out to eat, I leave it up to her. I can eat just about anything.

I have also never been fed by a bird. I bet Elijah hadn't either—before the events in this chapter. So, when the Lord said to go to the brook, "and I will send the ravens to feed you," he was probably thinking, "I can't wait to see this." Remember, ravens are not the most generous birds. In fact, they are quite stingy and are even known for scavenging food. For God to use this bird to feed someone was quite a miracle.

TEACHING MOMENT

The next time your children have to share a piece of cake or pie, tell them this story. Tell them how God even instructed the ravens to share food with Elijah. God sustained him for a long time with the bread and meat. So, surely, they can share a little food with each other.

But the main point of the story is that God is the source, not the birds. God provided the bread and meat. It was just delivered by the ravens. Perhaps you and your children could deliver some food to a needy individual or family. If God can use birds, He can certainly use you and your children.

Who can you help today? Is that person on the street corner holding the sign an object of scorn for you or an opportunity to be used of the Lord? You don't know their story. Maybe God has placed them there to test you, not them.

Provider of all I have, remind me daily how you are my source for everything. You are the one who provides my daily bread. Help me be an example to others of Your provision and grace.

TALKING BACK

Isaiah 45

BEST VERSE: 9

Woe to the one who quarrels with his Maker-an earthenware vessel among the vessels of earth! Will the clay say to the potter, "What are you doing?" Or the thing you are making say, "He has no hands"?

The absurdity of it all! Clay talking back to the potter? That is just dumb! The clay has no right to question the hands that are forming it. The clay doesn't know the intention of the potter. The clay has no idea the purpose for which it is being made. How dare it talk back!

Sounds funny, huh? But we are the same as the clay. We have no idea of the perfect plan God has for us. We have no right to question when He pushes and pulls us into shape. We may become a beautiful vessel to be displayed in a store window, or we may become a pot to cook in. The key is God is the one who knows best.

TEACHING MOMENT

Okay, it's time to get out the playdough again, either homemade or store bought. Let's get the kids to make something. (They are God in this scenario.) As they are forming it, start talking as if you are the playdough. Tell them to stop smashing you. Tell them that hurts. Tell them what you want to be. Make sure it's something that is impossible to make.

When your kids stop laughing, tell them how silly it sounds to God for us to do the same. We all have to trust the hands of God to form us into what He wants to use to accomplish His will. Now ask your children what they want to make with the playdough. It's the same with God. We need to ask Him what He wants to make us.

Aren't you tired of arguing with God about what He is trying to make you? Just let Him mold and shape you into His perfect image. When He is finished You will look more like Him and less like You. And that is a good thing since that will draw more people to Him.

You are the Potter. I am the clay. Help me remember that, Lord. Help me trust You to shape me and my children into whatever You desire.

APRIL 10

HOUSEHOLD FURNISHINGS

2 Chronicles 4

BEST VERSE: 10A

Solomon also made all the things that were in the house of God.

You may read 2 Chronicles 4 and start yawning. Don't! It's a short chapter. Read the whole chapter two or three times and then tell me what you read. Did you see it? God left nothing to chance when He gave all the details to David to give to Solomon. And then Solomon "made all the things that were in the house of God."

Look at the numbers. Look at all the furnishings. This was going to be God's house, and it was going to look right. How many times have you hurried to straighten your house when company was coming? You made sure everything was just right. Why? Because you wanted your house to look respectable. Solomon wanted to make sure God's house was the talk of the known world. He was honoring God by his actions.

TEACHING MOMENT

This is a perfect verse to read to your children when you send them to clean their room. Keeping their room clean is important. Why? Because cleanliness is next to godliness? Well, maybe. But that's not the reason. You are teaching them to care for their things. Everything they have in that room really belongs to God, right? Every toy! Every sock! Every piece of furniture. As believers, we believe that. It's all His. And if it is His, take care of it.

I truly believe if we teach our children that when they are young, they will learn to care for their possessions in a whole different way. They will learn to only purchase things that would give glory to God. That leaves those questionable cd's out. That leaves the wrong kind of clothing out. Just as Solomon took care of God's house, we need to take care of His stuff He is letting use.

Do you have a reverent respect for God's stuff? Don't you wish you could have made some of those items for the temple? Remember, all your stuff is God's too. Treat it that way! Honor God by seeing all your possessions as totally His.

Thank You, Father, for blessing me with all I have. I want to hold these as if I am holding Your possessions. I am truly in awe of how You have blessed me.

APRIL 11

RIGHTEOUS

Romans 4

BEST VERSES: 23–24

Now not for his sake only was it written that it was credited to him, but for our sake also, to whom it will be credited, as those who believe in Him who raised Jesus our Lord from the dead.

Abraham was declared righteous before he had the mark on his body (circumcision). The physical came after the spiritual. He was declared righteous because he believed God. We, too, are declared righteous, not from anything that we do, but because of our belief. Aren't you glad?

So many people try and try and try to please God through works or service. As long as they are serving, they feel God loves them. But when they "fall short" of their self-imposed service quotas, they feel unworthy and doubt God's love for them.

TEACHING MOMENT

It is so important for our children to know that there is nothing they can do to earn God's love. There is nothing they can do to become righteous—that is, except believing Jesus died for their sins and confessing Him as Lord. Our children must learn from us the simplicity of the gospel message. The last thing we want our children to believe is that they can earn their salvation.

How can you teach them this? How about modeling it in the way you love them? Love them unconditionally. Sure, we are always pleased when they obey, but their obedience doesn't earn them our love. Their obedience is a result of our love. Tell them that. Make sure they understand the difference. We obey God because He first loved us (while we were still sinners).

Can you say that about your walk with Christ? Are you so busy trying to please Him that you are not enjoying Him? Stop it! Rest in Him! Let Him have His perfect way in your life. Experience the joy of knowing His peace that comes from obedience to His Word.

O Lord, I obey because You love me, not to gain favor in Your eyes. Help me to keep that focus at all times. I am grateful for your gift of righteousness.

APRIL 12

WEDDING DAY

Song of Solomon 3

BEST VERSE: 11

Go forth, O daughters of Zion, and gaze on King Solomon with the crown with which his mother has crowned him on the day of his wedding, and on the day of his gladness of heart.

Wedding day! The bride is giddy. The groom is nervous. Oh, but the mothers! They are both besides themselves. And here we find Bathsheba, Solomon's mother, who has given him a special wedding day crown. Do you think she was proud of her son? Don't you know it!

Families should celebrate the wedding days in their families. Weddings are not just ceremonies. They are celebrations of two people's love for each other. And we all know that you don't just marry a wife or a husband. You marry a family.

TEACHING MOMENT

Get out your wedding album and share your day with your kids. If you have a DVD or VHS (yea, I'm that old), play it for them. They will love to see their mom and dad when they were much younger. They will love to ask you questions about your wedding day. "Did you have fun? Did you eat cake? What kind of cake?"

But make sure you talk about the holiness of the day. Explain to them exactly what a wedding is. If you get a chance to take them to a wedding, make sure they understand all that takes place. Weddings are special. You want them to know that and look forward to their own one days, should the Lord allow them to marry.

Perhaps you didn't have a wedding day. Maybe your marriage has broken up. Don't let that spoil the imagery you see today in this passage. God intends for marriage to be a holy occasion. He wants us to celebrate it. Hey, even Jesus performed His first miracle at a wedding celebration.

Father, today I thank You for my wife. I praise You for putting her in my life. I am grateful for the image I still have in my head of her walking down the aisle. You have truly blessed me.

APRIL 13

THE KING'S FRIEND

1 Chronicles 27

BEST VERSE: 33B

And Hushai the Archite was the king's friend.

All through chapter 27 of 1 Chronicles we see a list of appointments. This guy is over this. This guy is over that. And then, at the very end of the chapter we read, "and Hushai the Archite was the king's friend." He must have been a very special friend. Well, he was.

This is the same Hushai who confounded Absalom, who tried to overthrow his father David's throne. He protected David in the face of death if he was exposed. That's a true friend. That's a friend you can count on. Hushai was indeed the king's friend.

TEACHING MOMENT

As believers, we have a friend that sticks closer than a brother. Jesus, the very son of God, died for us. He was willing to give His life so that we might live. Hushai was willing to give his life to allow David to continue living physically. But Jesus gave His life so that we can live forever. That's a friend.

Your children are going to have lots of friends and be a friend to lots of others. I pray they have some Hushais in their life. But my prayer is more that they will have the true friend, Jesus, walking beside them every day. Parents, you are the one to introduce them to your best friend, Jesus. You are the one to show them how His "friendship" changed your life. You are the one to show them just how much Jesus loves them.

But let me ask you a question. Are you being a true friend to Jesus. Friends spend time together. Are you doing that? Friends talk to each other. Are you doing that? Friends will lay down their lives for each other. Would you do that for Jesus?

Father, thank You for sending Your Son, Jesus Christ, to be my Savior and my friend. What a friend we have in Jesus!

SLEEPY HEAD

Acts 20

BEST VERSE: 9

And there was a young man named Eutychus sitting on the window sill, sinking into a deep sleep; and as Paul kept on talking, he was overcome by sleep and fell down from the third floor and was picked up dead.

I have been guilty of falling asleep in church. I have also seen a lot of people fall asleep while I was preaching (which I am sure did not reflect at all on the quality of my preaching). But this young man, Eutychus, should have been more careful where he was sitting. He was not embarrassed for falling asleep, he died!

The story doesn't end there, though. Paul went down and raised him from the dead. He told the people "his life is in him." How did Paul do that? He didn't! God in him did. Paul didn't raise Eutychus to get fame and honor. He raised him to continue to live for Christ.

TEACHING MOMENT

Isn't it the cutest thing when your little daughter gets so sleepy she can't hold her eyes open? You may have even had a child fall asleep during a meal. Be careful where they lay their head. Ha Ha! Don't try to teach them our verse today at that moment. Wait until they wake up.

What's the lesson for this verse? I mean, why was this story recorded by Luke? One lesson, I think, is to let us know that falling asleep accidentally in church is not a sin. Kids should know that. Now, I don't mean stretching out on the pew and bringing a pillow. That wouldn't be an accident. But getting sleepy in church can happen. Kids should not be made to feel bad if that happens.

Eutychus will always be remembered as the boy who fell asleep during Pauls' sermon and died and was brought back to life. We don't know anything else about him. But I have to believe that he told of the power of God the rest of his life. He was dead and lived to tell about it.

Father, Your power amazes me. You bring life to the spiritually dead. Thank You for "raising" me.

DO NOT FEAR

Romans 13

BEST VERSE: 3

For rulers are not a cause of fear for good behavior, but for evil. Do you want to have no fear of authority? Do what is good and you will have praise from the same.

Why is it when we are driving down the highway and pass a police car we let off the gas? We fear getting a ticket, right? We may not even be exceeding the speed limit, but we naturally slow down. Let me give you a hint. Drive the speed limit and you have nothing to worry about.

Paul is telling the Romans here to obey those who are in authority. If they do, there is no need to fear. Speak well of them. He was telling them to treat ungodly, pagan authorities this way. We could learn a lesson here.

TEACHING MOMENT

If there is a lesson that must be taught, it's this one. Children have to be taught to respect and obey authorities. Police are getting such a bad rap right now. They are the good guys. We need to pray for them and obey them. There is never any reason to fear the police, if we are doing what we should be doing.

In fact, take your children down to the police department and introduce them to some officers. If you know an officer, take them out to lunch. Make sure your children feel comfortable around them and know they can go to them for help if needed.

Jesus respected the law. Jesus respected the government. Why? Because His heavenly Father had allowed them to be in power. As such, He would respect His Father's judgment. So should we.

Thank You, Lord, for those who are the authorities in my life. I may not always agree with them, but I must respect them. Show me ways to thank them personally for their sacrifice and service.

BE CAREFUL THE WORDS YOU HEED

Job 26

BEST VERSE: 4

With whose help have you uttered words, and whose breath has come out from you?

Job was sick and tired of hearing advice from his "friends" on what he should do to get right with God. He asked them, "Whose words are you using?" In other words, do you speak for God? Job discerned that they were not speaking truth to him.

People like to give advice. Christians are probably the worst. But not all advice given is from God. I pray you know that. Even Christian counselors can give wrong advice if they are not basing that advice on God's Word. Check it against Scripture—always.

TEACHING MOMENT

As we teach our children truth from God's Word, we need to make sure they know how to compare the world's advice and knowledge to it. When they come to you with something that was said by a teacher or friend, take them to the Word to find the truth.

If we can teach our children to do this early, they will avoid a lot of mistakes later in life. Taking someone's advice, just because they are a good person and respected by others, is not always a good thing. But any advice we get based on the Word can always be trusted. It will never fail us.

Are you in need of advice right now? Do you need a trustworthy counselor? Go to the Word. Go to Jesus. He will always counsel you right. If you don't hear from Him, wait. Don't make a decision just because time is running short. Bathe it in prayer and wait. He will come through.

Thank You, God, for giving me Your precepts to guide me. Teach me to trust them more. Let me point others to Your truth.

A GRAND ENTRANCE

Titus 2

BEST VERSES: 11-12

For the grace of God has appeared, bringing salvation to all men, instructing us to deny ungodliness and worldly desires and to live sensibly, righteously and godly in the present age.

Last year I had the opportunity to observe from a hotel balcony a Ugandan wedding reception. It was quite an elaborate event. The courtyard of the hotel was outfitted with three large white tents. There were tables and tables of food. But the main event was the arrival of the bride and groom. The wedding party marched in first to loud music. They actually danced into the courtyard. But then . . . the bride and groom arrived. Everyone stood and clapped as they entered. The main people of the celebration had finally arrived. Celebration!

We have witnessed the grandest entrance! The arrival of the grace of God in our lives! At least, I hope you have witnessed that. My guess is that all who were at that wedding reception knew either the bride or the groom. So, their arrival meant something. Unless you know the Giver of grace, its arrival means nothing. But if you do, well then, you celebrate its arrival.

TEACHING MOMENT

We have the opportunity to teach our children what this means to them and all believers. They have to have firsthand knowledge of the Giver of grace to appreciate it. With the grace comes the wisdom "to deny ungodliness and worldly desires and to live sensibly, righteously and godly." Wow! Isn't that better than the entrance of a wedding party?

We can't complain that we can't handle this world, because we aren't supposed to. God is! Through His wisdom we can handle anything the world throws at us. Our children, armed with this knowledge, can take on the biggest foes. They can defeat the enemies of the cross. They can make the right decisions as they face trials and temptations.

Will you allow the Lord to give you the grace you need today? Will you allow Him to teach you? Let Him instruct you today, and you will have the power you need to face anything hurled at you today. Amen? Amen!

Through Your grace, Lord, I can handle anything. It's Your grace that gets me through each day. How I desire my children to know the comfort of Your grace each new day!

APRIL 18

FATHERLY ADVICE

1 Chronicles 28

BEST VERSE: 20

Then David said to his son Solomon, "Be strong and courageous, and act; do not fear nor be dismayed, for the LORD God, my God, is with you. He will not fail you nor forsake you until all the work for the service of the house of the LORD is finished."

When my dad got up in years, I would call him often for advice. Now, I admit I really didn't need his advice on the topic I was asking about, but he needed to give it. Do you understand? My father needed to be a father. He needed to know he could still impart wisdom and advice to his son.

We see David here in front of all his leaders giving his son, Solomon, some advice. This phrase "be strong and courageous" was a familiar one. Moses had told Joshua these words, and the Lord had told Joshua the same words. They were recorded in the Holy Scriptures, and I am sure David had read them. What better advice than God's Word?

TEACHING MOMENT

How do you give advice to your children? Do you use your earthly wisdom (which is limited) or God's Word (which is limitless)? I recently told one of my children, "Your mother and I only know how to give you godly advice from His Word." We parents need to only give advice that is grounded in the Word of God.

Our job is to brainwash our kids! That's right, I said that. We are to fill their minds and hearts with Scripture. They should leave our home knowing the first place to turn when they face a trial is God's Word. This is a source they will always have. They should be taught to memorize Scriptures so that it rings through their mind daily. Brainwash may seem harsh. Maybe a better word is heartwash.

Are you heartwashed? Does your heart beat according to the Word of God? Does His words drive you? Let the Lord God speak to you today through His Word. This advice is good Fatherly advice. You can always trust it to be true and right. There is an answer to every issue you face right there in the Word.

Father, thank You for giving me Your Word. Thank You that it is timeless and perfect. Help me today to apply it to my life.

APRIL 19

HIDING FROM GOD

1 Kings 19

BEST VERSE: 13

When Elijah heard it, he wrapped his face in his mantle and went out and stood in the entrance of the cave. And behold, a voice came to him and said, "What are you doing here, Elijah?"

Man, Elijah was in a bad spot. Jezebel had threatened to kill him because he had killed all the prophets of Baal. So, he had fled and hid himself in a cave. Talking about scared? He was shaking in his boots, well, his sandals.

But God comes to him in a gentle wind and Elijah went to the entrance of the cave to hear from God. And what does God say? Did He say, "Don't worry about Jezebel"? Did He say, "Don't be scared Elijah"? No, He said, "What are you doing here, Elijah?" In other words, God was saying to him, "Why in the world are you hiding from that woman? She is nothing to fear. If you want to fear something, you should be fearing Me."

God had given Elijah the strength, boldness, and stamina to slay over four hundred Baal prophets, and now Elijah is hiding from one woman. Wow! But aren't we the same? We fear the things we can't control. We fear cancer! We fear betrayal of friends. We fear storms that bring tornadoes and hurricanes.

TEACHING MOMENT

As parents, we must teach our children that fear has no part in their lives as believers. First John 4:18 says perfect love casts out all fear. And what is that perfect love? Jesus. With Jesus by their side, they never have a cause for fear. With Jesus living within them through the power of the Holy Spirit, they can face the greatest dangers the world can throw at them, secure in the fact that Jesus is the one fighting their battles.

As you face the fears of life, let your children see you trusting Him! Show them that even though the future is not guaranteeing an easy path, you can face it fearlessly because of the confidence you have in our great Savior. As you lead courageously, your children will also trust Him with their fears. Rest easy in the strong arms of our God.

O God, I have no fear as I rest in You. No one can cause me to tremble, because You are my Victorious Warrior. You will defend me!

APRIL 20

RESTORATION

Nahum 2

BEST VERSE: 2

For the Lord will restore the splendor of Jacob like the splendor of Israel, even though devastators have devastated them and destroyed their vine branches.

Have you ever restored a piece of furniture? My grandmother had a 1908 Thomas Edison Diamond Disc Victrola that she left to my mom. It stands about 4 feet tall with cabinets for the records and the speaker horn. It has the handle on the side to wind it so it can play. My mother gave that to me because I had restored it for her. It was covered in a thick dark varnish that wouldn't allow the original cherry veneer to show. When I finished it, it looked like new.

In today's passage Nahum is describing the restoration of Judah after it has been destroyed. He says God will restore the "splendor of Israel." Can you imagine how encouraging those words were for the people? They had lived through the devastation of the city. They had seen friends and family murdered. And now they are promised restoration.

TEACHING MOMENT

Troubles come. Isn't that encouraging? But the Lord has promised those who love Him that He will restore us. Now, this is a truth we must teach our children. We must teach them to trust God's eternal plan. When all seems lost, God is there. When all seems hopeless, God is there. He promises that.

You're probably thinking, But Carl, you don't know what we are going through. Nope, sure don't. But neither do you know what I have gone through. We teach our children to trust God by not only living it out ourselves, but also helping those around us who are going through hard times. As God uses us to minister to others, we are fulfilling His plan for them. Let your children be a part of that.

Whatever you are facing right now, trust God to restore you. It may be a quick fix, or it may be a long process. During the testing, allow Him to open your eyes to the lessons He wants you to learn. There is always something to be learned.

God, You are always mindful of my situations. I know that. When I doubt that remind me with a gentle nudge. Show me Your presence.

APRIL 21

SHHHHH!

Habakkuk 2

BEST VERSE: 20

But the Lord is in His holy temple. Let all the earth be silent before Him.

Have you ever just sat and listened? I mean, have you ever really listened. Habakkuk is prophesying about the destruction of Judah by the Chaldeans, and right in the middle he says this. He wants them all to stop and listen for the Lord's word.

But look where God is. He is in His holy temple, where He belongs. He is still on the throne. No matter what we face, we can rest assured that God is still in charge. It may seem like He has deserted us, but He hasn't. He is still speaking. We must get quiet to hear Him.

TEACHING MOMENT

God's omnipresence is probably one of the most comforting attributes of God we can teach our children. Little Susie needs to know that God is always there for her. He will never leave or forsake His children. The key is, of course, do your children qualify as His children.

No amount of begging God can bring them into safety. Now hear me out. We must pray for their salvation and do everything in our power to usher them into the very presence of God. But ultimately, they have to believe on their own. And once they surrender, God will reign in their lives, just as He has in yours.

Are you being quiet today? Are you really listening to God today? Are you leading your children to hear God today? Remind them (and yourself) that God has NOT moved. He is still God. Nothing can change that. The world may seem out of control, but God is not.

God, You are the only God! You are on Your throne reigning supreme. Thank You for being my God and my Savior. Draw my children and loved ones into Your presence so they will hear You clearly.

APRIL 22

NO MORE WAR

Isaiah 2

BEST VERSE: 4B

And they will hammer their swords into plowshares and their spears into pruning hooks. Nation will not lift up sword against nation, and never again will they learn war.

Can you imagine? No more war! It seems the United States has been at war forever. This latest war against terrorism has stretched into two decades and soon to be three, unless the Lord returns. But what else can you expect as long as men are living for themselves or their ideologies.

There will come a day, according to Isaiah, when weapons of war will be no more. I cannot comprehend that. That seems too good to be true. But it will happen. God says so.

TEACHING MOMENT

Our children who are under sixteen eighteen years of age have never known a time when we were not at war. Do you realize that? Their world has been in chaos since September 11, 2001. We need to reassure them that God is in control. He is not caught unaware. He knows exactly what is going on and has a plan which has been in place since the foundation of the world.

Can we explain all the chaos? Sure, we can. It's called sin! Sin gives mankind the rationale to do as he pleases. Sin deceives mankind into thinking he is in charge. Sin leads mankind down a slippery slope. That's why we must teach our children to flee from it and run to Jesus. Only then will they understand.

I don't know about you, but I get weary of all the bad news. I am ready for some good news. Do you want to hear some? He is coming back soon. Jesus, our Redeemer, is on His way. He is sitting on "ready." The moment His Father, our Father in heaven, says, "Go get Your bride," He is here. Hallelujah!

God, I eagerly await Your return. I look forward to that day when there will be no more war. Thank You that, in the meantime, You are watching over us and leading us where You want us to go.

APRIL 23

WHAT ARE YOU BUILDING?

1 Corinthians 3

BEST VERSE: 10

According to the grace of God which was given to me, like a wise master builder I laid a foundation, and another is building on it. But each man must be careful how he builds on it.

My dad was a great carpenter. He could build just about anything. In fact, once he looked at a picture of a piece of furniture and then built it, without using one nail. He used wooden pegs, which he made, to put it all together. Amazing! I am doing good to drive a nail straight!

But my dad didn't lay his firm foundation until late in life when he gave his heart and soul to Jesus. That was something he couldn't build. Jesus had already laid the foundation stone. My dad realized he needed Jesus to be secure for his eternal home. He's enjoying that now.

TEACHING MOMENT

How do we teach our children to be wise master builders? We have to give them the tools they need. They need to know the Word. They need to have godly mentors in their lives to guide them. They need opportunities to sharpen their building skills. They need to see the "building" going up.

Have you given them any opportunities to build? Have you allowed them to "drive the nails" in their faith? Don't let your faith be their faith. They need their own faith, which they get from our Father directly. Our job is to give them the tools, to do some spadework in preparing the ground. But they must build their own faith.

At our Children's Camp last summer, several adult leaders had the opportunity to help some children build on their faith. But as much "construction" was done, the parents have to be the ones to really help the children build. It's not easy work. Construction requires some sweat. You can even bloody a thumb. But we build, as the verse says, to allow others to build on it. Is your foundation prepared and ready for building?

Father, I am so thankful that You are the foundation upon which I build my life. I know that foundation will never settle or crack. I can rest my life on You, knowing You will never move.

APRIL 24

EMBARRASSING STORY

Acts 19

BEST VERSES: 16–17

And the man, in whom was the evil spirit, leaped on them and subdued all of them and overpowered them, so that they fled out of that house naked and wounded. This became known to all, both Jews and Greeks, who lived in Ephesus; and fear fell upon them all and the name of the Lord Jesus was being magnified."

The sons of Sceva are trying to cast out demons in the name of Jesus without knowing Jesus. They want some attention. Well, they get it. The possessed man jumps up, whips them all, and they run out naked. Don't you know, for the rest of their lives, whenever they went to town, people would point and sneer? They got more attention than they bargained for.

Have you ever had an embarrassing moment? Most of us have. Sometimes we are lucky enough that only a few close friends witness it. Other times it seems the whole world knows. It's one thing to be embarrassed over an innocent mistake. It's another when it happens while we are caught doing something we shouldn't have. The sons of Sceva (notice we don't even know their names) are trying to do something they have no business trying. Their motive is all wrong.

TEACHING MOMENT

Our children must learn to rely on the Holy Spirit for their guide. He is the one who will lead them safely through life's challenging moments. As parents, we have to help them fine-tune their hearing. Listening to the Spirit is something that requires sacrifice. We must die to ourselves to hear from the Lord. When all we think about is self, the Spirit's voice is drowned out.

When your children come to Christ, their hearing is adjusted by the Spirit. He begins to speak into them the truth of the Word. He begins to direct them in life's choices. When they learn to trust the Spirit, those embarrassing moments are avoided. They aren't caught in situations that bring shame and reproach.

Won't you give your children a hearing test today? Won't you make sure they know the importance of listening to Him? How about you? How is your hearing?

Lord, I know I need a hearing test. I miss Your words way too much because my ears are listening. Help me, Jesus, to tune my ears to the frequency of Your voice.

APRIL 25

A CHANGING LANDSCAPE

Nahum 3

BEST VERSE: 7

And it will come about that all who see you will shrink from you and say, "Nineveh is devastated! Who will grieve for her?" Where will I seek comforters for you?'"

Cities and communities go through changes. Renovations are made. Streets are rerouted. Buildings are demolished, and new ones pop up in their place. But cities and communities also go through other changes. Nineveh, the city to which God sent Jonah to preach repentance, has turned into a wicked city. And now, God is not sending a prophet to preach. He is sending judgment.

Do not think you can say you love God and live any way you please. He will not tolerate that. He will hold you accountable. Sure, all your sins are under the blood of Jesus if you are a believer, but He does not excuse unholy living. And your faith doesn't get passed down to your children through your DNA. They, too, must come to their own salvation moment.

TEACHING MOMENT

That's the point I want to make crystal clear. Your children cannot get into heaven on your coattails. Nineveh had once been a repenting city. They had humbled themselves before God. But future generations turned from Him. You may be completely sold out for Jesus and doing your best to lead your family. But each individual has to come to that point of repentance.

Ask your child why they think you love Jesus. Ask them if they can see Jesus in you. Now, that may be a little scary to ask. But ask it anyway. Ask them to tell you how you can be more like Jesus. And then tell them why you are asking these questions. Because you want them to follow you in faith. You want them to be with you for eternity.

Are you preparing the next generation for faith? Don't forget Nineveh. A city that was once full of brokenness before God had become a city God destroyed because of their wickedness. Don't let that happen. Do all you can to lead others to Him.

I am reminded, God, that faith is only good one generation at a time. There are no guaranteed places in heaven for the children of believers. They must come to You on their own.

APRIL 26

HOW DARE YOU?

Romans 2

BEST VERSE: 1

Therefore you have no excuse, every one of you who passes judgment, for in that which you judge another, you condemn yourself; for you who judge practice the same things.

I know each of you have heard someone tell you when you have tried to correct or critique them, "You shouldn't judge me." Well, that may be partially true. We shouldn't judge someone for something we are guilty of ourselves. But we have become so careful to not offend someone that we don't say anything anymore.

As believers, we are not in the judging business, but we can be fruit inspectors. We should be able to recognize when someone is exercising their gift or just being fleshly. But in order to do that, we must first be in a position where we can hear the Spirit as He directs us.

TEACHING MOMENT

Your children may come home and tell what one of their friends did. Or perhaps they come home after visiting with someone to spill the beans on them. We have to teach our children to be observant and careful without being judgmental. We have to teach them how to discern God's movement in someone's life and when that person is acting out of their own flesh.

How can you know? Simple! If the action the person is taking will bring glory to the Father, He is pleased. We may have done it differently, but if the final result is God is praised, then we should celebrate it and not judge it.

But if that person's actions only exalt themselves you can almost bet on the fact that this is of the flesh. If what that person is saying or doing, brings the praise on them personally, what use is that to God. Only He is worthy of praise. Amen?

So, be careful as you observe others' actions. Check out your own life first. Make sure you are pleasing the Father. Then come alongside others to help them do the same.

Lord, help me be careful to only bring You praise. Let all my actions and my words point others to You. Help me teach my children to recognize the difference.

REDEEMED, HOW I LOVE TO PROCLAIM IT

Job 19

BEST VERSE: 25

As for me, I know that my Redeemer lives, and at the last He will take His stand on the earth.

Have you ever really suffered? I mean, really suffered? Perhaps you were extremely ill and saw no hope of recovery. Perhaps you had just suffered the third loss of a loved one within a short period of time. Perhaps you had gone through an extended period of joblessness. We can suffer in many ways.

How did you come out of that pit? Who lifted you? We can rely on friends and family for only so much. The only true and reliable source is God, our Redeemer. Job knew this. No matter how long God wanted Him to stay in this suffering, he knew that His Redeemer lives.

TEACHING MOMENT

How do we teach this concept to our children? How do we teach them that suffering will come and will last for a season? It could be a long season, or it could be brief. But how do we teach them to trust through it? Simple! Easy Peazy! You have to model it.

That again! Come on Carl! Yep! There is no other way. When your children suffer you suffer, right? Use that opportunity to show them how you are trusting your Redeemer. Trust His perfect will. Show your children that you are right there beside them, suffering and trusting.

God may allow you to suffer in order to teach them to trust in a future suffering. What? Seriously? He will because He knows your affliction will be comforted by Him so you can use that same comfort to comfort others (2 Corinthians 1:3–5).

Stop complaining in the midst of your suffering. See it as a preparation period for your children or others. Learn and then teach!

Lord, I don't want to suffer, but if You allow it I will receive it. If You think I can handle it, then I know I can. But Lord, when I get low and discouraged, remind me whose I am.

APRIL 28

WHOSOEVER

Acts 26

BEST VERSE: 29

And Paul said, "I would wish to God, that whether in a short or long time, not only you, but also all who hear me this day, might become such as I am, except for these chains."

Don't you just love the boldness of Paul? Even while standing before Agrippa and Festus in chains, he is proclaiming the truth of the gospel message and begging them all to come to Christ. He knew these men held his life in their hands, but that did not matter. What mattered more is the eternal condition of their soul.

What Paul had discovered through his own conversion and subsequent journeys is that nothing is more important than knowing Christ as Savior and telling everyone about Him. He wanted to spread the news of Christ to as many as he could. Perhaps that is part of the reason he appealed to Caesar. He wanted to share Jesus with Caesar himself in Rome.

TEACHING MOMENT

How important is sharing your testimony? Do your children know how you came to Christ? Have you told them your salvation story? They need to know that. They need to see how you have grown in your faith. They need to know their own faith heritage.

Educating your children about your family's faith is so important. They need to know who in your family loves the Lord and who is trying to live for Him. They need to know which of their uncles, aunts, cousins, or grandparents are lost so they can pray for them and perhaps share with them. I have known grandparents who were saved through the witness of a grandchild.

Witnessing can be hard sometimes, especially when it is to a family member who knows all your faults. But who deserves your witness more than those who are closest to you? Pray for your family, but also be diligent with your children to win them all to Jesus.

O God, let me be diligent to share the love of Christ to all those in my family who have never bowed their knee to You.

APRIL 29

HOPE FOR THE HOPELESS

Romans 15

BEST VERSE: 13

Now may the God of hope fill you with all joy and peace in believing, so that you will abound in hope by the power of the Holy Spirit.

This is probably one of my favorite verses in the Bible. I know, I've said that before, but this time I mean it. This verse is so full of truths that it is hard to pull just one thought out of it. But I will try to do that.

Have you ever wanted to give someone else hope? They have come to you with an impossible situation or problem, and they just want to see some light at the end of the tunnel. What do you do? Do you pray with them? Do you give them the name of a good, Christian counselor? Both of those are good ideas. But for you to give them hope you must have hope.

Look at the last part of the verse, "so that you will abound in hope by the power of the Holy Spirit." That word "abound" literally means to overflow, to spew over. Do you have that much hope? If you allow the God of Hope to fill you with all joy and peace by the power of the Holy Spirit, you will.

TEACHING MOMENT

How do we teach our children hope? There is only one way. We have to be hopeful! We have to show them that we know the source of all hope. When we are facing hard times in the family (sickness, employment, money, etc.) we have to give our children hope. This is another one of those attributes that is caught and not taught.

By teaching our kids this truth in our lives, they are prepared to reach out to the Hope Giver when they face their own uncertain times. They will face them. That is for certain. Don't you want them to have hope? Then be hopeful!

You are the God of hope, God. I thank You for giving me hope when I was hopeless. Thank You for giving me hope when I saw nothing but defeat.

APRIL 30

DID YOU HEAR THAT?

Nehemiah 1

BEST VERSE: 6A

Let Your ear now be attentive and Your eyes open to hear the prayer of Your servant which I am praying before You now, day and night, . . .

Our family used to have a dog named Reese. He was a good dog, and we all loved him. Reese would lay in the floor near where we sat, and if we called his name, his ears would lift up and he would turn his head to look at us. Sometimes, when he was sleeping near me on the floor, I would whisper his name just to see his ears twitch. It seemed he was listening even in his sleep.

Nehemiah is beseeching Jehovah God to listen to his prayers. Remember, Nehemiah is in captivity in Babylon. He was the king's cupbearer, a servant. He probably felt most of his life that God had stopped listening to him. But with the news of the condition of Jerusalem, he was begging God's ear.

TEACHING MOMENT

Children need to know that they always have our ear. They need to know they can always talk to us, no matter what they may have done. They also need to know that as a child of God they always have God's ear. This story of Nehemiah is a great story of how God heard and responded. He stirred King Artaxerxes' heart to let Nehemiah return to Jerusalem to rebuild the walls. God can do anything.

Listening is an art. I often do not listen closely when my wife speaks to me. We may be watching television, and I am engrossed in a show. I simply don't hear her until she throws a shoe at me. Just kidding. She will usually ask, "Are you listening?" I need to be better about hearing her, right?

Aren't you glad we don't have to wave our hands and jump up and down (or throw a shoe) to get God's attention? He is always listening. He is always ready to respond to our need, if we come to Him with humility, acknowledging His place in our lives. He wants to hear us. He wants to listen to us. But we have to be deliberate about talking to Him. Have you been deliberate lately?

Father, help me to focus my prayer time and not be distracted by other things. Thank You that You are always listening. Your ear is always bent earthward to hear the prayers of Your children.

MAY 1

DOOR OPENER

1 Chronicles 9

BEST VERSE: 27

They spent the night around the house of God, because the watch was committed to them; and they were in charge of opening it morning by morning.

Upon first reading of this chapter, my initial thought was, "How boring!" I mean, come on, every day their job was to open the doors of the temple. That's it! I immediately had the image of the guys you see at the door of a fancy hotel opening the door for people.

They were so committed to this role that they would sleep near the temple every night so they could be close to their jobs. They took their jobs seriously. It may not have seemed important to others, but it was to them. I bet they kept the doors polished and shining. I bet there was no trash lying around the doors.

TEACHING MOMENT

Our children need to learn there is no task too small in the service of the King of kings. Whatever He asks you to do, you need to do it. If He is asking it is important. We should show them this by how we treat His requests on our lives. Whether we are "opening the doors to the temple" or sweeping up after a church event, our children need to see us modeling a servant attitude.

Why not get your kids in on the action? The next time you are asked to do something at church take them along. Let them have a part in it. Children love to serve, especially when they can see the "finished product." And when they assist you, brag on them to others. Let them know that you are proud of them.

How low will you go in service? Will you do anything to serve the Lord? Or do you demand the spotlight jobs that everyone can see?

Just recently I arrived at church for a Sunday morning service in which I was preaching. When I walked into church, I noticed some dead leaves all over the floor at the front entryway of the church, and so I picked up a broom and dustpan to sweep those up." I thought, "I'm preaching today.

Why should I do that?" But I did it. No one knew I did it. That didn't matter. I just did it.

Will you humble yourself to do whatever you are asked? And when you do it, know that you are pleasing the Master. He is the one whom you serve.

It is my joy to serve You, O Lord. Help me be more observant of the needs around me. Let me be the first to pick up that broom.

MAY 2

AN EVERLASTING LIGHT

Isaiah 60

BEST VERSES: 19–20

No longer will you have the sun for light by day, nor for brightness will the moon give you light; but you will have the LORD for an everlasting light, and your God for your glory. Your sun will no longer set, nor will your moon wane; for you will have the LORD for an everlasting light, and the days of your mourning will be over.

I don't know about you, but I am not a fan of the new light bulbs. For decades we could buy inexpensive incandescent light bulbs. For some reason, it was decided we needed a better bulb. We needed LED bulbs. They are marketed as lasting longer, years in fact. What I do know is they cost a whole lot more.

Well, one day we won't need those light bulbs. One day we won't even need the sun or moon for light. God will be the everlasting light that shines on us forever. No need for LED when you have the L-O-R-D. That will be incredible.

TEACHING MOMENT

The next time you have to change a light bulb, get your child involved in the action. If all you have are LED bulbs, they may never see you change a light bulb in the house. Don't miss the opportunity. As you change the bulb, talk about these verses. Ask them what they think God's light will be like.

Children have such amazing imaginations. I wonder if they will see God's light as cool, warm, or bright. I have to believe that God's light won't cause us to squint or shield our eyes like we do outside. We will be able to stare directly into His incredible, perfect, pure light.

Now, let me ask you something. Are you in need of some light in your life? Are you walking in darkness? Let the light of Christ illumine your path today. And use that light to shine on others. Let Him shine through you.

Father of lights, I cannot imagine a world without the need for the sun or moon. Your light gives not only light, but it also gives life. Shine on me!

MAY 3

DO WHAT'S RIGHT

Isaiah 56

BEST VERSE: 1A

Thus says the Lord, "Preserve justice and do righteousness."

Sounds pretty simple, right? Wrong! We can't do this. There is nothing in us that will preserve justice or do righteousness. Nothing! Our flesh wants what it wants. We want to see justice according to our desires. We think what we want is righteous.

But God tell us to "preserve justice and do righteousness." Notice He says to preserve justice. You see, He is the only just one. Only He can dispense justice. Only He has the wisdom and knowledge to show justice. Our job is to preserve the justice He exhibits. And that is done by doing righteousness, by being righteous.

TEACHING MOMENT

The next time you have to dispense justice to your kids (and there will be a next time), remember this verse. Any justice you issue must be God's justice. You must apply His Word. As a parent, you should only correct your children as it relates to the justice you see in Him. If we all did that as parents, this world would be a much better place.

But it is paramount that as you do that, you let your children know you are only following God's commands. Any advice you give them as they get older should be centered in His Word. Any directions you give have to be done according to His righteousness. They can depend on that to be always true.

Are you doing this? Are you preserving justice? Are you doing righteousness? As a believer, the Lord is directing you to do these things. You do not have the luxury of not doing them. Because when you don't, you are just asking for trouble, trouble which could have been prevented.

Lord, I am incapable of preserving justice. But with You doing it through me, I can. Help me live a righteous life and point others to You in all I do.

MAY 4

CROCODILE HUNTERS

Job 41

BEST VERSE: 1

Can you draw out the crocodile with a fishhook? Or press down his tongue with a cord?

Chapter 41 is a full description of the strength and ferociousness of the crocodile. I've seen these creatures. They make the American alligator look tame. They are huge and monstrous. God describes it to Job in complete detail and says, "I made that!"

God's power is exhibited throughout creation, but nothing He created can compare to the Creator. He is more powerful than anything that exists. He is the energy source behind everything. He powers the universe. Job seems to have forgotten that in his misery. God is just reminding him that He knows and can take care of the trials Job is facing.

TEACHING MOMENT

If you read this chapter with your children, find a good National Geographic video that shows the crocodile. Let them see the power and force they have to take down a full-grown wildebeest. And once they have seen that, explain that God's power goes way beyond that. It is immeasurable.

My kids always liked flexing their muscles when they were little. I would brag on how big their muscles were. Then they would want to see my muscles, as puny as they were. But in comparison to theirs, it was huge. Power belongs to God, not us. Real power belongs to the Power Maker. He is reliable and sustainable energy at its best.

Are you feeling powerless right now? Let Him energize you. He will. He wants to. Plug in to Him today.

Lord, You are all powerful. I know that. Remind me today just how powerful You are.

MAY 5

WHO DRINKS VINEGAR?

Psalms 69–70

BEST VERSE: 69:21

"They also gave me gall for my food and for my thirst they gave me vinegar to drink."

Many people drink vinegar for their health. Even I have fallen into the habit a time or two. But man, that stuff is nasty. I know what they say. Vinegar can cleanse your system. It can help regulate your body's Ph. It can…do miracles. But getting it past the nostrils is a challenge.

You may read this verse and think of Matthew 27:34 where Jesus is being crucified and was offered vinegar to drink. Many commentators point back to this verse as a Messianic prophecy. Whether it is or not, the picture is clear. Those who offered the vinegar were not trying to quench Jesus' thirst. As the saying goes, "With friends like that . . ."

TEACHING MOMENT

At your next family dinner why don't you pour everyone a little sip of vinegar in a cup? Read this verse and talk about the prophecy. Then ask all those who are brave enough to drink the vinegar. It's not going to hurt them. Promise them that. See who can drink it and keep it down. (You might want to have a spit pail handy.)

Vinegar is bitter and can cause a burning sensation in your throat and mouth. People can be bitter as well and cause you to want to spew that bitterness right back at them. This is the lesson for today. But like Jesus, we should not receive that bitterness. (Note that Jesus didn't drink it when offered.) Just like Jesus, we should not return bitterness with bitterness. What did He do? He died for them. He gave His life for those who offered Him that vinegar. We should be willing to do the same.

Is there someone in your life who is causing you to be bitter? Now, hang on. No one can make you bitter. That is your choice. Don't fall into that trap. Don't receive that bitterness from them. Don't return it. Pray for the sweetness of Jesus to come out of your mouth. Bless those who curse you.

O Lord, it is hard to return sweet words to those who spew bitter ones. But Lord, I know if I die to myself and allow Your Holy Spirit to control my tongue, I can do that. Thank You!

MAY 6

HAIRLESS

Isaiah 15

BEST VERSE: 2C

Everyone's head is bald and every beard is cut off.

This may seem like a strange verse. Bald and beardless? What is Isaiah talking about? Well, during those times, men would shave their heads and cut off their beards as a sign of mourning. I am sure glad that practice stopped.

Moab was mourning because of the encroaching judgment of God. They were wailing and crying out. They wanted deliverance, but they were not remorseful. They just wanted relief from the suffering. Hmmm, sounds familiar. We are just the same but with hair, well, most of us anyway.

TEACHING MOMENT

Our children will face times of mourning, hopefully few and far between. But we need to teach them about mourning. There are right ways and wrong ways. Shaving our heads is probably not the right way to go about it today. But neither is staying perpetually dressed in black. How should we mourn?

We teach our children to grieve and mourn by the way we do it. It's okay to grieve the loss of a pet, but it does not compare to the loss of a grandparent or sibling. Our world today confuses our grief. Everything seems to involve tears. I am not sure about that. I want to be known as someone who knows how to show sadness without making someone sad.

Do you grieve as unto the Lord? When we are focused on the Master of the Universe, all grief seems trivial. Sure, we will have tears. That's normal.

But let your grief spring forth joy. Show the world how a believer grieves and mourns.

Father, I grieve in Your Spirit. I have hope in You, therefore, my grief shall be short-lived and end in joy.

MAY 7

LIKE JESUS

Isaiah 50

BEST VERSE: 6

I gave My back to those who strike Me, and My cheeks to those who pluck out the beard; I did not cover My face from humiliation and spitting.

Who would willingly stand there and let someone beat them, pluck out their beard and spit on them? Who? Jesus! I know you are going to say, "Well, He had been arrested. He didn't have a choice." Oh really?! He was God. He could have called ten thousand angels to defend Him. He could have just spoken and slain His oppressors. Instead, He stood there and took it—for you and for me.

I get upset when someone cuts me off in traffic. How would I respond when spit upon? How would I respond if someone pulled out my hair or beard? How would I respond if someone lashed my back? Would I be like Jesus? Can I truly say I could handle the humiliation? That is the question for all of us.

TEACHING MOMENT

How do you apply this verse to your children? Teaching humility is hard. You really just have to model it. Now, I don't mean you should let your children watch as you are beaten, spit on and have your hair plucked. That would be silly (and painful). I mean, when someone wrongs you in front of your children, remember this verse and respond as Jesus would. Be humble. Be gentle. Let the Lord be your strength.

I've said it a hundred times at least – you've got to live it out for your kids. They learn best by watching you, not listening to you. When they see you live it out in your own Christian walk, they get a glimpse of what you mean. Just telling them won't cut it, especially when you are talking about humility. Be like Jesus.

I don't know about you, but this is a hard lesson. I don't want to be humble. I want to be proud. I want to stand up for myself. I have been spat on, and I did not like it. But if the God of the universe could stand there and take this for me, I should be willing to suffer for Him. Will you?

Suffering, Lord, is not on my agenda today. But I am willing to do whatever You ask of me. I know that is a dangerous statement, but today I mean it.

MAY 8

FIRSTBORN, BUT NOT FIRST

1 Chronicles 3

BEST VERSE: 1

Now these were the sons of David who were born to him in Hebron: the firstborn was Amnon, by Ahinoam the Jezreelitess;

Do you remember who followed David as king? That's right—Solomon. Do you know where he fell in line with the rest of David's sons? Way down there. Solomon was not the firstborn son, who would normally be expected to follow in succession to the throne. The firstborn son of David, according to this verse, was Amnon. Who was he? We know nothing about him.

Don't you wonder why? I do. Why wasn't Amnon made king after David? Why wasn't he groomed to take over? That was pretty customary. Perhaps he died young. Perhaps he was rebellious. We just don't know.

TEACHING MOMENT

My point is position doesn't equal power. Your children need to know that. Your firstborn may not be the most influential. Your children all have unique gifts. God doesn't just choose to bless the oldest or the smartest. God calls each of them separately and only when they surrender to His will.

How do you see God using your children? You probably don't have a kingdom to pass down, but you do have a legacy to leave with them. How are you preparing your children to carry on your legacy of faith? David may have done his best with Amnon, and he still didn't follow the Lord. We just don't know. Neither do you. You have to trust the Lord and allow Him to direct your children.

Are you allowing the Lord to direct you? What would the Lord have you do for Him today? Perhaps the Lord has a "kingdom" for you to rule over. Maybe He has another task planned for you, but He can't give you the task until you are willing to do whatever He asks. We must surrender ALL.

All to Jesus, I surrender. All to Him I freely give! . . . I surrender all. I surrender all. All to Him, my precious Savior. I surrender all.

MAY 9

FOOLISH DECISIONS

2 Chronicles 10

BEST VERSE: 13

The king answered them harshly, and King Rehoboam forsook the counsel of the elders.

Rehoboam may have been a grown man when he became king, but he wasn't very wise. He sought the advice of his father Solomon's advisors and then forsook that advice to follow the advice of younger men. While it is not true that every "older" elder is wise, it is usually true that the older men have learned more and can give better advice that a younger man. Again, I say, that is not always true, but generally it is.

But Rehoboam decided to ignore the advice given him, thus splitting the kingdom into two kingdoms, which lasted until the end of both. What might have happened if he had taken the advice he was given by the elders? We will never know.

TEACHING MOMENT

Your children will come to a point when they will reject your parental advice. They will follow the lead of their friends or others who are younger than you. This is a heartbreaking time for parents. Is there anything you can do to avoid this? Short answer—no. Better answer—with God's help you can continue to give input into their lives.

Teach your children how to make decisions by letting them make some when they are young. These normally will be decisions that are simple and non-life threatening. But making these small decisions gives them confidence to make more serious decisions later.

Give them guidance when they are young that they can trust. Own up to your own bad decisions so they can learn from your mistakes. Help them through the bad decisions they make without judging. These are all ways to prepare them for the future.

Solomon was the wisest man on earth, but he failed to teach his own son how to make wise decisions. Don't repeat that mistake. Learn from Solomon that it does not matter how smart people think you are. Let your children speak for you when you are gone by preparing them to be your legacy.

I know my children are my legacy. Help me leave them ready to serve. They need to know the depth of my love and the willingness to serve You.

MAY 10

TICK, TOCK

Psalms 89–90

BEST VERSE: 90:4

For a thousand years in Your sight are like yesterday when it passes by, or as a watch in the night.

Have you ever been awake all night listening to the clock tick? Boy, I have. Some nights I am awake more than I am asleep. But I have found those nights to be sweet times with the Lord. That's a whole other story.

This verse, especially the last phrase, reminded me of that. God's clock runs differently than ours. He can see all of eternity at the same time. Our finite minds can't comprehend that. We simply have to trust that time is in His hands, not ours.

TEACHING MOMENT

Teaching time to our children is a challenge, isn't it? Do you remember learning to tell time on the old analog clocks? Now everything is digital, but the challenge of understanding time is still there. Our children have to learn to look at time with biblical eyes though. Time isn't just time. It's a spot on the line of eternity.

Do some math with your kids. Count up the number of seconds in a minute, then an hour, then a day, then a week, then a month, then a year, since the days they were born. That will blow their minds. Every second counts. Teach them to make the most of each second.

But, are you doing that? Are you aware of how much time you waste watching tv or piddling around? I am guilty of that. Show your kids by your actions that time is important to you and to the Lord.

Maker of time, remind me of my place in eternity. Every minute You bless me with is a minute I should use to glorify You. Thank You for giving me this day.

MAY 11

BETRAYED BY A FRIEND

Psalms 55–56

BEST VERSES: 55:12-14

For it is not an enemy who reproaches me, then I could bear it; nor is it one who hates me who has exalted himself against me, then I could hide myself from him. But it is you, a man my equal, my companion and my familiar friend; We who had sweet fellowship together walked in the house of God in the throng.

It's one thing to be hurt by an enemy. It's a whole other matter when the hurt comes from someone close to you. We don't know who this person was in David's life who betrayed him. Many speculate it was Absalom, the son who tried to overthrow him as king. Maybe, maybe not. We do know whoever it was deeply hurt David.

Have you been hurt like that by someone you thought loved you? Maybe they even attended church with you. You thought they were your Christian brother or sister. But then they turned on you, seemingly for no reason. Flesh is flesh, and this side of eternity, people can do anything.

TEACHING MOMENT

Your children need to be prepared to handle hurts like this. But, in reality, the only way to learn how is to go through it. That sounds bad, doesn't it. We don't want our little Johnny or Susie to be hurt. We would do anything to shield them from heartache. But some things just can't be taught. They have to be caught. This is one of them.

You can, however, teach them, as they are going through this hurt, to rely on Jesus. He is the Author and Finisher of their faith. He is the Healer of the brokenhearted. He is the Balm of Gilead. You get the picture. Point them to Jesus.

Father, thank You for helping me through those times in my life when I have been wounded. You have been my support and my defense. I can always depend on You.

MAY 12

STRENGTH IN WEAKNESS

2 Corinthians 12

BEST VERSE: 9

And He has said to me, "My grace is sufficient for you, for power is perfected in weakness." Most gladly, therefore, I will rather boast about my weaknesses, so that the power of Christ may dwell in me."

This statement by Paul is really confusing. He says here that the Lord told him that His "power is perfected in weakness." That really makes no sense to us. How can something that is weak have power? How can the Lord exhibit His power through weakness?

Only He can! He takes our emptied vessel, our surrendered will, and fills it with His Spirit which empowers us to do amazing things in His name. Our strength gets in the way. Our abilities can get in the way. He needs to show others that it has nothing to do with us. It has everything to do with Him.

TEACHING MOMENT

Has your little Susie ever said, "I just can't do it!"? What a perfect time to share this verse! Perhaps they are trying to do something for the first time and are struggling. You step in and help them. Explain to them how the Lord does the same for us when we turn to Him for the help that only He can give. He wants to work through us, but we have to let Him.

In the same way you can't help your Johnny unless he allows you to, God will not intervene in our lives unless we allow Him. He wants to help, and He is watching us struggle, but He won't step in unless we yield to His authority. Our children need to learn that at an early age. They can't blame God for their failures. He is always there to assist and guide, if they will let Him.

How about you, Mom or Dad? What are you struggling right now to achieve in your lives on your own? What are you refusing to turn over to the Lord? Stop it! Give it up to Him! He wants to come alongside you through His Spirit. He gets joy out of being with us. He gets joy in seeing us surrender to His Will.

I don't know about you, but I'm tired of trying all this stuff on my own. I have learned that it is much easier to relinquish control of things to Him to begin with. That way He can make it what He wants to make it. I can just step back and watch Him work. He will expect me to do my part (what He tells me to do), but He is the one who decides how and when. What a relief!

Lord, use my weakness today! Burst through with Your strength and give me real power.

MAY 13

BLINDED

2 Corinthians 4

BEST VERSE: 4

In whose case the god of this world has blinded the minds of the unbelieving so that they might not see the light of the gospel of the glory of Christ, who is the image of God.

Do you ever wonder why people you know just don't understand the love of God? They doubt His existence. They ignore His Word. Well, this verse tells us why. The "god of this world" has closed their eyes to the things of the Lord. That "god" does not want them to see the truth, and the only way he can prevent that is by blinding them.

Think about it. If you were blindfolded where you could see absolutely nothing, how helpless would you be? I recently saw a blind man in Uganda. He was being led around by another man. Where we were walking was riddled with steps, ditches, and small walkways over those ditches. Without his friend, he would have been hopelessly lost and probably hurt.

TEACHING MOMENT

Our children love to play blindfold games. What a great way to teach them this verse! Make an obstacle course in your house or on your lawn and have them walk through it without assistance. Make sure they can't see at all with those blindfolds and turn them loose.

After failing, take off the blindfold and have them walk it again. They will probably say, "Mom, that's silly. Of course, I can walk it now. I can see." Bingo! Now give them this truth from God's Word.

But let me ask you something. How many days do you tie on the blindfold? How many times do you try to maneuver through life without allowing the great Guide to guide you? We think we can handle it on our own, but we can't. We need a guide. We are blind and helpless without Him.

Will you open your eyes? Will you trust the All-Seeing One? Will you tell the "god of this world" to take his blinders elsewhere? You know the truth. Now live it!

Open my eyes that I may see glimpses of truth You have for me. Place in my hand the wonderful key that shall unclasp and set me free.

MAY 14

DIRTY WATER

Job 14

BEST VERSE: 4

Who can make the clean out of the unclean? No one!

When I was growing up, I worked part time at a local gas station. I started working there when I was 14. Yep, back then you could do that. I was put in the side alley where all I did was wash cars. They would pull one in, I would wash it, and they would pull it out. Wash, Rinse, Repeat! I got pretty good and fast at washing cars.

I learned something quickly though. You had to change the wash water after every car. You could not get a car clean if you used dirty water. I had to rinse out my wash mitt and pour out the old dirty water before I could begin the next car.

TEACHING MOMENT

There is not a thing we can do to clean up our child's life. That is all up to the Lord. He alone has the power to clean them up. In our passage today, Job is talking to God. He knew no one on earth had the power to cleanse the wicked. But God. . .

Our job as parents is to make sure our children are in the right environment where they can hear from God. We have the responsibility to prepare them so He can cleanse them. We can pray for them and teach them the Word. But we cannot clean them. That is God's job and His alone.

Are you clean today? Have you allowed the Lord to cleanse your heart and mind today? Do you think He can't cleanse you? He can! He is so much more powerful than Mr. Clean®. He cleanses us so we reflect His Son. And we know that He is clean.

Lord, have Your cleansing way today. Throw out all my efforts I have made (the dirty water) and cleanse me with the cleansing power of the Holy Spirit (the clean water). I promise You I will shine for Jesus!

MAY 15

TRUE CORNERSTONE

Isaiah 28

BEST VERSE: 16

Therefore thus says the Lord God, "Behold, I am laying in Zion a stone, a tested stone, a costly cornerstone for the foundation, firmly placed. He who believes in it will not be disturbed."

Most people have no clue about the purpose of the cornerstone of a building. According to Wikipedia (that totally trustworthy source, ha!), "the cornerstone is important since all other stones will be set in reference to this stone, thus determining the position of the entire structure." Well, this time Wikipedia got it right. I have seen a lot of cornerstones on buildings but normally fail to recognize their importance.

But this cornerstone, laid by the Lord, is the most trusted cornerstone ever laid. The Master Mason put this stone in place as the stone upon which all will be measured. If we are out of line with this stone, our buildings (lives) will crumble. If we are not attached to this stone, our walls (lives) will not be plumb and stand straight.

TEACHING MOMENT

Now this is definitely a fun verse to teach our kids. I hope you have some building blocks or tinker toys laying around your house. (I loved tinker toys.) If not, get some rocks and boards from the yard or garage. Then plan a building with your kids. Build the first one with a soft sponge as the cornerstone. Let them see how high they can build their tower on that sponge. It won't take long to watch it tumble.

Then build the same structure on a solid board or flat stone, like a paving stone or brick. You will all be amazed at how high you can go. You may even have to get on a chair to place to the top blocks. What a picture for your kids to see!

More importantly, what can you show your children you are building your life upon? Is it your job or your family or your health? You name it. It doesn't matter. Nothing will stand the test of time except the true Cornerstone, Jesus Christ. He is the One we place first and build upon.

Thank You, Father, for placing Your Son down as the cornerstone for my life. I rest assured of His steadfastness and faithfulness. Help me show my children the importance of this firm foundation.

MAY 16

DOUBLE DOSE

2 Kings2

BEST VERSE: 9

When they had crossed over, Elijah said to Elisha, "Ask what I shall do for you before I am taken from you." And Elisha said, "Please, let a double portion of your spirit be upon me."

What a request! Elisha knew the acts of Elijah. He had been a bold prophet of God and had been used greatly by the Lord. Now, as his apprentice, Elisha is asking for twice the spirit. Sounds kind of cocky, doesn't it? Maybe not.

Have you ever been around someone who just shows signs and evidence of Jesus? I mean, you can just see Jesus all over them. If you could, wouldn't you want to be just like that, in fact, even more so?

TEACHING MOMENT

Have your kids ever said, "When I grow up, I want to be just like you, Mom"? Chances are they have said that when they were little. Don't you want them to be better than you? Don't you want them to love Jesus even more than you? As a good parent, we should all want that. We should want more for our kids than we have ourselves. We want them to walk with Christ in a way that makes our walk look futile.

Well then, you have to walk in a manner that reflects that to them. You have to be so intent on leading them to Christ that it is just a normal part of their life. They should want to follow you because you exemplify Christ. They should want to follow you because they want to be . . . just like Jesus.

Just like Elisha had to see Elijah being taken up to receive the double portion of the Spirit, we have to be watching Jesus to be like Him. We have to keep our eyes on Him, not on others.

My eyes, O Lord, should always be looking toward You. I do want more of You, but not for myself. I want more of You to share with others.

MAY 17

ALL I NEED

1 Kings 3

BEST VERSE: 9

So give Your servant an understanding heart to judge Your people to discern between good and evil. For who is able to judge this great people of Yours?

Okay, let me ask you, "What would you have asked for?" Be honest. If God had asked you to ask for anything, what would you have asked for? Here was Solomon, the king of Israel, who already had everything. What does he ask for? Wisdom. And God gave it to him, along with a lot of other stuff.

It is tempting in our prayer lives to ask for stuff. It is permissible to ask God to help meet our needs. He wants to bless us. But He had much rather hear us ask for things that will glorify Him and bless others. I truly believe He had rather hear us begging for the salvation of others than asking Him to get us out of debt. God hears every prayer of His children. He will answer every prayer. We just might not like His answer.

TEACHING MOMENT

Do your children have their prayer list that they pray through each night? Now is the time to teach them to make sure that list includes more about others than their wants. As we kneel beside them in prayer, we have the perfect opportunity to guide them. In fact, before you pray, write out their list and talk about each person or thing.

Remember, we are not raising children. We are raising child raisers. What you teach them now about prayer will be passed down to their children and hopefully their children. Prayers change things. Look at how wise Solomon was in the beginning of his reign. He was known as the wisest king on earth. But he obviously neglected his prayer life later in his life. Just look what happened to his kingdom. He took wives who spiritually led him astray. His son, Rehoboam, lost the kingdom quickly.

Don't stop praying. Pray when you feel like it and when you don't. Pray when you are tired and when you are rested. Pray! Pray for others. Pray for the lost. Pray for your needs. Just pray! God hears and wants to respond. Just pray.

I am thankful, God, that You are listening all the time. You know my needs well before I even ask. Help me to prioritize my prayer life to put others before me. I trust You to give as You see fit.

MAY 18

DEATH OF A CHILD

1 Chronicles 24

BEST VERSE: 2A

But Nadab and Abihu died before their father and had no sons.

If you read only this account of Nadab and Abihu's deaths, it may appear that they just died young. You have to go back to Leviticus 10 to find out why they died. As sons of Aaron they were anointed as priests, but the Word says they offered "strange fire" at the tabernacle. They obviously were not following the Law as given by God through Moses, and God killed them there on the spot.

It is always sad when a child dies before their parents. That's not the way it is supposed to happen, right? No parent should have to bury their child. But here we see that Nadab and Abihu were being disobedient and rebellious, which resulted in their untimely death. The same can happen today.

TEACHING MOMENT

Children who deliberately spit at God and deny His supremacy risk punishment and the consequences of sin. No parent wants to hear that, I know. No parent wants to see their child suffer or even die for their sins. But I bet you can name people you know who have lost children to drugs, driving under the influence, violent lifestyles, or other destructive patterns. Sin has consequences. That hasn't changed.

How do you, as parents, protect your children from making these kinds of wrong choices? How do you guard their hearts from being lured away by the world? All you can do is pray and saturate their minds with His Word. You have to live it yourselves. And once you've done all that, give them over to God. Don't be a hyprocrite. Don't say, "Do as I say, not as I do."

This may sound harsh for a devotional. I guess it is, but it is what the Word says. God is still a holy, righteous, jealous God who requires us to honor and uphold His name. We can't be called His child and live like the devil. If that is you today, repent and return to righteous living. Amen?

Lord, I know I come short too many days of living up to Your standards. Help me to honor Your name by living a life that exemplifies You. Help me teach others to do the same.

MAY 19

BIRTH RECORD

Psalms 87–88

BEST VERSE: 87:6

The Lord will count when He registers the peoples, 'This one was born there.' Selah.

Isn't it amazing when you read God's Word how many times you see a verse that strikes you in a completely new and profound way? This verse, for instance. I have read Psalm 87 many times, but today this verse hit me in a way I had never considered before. God is counting us! He knows when and where we were born. Now, I've always known that, but I had never seen it written. Well, I had seen it, but it never registered like this before.

Where were you born? I was born at Phoebe Putney Hospital in Albany, Georgia, on a Friday evening around 6. I only weighed a little over five pounds (I have been trying since then to gain weight. Ha!) That evening, God counted me. Selah!

TEACHING MOMENT

When you help your children with their math and they are complaining, read them this verse. Tell them that even God counts. And think of how high He has to count to count everyone who ever lived. Hmmm, I wonder how many that is? Some estimate over one hundred billion. Only God knows for certain.

Remind your children that they are important if God counted them. He knows them intimately. He not only counted them, but He also counted every hair on their heads. Wow! Now that's a good counter.

What are you counting right now? Are you counting the number of days until vacation? How about the number of days until you can retire? How about counting something important like the number of your neighbors or friends or family members who don't know Christ? Then start subtracting from that number by being deliberate to share Christ with them.

Lord, You are the ultimate mathematician. Nothing escapes Your keen eye. Thank You for counting me and knowing me like You do.

MAY 20

REJECTING GOD

2 Chronicles 28

BEST VERSE: 24B

And he closed the doors of the house of the Lord and made altars for himself in every corner of Jerusalem.

Ahaz was, to put it simply, a very bad king. Just read 2 Chronicles 28 and you will see. It's a wonder God didn't just strike him dead with a lightning bolt or something. That's why I am not God. Ha!

This verse caught my eye when I read it, "and he closed the doors of the house of the Lord and made altars for himself in every corner of Jerusalem." He just shut up the temple. He was done with God, so it seemed. And he didn't want the people going either. That's bad.

TEACHING MOMENT

We do the same thing, in a way, when we neglect our church. Did you know that today someone who attends church just forty percent of the time is considered a regular attender? Now don't hear me wrong. I am not saying you have to be at church every single time the doors are open. But we allow too many things to get in the way of worship.

Your children need to know that worshiping with fellow believers is more important than soccer, swim meets, or camping trips. If they grow up thinking church is something you do on the weekends when you have nothing else planned, that's exactly how they will treat God. You might as well be like Ahaz and close the doors.

Church attendance is a sign of obedience to our Lord. We should want to be in His house with other believers worshiping and praising His name. We should crave the fellowship we get when we are together. Look at your family calendar today and make sure you have your day of worship prioritized.

Father, I do not want to become legalistic about church attendance, but I do want a desire to be in God's house more. I need other believers in my life to encourage and strengthen my faith. Help me, Father, to make my church a priority in my life.

MAY 21

PLAYDOUGH

Romans 9

BEST VERSES: 20-21

On the contrary, who are you, O man, who answers back to God? The thing molded will not say to the molder, "Why did you make me like this," will it? Or does not the potter have a right over the clay, to make from the same lump one vessel for honorable use and another for common use?

Don't you just love playdough? When I was little, we had the playdough fun factory where you could make all kinds of cool things. You would stuff the playdough into the machine and attach forms to the other end. By pressing the playdough through it would come out in shapes.

The one key thing was you had to keep your playdough soft and pliable. If you didn't seal your container well, it would get hard and brittle. Then it would not make shapes. It was stuck in a shape that usually wasn't very fun.

TEACHING MOMENT

I am sure your children have played with playdough. This is a perfect passage to share with them while you are making stuff. Just like they have the power to shape the playdough into whatever shape they want, God has the authority to do the same to us. But unlike the lifeless playdough, we have a choice, a free will. We can refuse to be molded. We can get rigid and stiff and not useable for anything.

And what happens to hard playdough? It has to be discarded, thrown away. God wants to use us, but we have to be willing. If we refuse His hands to mold us into the perfect shape He has in mind, He won't and can't use us.

Mom and Dad, are you moldable? Are you willing to let God get a hold of you and shape you into whatever He wants? You may think you are too old to be reshaped. Hardly! God can take anyone who is pliable and use them to complete His purpose in this world. Let Him shape you!

Great Shaper of Souls, mold me into Your perfect image. Take me and make me what you want me to be. If I resist, press harder.

MAY 22

HOUSE OF THE WICKED

Job 18

BEST VERSE: 21

Surely such are the dwellings of the wicked, and this is the place of him who does not know God.

Bildad is assuming, due to Job's suffering, that Job is a wicked man and is getting his just desserts. He rattles off a list of punishments and judgments that fall on the wicked and ends his rant in chapter 18 with the verse above.

But I have seen really wicked people living in the lap of luxury. They seem to have life by the tail. Everything they touch turns to gold. Yet they abhor God and have nothing to do with righteousness. We can't assume poverty and suffering is equated with wickedness. It just doesn't work that way.

TEACHING MOMENT

The next time little Johnny comments about someone you see on the street, make sure he understands that outward appearances do not always portray the whole story. You may have heard the expression "before you judge a man, walk a mile in his shoes."

How do you get your children to not judge when they see or hear someone who appears to be down and out? You do it by being Jesus to that person. They need to be taught to see everyone through the eyes of Christ. When we do that, we can love them no matter how they look or smell.

Have you been judgmental this week? Have you made assumptions about someone? Confess that and then make it right. If possible, go to that person. Ask the Lord what He would have you do.

Give me Your eyes, Lord. Let me see everyone through the eyes of Jesus. I want to see their eternal worth, not what they appear to be here on this earth.

MAY 23

KEEPING SUNDAY HOLY

Nehemiah 13

BEST VERSE: 19

It came about that just as it grew dark at the gates of Jerusalem before the sabbath, I commanded that the doors should be shut and that they should not open them until after the sabbath. Then I stationed some of my servants at the gates so that no load would enter on the sabbath day.

I am not going to argue about whether the Sabbath is Saturday or Sunday. At the time of Nehemiah, the Sabbath was from sunset on Friday to sunset on Saturday. Today, the vast majority of Christians recognize Sunday as the day of worship. Enough said about that.

The reason I chose this verse was more about how we treat our Holy Day. I am not a legalist. I don't have a problem with people who have to work on Sundays. Society has changed since I was a boy in Pelham, Georgia. I remember on Sundays every store in town was closed. There was a "Blue Law" which required businesses to close that day. Our downtown was a literal ghost town on Sundays, except for church traffic. This allowed everyone a chance to rest and recognize that this day was different.

TEACHING MOMENT

We do need to teach our children that every day is holy to the Lord. However, there is a day we choose to meet with fellow believers to worship. Your day may be Saturday or Sunday, but whatever day it is, make it special. Set aside some time that day to gather with other believers. The Word tells us not to forsake the assembling of ourselves together. We need fellowship with other believers.

Your children will learn the joy and peace that comes from worshiping together as they watch you doing the same. Explain to them why you are going to church this Sunday. There will come a time when they will have to choose on their own whether church is important to them. But while they are with you in your home, they need to know how important it is to be there.

Let God lead you this week as you seek to serve Him. He gets pleasure in seeing His children worship Him.

Thank You, Lord, for setting aside a day to rest and worship. I look forward to seeing my brothers and sisters this Sunday. Help me teach my children the importance of worship without sliding into legalism.

MAY 24

CLEAR CONSCIENCE

Acts 23

BEST VERSE: 1

Paul, looking intently at the Council, said, "Brethren, I have lived my life with a perfectly good conscience before God up to this day."

You have probably heard the statement "I have a clear conscience." Here in this verse we see Paul saying that very thing. But what does that mean? How can someone really have a clear conscience? Isn't there something in everyone that they feel badly about?

Think of all the evil Paul did before he came to Christ. He stood by while Stephen was stoned. He pursued believers to throw them in jail and even kill them. But when he met Christ on the road to Damascus, all those sins were forgiven. He was completely cleansed, not just his heart but also his conscience. The Lord gave him a new mind with instructions not to dwell in the past.

TEACHING MOMENT

Our children sin. Let's admit that. Most of us see them make bad choices daily. Usually their sins at an early age are "little" sins, like lying or hitting their brother or sister. But sin is sin, and the devil wants them to feel badly about it. So badly in fact, that they can't forgive themselves sometimes.

But if your child is a believer, every sin they have committed in the past and all those they will commit in the future are under the blood of Christ. What a conscience clearing statement! Moms and dads, you have to teach your kids that. They need to know that no matter what they do, Christ loves them and has died to forgive them.

That doesn't give them (or us) the license to do as we please though. You have to make that distinction with them. As a believer, the Holy Spirit will convict them when they have sinned to drive them to repentance, not to guilt. We are free as believers to do as we should.

The next time your child sins and you have to correct them, afterwards celebrate the fact that the guilt is gone once they repent. There is no burden to bear. Hallelujah!

O God, I know I am forgiven, but it is so hard to live with a clear conscience. Satan attacks me with accusations. Let me only hear You whisper, "You are forgiven."

MAY 25

HIGHWAY OF HOLINESS

Isaiah 35

BEST VERSE: 8

A highway will be there, a roadway, and it will be called the Highway of Holiness. The unclean will not travel on it, but it will be for him who walks that way, and fools will not wander on it.

I don't know if you have ever traveled on a bad road, but it can be tiresome and dangerous. Dodging potholes can prove to be more than you can handle, especially at a higher speed. I truly take for granted a good highway until I come across a bad one.

Isn't it good to know that God's highway, the highway of holiness, is perfect? Only the righteous will be on it. That means you are free from the threat of robbers or those whom want to harm you. It is not always smooth, but that does not matter because God is with you. He will help you navigate the potholes.

TEACHING MOMENT

The next time you are in the car with your kids and hit a pothole or a bad spot in the road, talk about this highway of holiness. Ask your kids what they think that highway is like. When you get home, tell them you want them to draw you a picture of God's highway.

Ask them where they think it leads them. Ask them who is on the road with them. Children have such wonderful imaginations. It will be interesting to see what they come up with. Do they think the road will be barren or full of beautiful things? Do they think it will be narrow or wide?

How is your highway experience? Do you trust the road builder to prepare the road for you? Unless you are traveling on God's highway, you are one miserable person. Stop taking the detours. Follow His highway to peace. He will keep you as long as you are traveling with Him.

Lord, I like to choose my own route, and that gets me into trouble. I know that. Teach me to follow Your highway. I want to be holy as You are holy.

MAY 26

JELLO MOLDS

Romans 12

BEST VERSE: 2

And do not be conformed to this world, but be transformed by the renewing of your mind, so that you may prove what the will of God is, that which is good and acceptable and perfect.

I remember when I was growing up my mom would make a lot of jello for us kids. It was cheap, and we loved it. Sometimes she would put fruit cocktail and nuts and even cheese in it. I loved the creations she would come up with.

But what was even cooler was when she had some different molds she used to make it. They had a shaped side and a replaceable shaped bottom. After the jello jelled overnight she would dump it upside down and remove it, thus revealing the shape of the bowl in the jello. As a kid, I thought that was just cool. The jello took on the shape of the bowl.

TEACHING MOMENT

As believers, we need to make sure we do let our children take on the shape of the world. It is so easy to compromise a little here and a little there. Before we know it, they look just like the world. How do we prevent that?

Pour them into the mold of God's Word. Pour them into the lives of godly men and women. Pour them into the mold of an environment that exudes Jesus. If you don't, the world will pour them into its mold.

When we pour them into the correct molds, they will begin to take that shape. They will look more and more like Jesus. When they are exposed, all others will see is Jesus.

And when others tell you that you shouldn't force that mold on them, quote this verse to them. By pouring them into God's mold you help prove what is good and acceptable and perfect.

O Lord, I want to have Your shape and Your image on me. I want others to see You first when they see me. Most of all, I want my children to reflect You to others.

MAY 27

SPIRITUAL DISCIPLINE

1 Corinthians 4

BEST VERSE: 14

I do not write these things to shame you, but to admonish you as my beloved children.

Why do we think being disciplined or admonished is a bad thing? Look at the verse for today. Paul is really coming down hard on the Corinthians. There were a lot of problems in that church, and he was not pleased with their behavior. He could have just let them work out the issues without his interference, but he loved them too much to do that.

He said, "admonish you as my beloved children." Do you get that? He chastised them because he loved them. I truly feel we have failed in our churches today in this area. We do not hold people accountable for their actions. Admonishment is not a bad thing. It is a godly thing when done to correct a believer and warn them of their straying.

TEACHING MOMENT

How do you think your children will turn out if you never discipline them? Do you think they will be good parents? Remember we are not raising children; we are raising child raisers. We have to teach them the importance of good and evil, right and wrong, belief and unbelief, obedience and disobedience.

I never enjoyed disciplining any child, whether they were my own two or someone else's child. I don't enjoy seeing tears or hearing them cry. But I had rather see and hear that than see them making horrible decisions because I failed to teach them the principles mentioned above.

The next time you have to discipline your children, take a moment to teach them why. They need to understand why they are being corrected. It's not "just because." It's because there is a cause—His cause. He loves us so much and wants us to follow Him. We cannot do that unless we are willing to submit to His chastisement when necessary. Be a good student and a better teacher!

You know, I don't like to get spanked, God. But sometimes I just need a good "whooping." Keep me on the straight and narrow path.

MAY 28

CIVIL DISOBEDIENCE

Acts 5

BEST VERSE: 29

But Peter and the apostles answered, "We must obey God rather than men."

Don't you just love Peter's response here? What a change in a man who just a few weeks prior had gone back to fishing. Now, here he stands before the religious leaders of his day, telling them he is boldly representing Jesus—whom he had denied three times on that fateful night.

There are times when we must choose obedience to God over obedience to man. Those times may become more and more frequent in the days ahead. We must be ready. What will you choose? When you are faced with that decision that could cost you your job or maybe even your life, what will you do? (Notice I said "when" not "if.")

TEACHING MOMENT

Our children are more than likely going to face these same decisions. They may face these decisions in school when faced with a project that flies in the face of their faith. With your knowledge and support, will they choose to take the zero and voice their opposition respectfully? Or will they silently just do the project even though they know it is against everything they believe?

We must help them be bold in the face of a world that is doing everything it can to tear down and destroy our faith. Our children are being bombarded by ideas and words that tell them their faith is stupid, ridiculous, and intolerant. What will they do when faced with the tough choice? Will they be strong or weak?

I will ask you again. What will you do? What example will you give them? How far will you go to take your stand for Christ?

The Holy Spirit will lead me to obey You God rather than men, but I have to do my part and surrender and obey Your voice. Help me to be ready and train up my children to be the same.

MAY 29

DON'T LOOK BACK

Isaiah 38

BEST VERSE: 17B

It is You who has kept my soul from the pit of nothingness, for You have cast all my sins behind Your back.

Let me ask you a personal question. How do you feel when you know you have sinned against God? I feel horrible. I feel like Hezekiah who said in verse 17a of this chapter, "Lo, for my own welfare I had great bitterness . . ." That sounds pretty bad, doesn't it?

But then look what he says in the rest of the verse. He recognizes that it is God who keeps him. He says God has cast his sins behind His back. What? God forgives us and then forgets it. Why can't we? If God can forgive eternal mistakes, why can't we forgive others?

TEACHING MOMENT

Children can beat themselves up over mistakes. When your little Johnny or Susie gets in the dumps over a failure, read them this verse. Remind them God forgives them and so do you. They need to hear, that and they need to feel that. How can they feel that? By the way you treat them once they have confessed and accepted responsibility.

Don't get historical when they make a mistake or sin. You know what I mean. "Johnny, that's the tenth time you've done that this week." "Susie, I have told you every day this week not to do that." Now, I am not excusing their behavior. But kids learn by doing. We have to walk with them in the process. More importantly, they need to understand that God forgives them and forgets the sin. Drive that home.

Have you forgiven yourself? We ask the Lord to forgive us but hold on to the guilt. Why don't you let it go today? Let the Lord have it. He can handle it.

Thank You Father for Your mercy and grace. Your forgiveness washes over me, and I am thankful. Remind me today of the distance you remove my sins from Your thoughts. They are behind You.

MAY 30

WHO DOESN'T LIKE A PARADE?

Nehemiah 12

BEST VERSES: 31, 38

Then I had the leaders of Judah come up on top of the wall, and I appointed two great choirs, the first proceeding to the right on top of the wall. . . . The second choir proceeded to the left.

These probably seem like strange verses to write a devotional about. Well, I'm just strange like that. Seriously, you have to read all of Nehemiah to understand why I selected these verses. They had been rebuilding the wall and getting everything prepared to re-establish worship in Jerusalem. What better way to celebrate than to have a parade?

So, Nehemiah gets two choirs on top of the wall, and they begin to march around the city singing and praising God. Everyone in the city could see them and hear them. He wanted to make sure everyone could take part in this celebration of praise. Walking the wall also was a strong visual of what the Lord had done through them. Rebuilding that wall was a huge!

TEACHING MOMENT

Teaching our children to celebrate big movements of God in their lives is important. They should let everyone know it was God who did amazing things through them! Giving praise to Him can encourage others to trust Him. Giving praise to Him encourages their hearts to continue to trust Him. And giving praise to Him can point the lost toward Him.

What spiritual victories have your children experienced lately? How can you help them direct all the praise to the Father? Why not have a parade around your house? Get some "instruments" and come up with a song you all can sing to praise God. I guarantee your children won't soon forget that parade.

Are you marching in praise today? Or are you sulking about what God "hasn't done" for you? Take a moment and reflect on all that He has done. Then have a parade in your own mind. Praise the one who is able to do more than you can ever imagine. Let Him be your object of praise today.

God, You are the one who has brought me through. You are the one who defeats my enemies. You are the one who gives me strength. For that, I will praise You!

MAY 31

POPPING UP

Acts 1

BEST VERSE: 3

To these He also presented Himself alive after His suffering, by many convincing proofs, appearing to them over a period of forty days and speaking of the things concerning the kingdom of God.

Have you ever had the experience when you kept running into the same person everywhere you went? You go to the grocery store, and there they are. You stop off to get gas for your car, and they pull up beside you. You go out to eat and, lo and behold, there they sit. You finally begin to look for them wherever you go.

I bet people started feeling that way about Jesus during this forty-day period. It says He was "appearing to them over a period of forty days and speaking of the things concerning the kingdom of God." They not only saw Him, they heard Him. He was still teaching. But now, since He was in His resurrected body, they were listening even more closely.

TEACHING MOMENT

The next time you "pop in" and surprise your child, mention this verse to them. They need to know that Jesus' physical body is not necessary (like yours is) to be present among them. He is there all the time, through the presence of the Holy Spirit in their lives (if they are a believer). They don't have to look for Him. They don't have to search for Him anymore.

But that also means that everywhere they go, they take Him with them. He is aware of everything they say or think. He knows which friends are best for them. He knows the words they should use when someone is mean to them. All they have to do is talk to Him, and He will direct them.

I don't know about you, but I forget that sometimes. I get so frustrated with my situation that I start to "figure it out" for myself instead of pushing the pause button and asking the Lord to guide me. Jesus doesn't have to "pop in" unannounced in my life. He is there. I just have to listen.

Will you listen today to the ever-present Christ in you?

Often, I get so busy that I cannot hear or see You Father. My prayer is that I will choose to be still and know that you are God. Thank You for being ever present!

JUNE 1

HOLY GRIEF

2 Chronicles 34

BEST VERSE: 19

When the king heard the words of the law, he tore his clothes.

Every time I hear the expression "Good Grief," I think of Charlie Brown. I can just hear Lucy saying, "Good Grief, Charlie Brown." Okay, I'm telling my age again.

But here in this passage we see a true expression of good grief by Josiah. It would be better called holy grief. When he heard the words of THE WORD, his heart was grieved over his and the nation's disobedience. He obviously had never heard these words and was appalled that they had not kept God's commandments that were so simply spelled out in the Word.

TEACHING MOMENT

This is a beautiful example of how easy it is to find out what God wants you to do. Your children simply have to read God's Word to find out how to live their lives. Without it, they have no clue. Josiah was trying to do all the right things, but until he heard God's Word, he didn't realize all that was commanded.

Now, I am not saying that little Johnny and Susie have to be legalist and spend all their time making sure they are following every command of God. As Christians, we have the Holy Spirit to guide us too. Josiah didn't have that. But we still need to read and study the Word to find out how God would have us live.

How is your study of the Word going? There are so many truths hidden in the Word of God. It is somewhat like a treasure hunt each day as we turn to it. Ask the Lord each time you pick up the Bible to show you a new truth to live by. He is faithful to disclose Himself to those who truly seek Him.

O Lord, my God, You are faithful to reveal Your truths in Your Word each time I seek You. Thank You for leading me in Your path of righteousness. Help me seek You earnestly each day.

KEEP SILENT

Job 16

BEST VERSE: 2

I have heard many such things; sorry comforters are you all.

Recently I was called to a home where someone's brother had just died. I have known this person for ten years. I needed to be there to lend comfort, but words were not necessary. There were no words that were good enough to ease the pain. So, I told them that. I did pray, but I did not quote a bunch of verses and wax eloquently. I just prayed.

Job needed friends to be with him, not try to figure out what he did wrong. I love his words here. "I have heard many such things; sorry comforters are you all." Haven't you wanted to say that sometimes? He is trying to tell that he doesn't want their advice, just their love and friendship.

TEACHING MOMENT

How do we teach comfort to a child? They will only learn this firsthand. When you comfort them, they will learn. When they see you comfort others, they will learn. Comfort is not taught—it's caught. Sometimes we just hold them tight and love on them. That's comfort. Sometimes we pat them on the back. That's comfort. Sometimes we cry crocodile tears with them. That's comfort.

Whenever your child is hurting, remember they are taking mental notes of how you comfort them. Over the years they will fine-tune their comforting skills by watching you. If you want a hardhearted child, then be stoic and hard on them. That's what you will get. But if you want a child who recognizes the hurt in others and seeks to comfort them, then be that to them.

Are you hurting today, Mom or Dad? Are you seeking comfort in something or someone that is not healthy? Were you brought up to not cry? Stop right where you are and seek the Great Comforter. He is always listening to His children. He wants to use His Holy Spirit in your life to not only convict you but to also comfort you. Won't you let Him?

Father, let me never forget that my children are watching! I want to show how to rest in You. I want them to learn how to walk with You daily.

BLESSING YOUR HOME

1 Chronicles 16

BEST VERSE: 43

Then all the people departed each to his house, and David returned to bless his household.

First Chronicles 16 is a beautiful chapter on the return of the ark to the tent of meeting in Jerusalem. David sets it back up and then establishes the men who will attend to the sacrifices and worship. Verses 8–36 are a must-read. It's a psalm of thanksgiving and is full of beautiful imagery.

But it's the last part of the last verse of this chapter that struck me. After this day of worship and celebration, "David returned to bless his household." The king of Israel goes home and blesses his family. Why didn't he just let the priest do that? Wasn't he too busy to do that? No, David knew the importance of leading his family well, and that begins with blessing them.

TEACHING MOMENT

If you have not done that, dads, do it today. Gather your brood together tonight and pray a blessing over them. Lay your hands on their heads and ask the Lord to guide and strengthen them. Ask the Lord to give them wisdom and discernment to follow Him. Ask the Lord to direct their every step as they go to school or play. Ask the Lord to bless them with a godly spouse.

Then turn to your wife and bless her. She needs that. Ask her how you can bless her in the name of Jesus. Get on your knees before her and lay your hands on her and pray over her. I promise you she will let you. This will bless her socks off.

This devotional today is addressed towards men and dads, but ladies you also can get a takeaway from it. You too can bless your children daily. Don't just pray for protection over them. Pray for the Lord to use them how He wants to.

O God, You bless me every day. Help me to be faithful to bless my family daily. Let me show them the power of prayer in their lives as they see these blessings come to fruition.

JUNE 4

A FRIEND'S COUNSEL

Job 4

BEST VERSE: 5

But now it has come to you, and you are impatient; It touches you, and you are dismayed.

I have often wondered what I could get out of Job's chapters in which his friends speak. Their counsel was so misinformed. They truly believed, because Job was suffering, he had some secret sin that he just refused to confess.

But here, Eliphaz, one of his friends, says something that can be so true, even today. Have you ever encouraged someone who was suffering, but when the tables are turned you forget the comforting words you shared with others? It's one thing to see others hurting and to reach out to them. It's a whole other world when it's you. Right? That is what Eliphaz is saying to Job. "Take your own advice."

TEACHING MOMENT

I have seen this so much in children through the years. When a child's friend is hurting, they are quick to come alongside them and try to comfort them. But when they get hurt, say, by being dumped by a boyfriend or girlfriend, their whole world crumbles.

Mom and Dad, you must be like Eliphaz here and remind your children how compassionate they were for their friends. Remind them of the words they used to comfort their friends. Allow them to grieve appropriately, but remind them of their greatest friend, Jesus. He always has the right words to say.

How about yourselves? Are you allowing the comforting words of the Lord to advise you? Are you seeking wisdom from His Word daily? There is no better source of guidance and truth. Friends can help you through hard times, but there is one who sticks closer than a brother, remember? Let Him be your advisor and comforter.

O Great Counselor, hear my cries. And let me hear the cries of others so that I may be a comfort to them. Let my ears be Your ears.

JUNE 5

PUT IT BACK

2 Chronicles 35

BEST VERSE: 3

He also said to the Levites who taught all Israel and who were holy to the Lord, "Put the holy ark in the house which Solomon the son of David king of Israel built; it will be a burden on your shoulders no longer. Now serve the LORD your God and His people Israel."

Have you ever been told, "Put that back!" Oh, I remember well being told that when I was little. I would go down to my dad's shop with him to watch him work on something. He had every kind of tool a little boy could want—drills, saws, hammers, you name it, he had it. But if I ever picked up a tool that was beyond my ability, my dad would say, "Put that back!" He wanted me to be safe, and he wanted his tools in their right place.

After Josiah had restored the temple, he commanded the Levites to return the Ark to the Holy of Holies. What?! Why wasn't it there to begin with. Well, it had obviously been moved. Perhaps it was moved to keep it safe from the rebellious kings in the past who had tried to stop the people from worshiping. Perhaps it was moved to keep it safe while they renovated the temple. Whatever the reason, it now belonged back in its rightful place.

TEACHING MOMENT

Everything belongs in its rightful place. That includes your kids. Your kids belong to God. He gave them to you for a short time to invest in them, to teach them about Him, to love them and to give them back to Him. You need to teach them that their heart belongs to God. He longs to have them come home.

Your children will only experience true peace when they place their hearts back in the rightful place—the hands of God. When they surrender to Jesus, He restores them to their spots in His heart. He has a spot for all of us. I don't understand how He can absorb everyone into His heart, but He can.

Where is your heart right now? Is it in its rightful place? Put it back where it belongs. Keep your heart safe. There is no safer place for your heart to rest than in the capable, loving hands of God. He will NEVER break your heart. He will never desert you. Put it back.

O God, lover of my heart, take my heart back where it belongs. Show me the love it desires has always been there. Thank You for loving me so well.

JUNE 6

LONG LIVE THE KING

2 Kings 15

BEST VERSES: 1-2

In the twenty-seventh year of Jeroboam king of Israel, Azariah son of Amaziah king of Judah became king. He was sixteen years old when he became king, and he reigned fifty-two years in Jerusalem; and his mother's name was Jecoliah of Jerusalem.

King Azariah (Uzziah) was the longest ruling king of Judah or Israel. He was a good king. He followed the Lord, or at least tried to. He began his reign at sixteen! Wow! And he reigned fifty-two years. But the verses go on to say the Lord struck him with leprosy. We don't know exactly when that happened, but it must have been later in his reign because his son ruled in his place and eventually took over when he was twenty-five.

Why am I recounting all of this? Just to show you that God can use anyone who is willing to be used. He took a teenage boy who became leprous and made him the longest ruling king of the nation. God can use anyone, anytime, anywhere, anyhow He chooses. We just have to be willing.

TEACHING MOMENT

Many parents tell their kids, "You can be anything you want to be when you grow up." I understand the sentiment and respect their desires for their children, but that is just not true. A short child will most likely not succeed in the NBA.

Instead, we should be telling them, "Johnny, we need to pray that the Lord shows you what He has for you to do to honor Him." That's the most important thing. So, whether he is a banker, soldier or astronaut, he can honor God. Push them to excel, not for self, but for God. Give them opportunities to thrive, not for you, but for the glory of the Lord.

Do you know what the Lord has called you to do? So many of us are still seeking that. Ask Him. He doesn't want to hide this from you. He is preparing you every step of the way to be His instrument in His master plan for mankind.

Open my eyes, Lord, to what You have for me. Let me see the opportunities plainly. Help me point others to Your plan for their lives.

JUNE 7

A WHOLE WEEK

1 Kings 16

BEST VERSE: 15A

In the twenty-seventh year of Asa king of Judah, Zimri reigned seven days at Tirzah.

If you were elected President of the United States, what could you get done in seven days? Not much. It takes a while to get yourself established and set up to rule. Seven days just isn't long enough to make a huge impact on the country, is it?

That's how long Zimri had to rule Israel. He had taken over by killing the previous king, which didn't sit well with the army, especially Omri, who came and killed him. Wow! Justice is swift and brutal. I wonder what Zimri might have done as king if he had lived longer. We will never know.

TEACHING MOMENT

What can we learn from such a lesson to teach our children? Well, we know that treachery against another person is wrong. Zimri paid the ultimate price for his treachery—death. Our children must see that dealing harshly with others will not be received well. Now, I doubt they will face a threat on their life, but it can cost them dearly in other ways.

What else can we learn from Zimri? Nowhere does it say God had chosen him king of Israel. He had proclaimed himself king and took the throne.

Our children should learn that self-proclamations seldom last long. We should teach them to allow the Lord to exalt them in His time.

Are you guilty of proclaiming your greatness? Are you known as someone who brags on yourself? You may be one of those who says, "If I were in charge . . ." Allow the Lord to raise you up. Those whom He raises up are blessed by Him. He will sustain you.

Lord, I will wait on Your recognition of me. I will allow You to be the one who puts me forth. I will trust that You know exactly where I need to be and what I need to be doing.

JUNE 8

GETTING GOD'S ATTENTION

2 Chronicles 6

BEST VERSE: 40

Now, O my God, I pray, let Your eyes be open and Your ears attentive to the prayer offered in this place.

You really should read the entire sixth chapter of 2 Chronicles to get a glimpse of what is happening here. Solomon had just finished building and furnishing the temple. God's glory had filled it, and now Solomon is offering a prayer of dedication.

I have attended a lot of dedication ceremonies in my life. But I have never heard a prayer offered like this one. Verse 40 caught my eye though. Solomon says, "Now, O my God, I pray, let Your eyes be open and Your ears attentive to the prayer offered in this place" (emphasis added). That is so important! We need not even pray if we don't believe God is looking and listening. But because we know He does, we pray.

TEACHING MOMENT

Your children may ask you, "Mom/Dad, how do I know God is listening? How does He hear all the prayers of all the people all over the world at the same time?" How do you answer? You answer by telling how God has answered your prayers and the prayers of others you know. You answer by telling them the peace you get when you pray. You answer by telling them that although you don't understand, you trust.

Each time we take a breath we don't wonder if there is oxygen out there to breathe in. We just breathe, most of the time involuntarily. We breathe knowing that the oxygen in the air around us is enough to keep us breathing. Prayer should be the same. We should pray without ceasing, knowing that the Almighty God of the universe is listening. He is prepared to answer all our prayers according to His perfect will for our lives.

Pray, believing that even before you utter the first syllable of the first word, God is listening.

What joy I have knowing that You, the God of the universe, listen to my every word. Your Word tells us that when we don't understand, You do. You are the one who hears and responds.

JUNE 9

OUR BELOVED

Song of Solomon 5

BEST VERSE: 9

What is your beloved more than another beloved, O most beautiful among women? What is your beloved more than another beloved, that you thus adjure us?

This verse is part of the discourse between the woman/maiden in the Song of Solomon and her handmaidens. She is asking them to go look for her bridegroom, her beloved. They ask a simple question. "Why is he so great?"

May I ask you a question? What would you tell someone if they asked that about your Lord? "Why is He so great?" I could tell you story after story of how I have seen Him work in my life. I could tell you how I have seen Him change lives. I could tell you the love I feel each time I bow before Him in prayer. But what would you say? Have you thought about that?

TEACHING MOMENT

Our children need to hear the stories of the works of God in our lives and in the lives of others. They need to be told about the wonderful works of grace we have experienced. Write these events down so you won't forget. Give your children that legacy of faith that you have witnessed firsthand. Show them how your Beloved has come to visit you in your darkest moments.

Then help them develop their own life story with Christ. When something happens in their lives that only God could have done, record it for them. When they are grown, they will appreciate it.

I will never forget one of our experiences with our son. He was still going through his immunizations and needed the Measles, Mumps, and Rubella (MMR) shot. The only problem was the vaccine contains egg, and he is egg-intolerant. After a week of fasting and praying together, my wife and I took him for the shots. Through a series of increased dosages with no reaction, they gave him the shot. No reaction. A few weeks later, we decided to see if God had just healed him of that allergy, so we gave him a little egg (we had the Benadryl on standby). He reacted immediately.

Now you may blow that off as just coincidence. But we know that God protected him that day of the shot so he could receive it. Our Beloved cares for the smallest things in our lives. He is greater than all the rest. In fact, there is no other. He is the only true God! Amen?

You are the God of greatness. You are the Almighty God who is over all. Thank You for showing me Your greatness personally. Help me tell Your story to my children.

JUNE 10

THE GREATEST

1 Corinthians 13

BEST VERSE: 13

But now faith, hope, love, abide these three; but the greatest of these is love.

In 2016, one of the greatest boxers of all time died, Muhammad Ali. He was, without a doubt, a showman. He talked big but delivered once he got in the ring. He even called himself "The Greatest." And he very well was the greatest when he was in his prime. But guess what? He wasn't the greatest forever! Like all of us, he was mortal, and in the end his body became frail and eventually gave in.

Why is "love" called the greatest of these? What makes it better than faith and hope? Because God is love. He is, in His purest form, love. Everything He does is because of His love for us. Everything He created was because of love. And He wants us to be the same.

TEACHING MOMENT

Have you ever asked your children, "Who do you love?" We all have done that, especially when they are just learning to talk. We love hearing them say "Mama" or "Dada." And we love telling them over and over again just how much we love them.

But do you tell them daily just how much God loves them? Do you tell them repeatedly that, in comparison, your love is weak? Do you show them in His Word the wonderful stories of love He has written for them through the Holy Spirit?

Our children need to know they are loved by us. But it is so much more important that they know they have a loving God who loves them beyond measure. They need to know that He will never stop loving them. Others in their lives may stop loving them for one reason or another. But God is forever faithful, forever hopeful, and forever loving.

If you haven't read the entire 13th chapter of 1 Corinthians lately, do that now. Read it to your child. Help them understand the love you have and the love God has for them. And don't forget—YOU ARE LOVED!

Love! Love! Love! That really is all I need, O God. Will You show me true love today?

JUNE 11

UNENDING POWER

2 Kings 13

BEST VERSES: 20–21

Elisha died, and they buried him. Now the bands of the Moabites would invade the land in the spring of the year. As they were burying a man, behold, they saw a marauding band; and they cast the man into the grave of Elisha. And when the man touched the bones of Elisha he revived and stood up on his feet.

Pardon me, but I find a little humor in this story about Elisha. Elisha was dead. But God's power was still evident. What do you think these men were thinking when the guy they just threw in the grave jumped up on his feet? That must have been a little bit surprising. And how about the dead man? What do you think he thought? He had no idea what just happened.

God's power is never ending. Elisha possessed God's power in life and obviously even in his death. There was nothing special about Elisha. It was all God. God used him to bring life to a dead man even beyond death. But it was all God, not Elisha.

TEACHING MOMENT

Our children need to learn that God's power is never ending. He will be with us forever, even in death. When they need encouragement, they need to go to Him. When they need counsel, they need to go to Him. When they feel they can't go on, they need to go to Him. Because God will never leave them.

But there is one catch. They have to be His. They have to surrender their lives to Him to receive that never-ending power. So, our task as parents is to do everything within our power to lead them to Him. God will do the rest. We need to provide the environment, though. Our actions and lifestyles should always point to the Father.

Are you feeling weak and powerless? Are you feeling defeated? Turn to Him whose power is endless. Turn to Him who has the power to supercharge you. You have to plug into Him to receive it. He won't force-feed you.

O God, the Almighty One, give me Your power today. When I am weak, be my strength. Fill me with Your energy and strength today so that I can draw others to You.

JUNE 12

I KNOW YOU'RE UP THERE

Psalms 61–62

BEST VERSES: 61:1–4

Hear my cry, O God; give heed to my prayer. From the end of the earth I call to You when my heart is faint; lead me to the rock that is higher than I. For You have been a refuge for me, a tower of strength against the enemy. Let me dwell in Your tent forever; let me take refuge in the shelter of Your wings. Selah.

I just love the hymn "A Mighty Fortress." I couldn't help but think of it when I read these verses today. God is our refuge and tower of strength. He is our bulwark. He defends us. How? Through just His spoken word. He speaks, and Satan flees. How awesome is that?

So, when I cry out to God, He listens and responds. He doesn't do it just because we ask, though. He does it because He loves us and wants to see us thrive. He wants to lift us up. He wants to conquer our enemies. He wants us to see Him work in our lives.

TEACHING MOMENT

Teach your little Johnny to cry out to God first. They should not wait until it gets unbearable. Teach them to cry out at the first hint of the enemy. Don't let the enemy approach. Keep them at a distance. We cannot defeat them—on our own. And we don't have to.

If our children can learn this life lesson early, they will have such a deeper walk with Christ as they get older. Seeing the Lord work builds our trust in Him. He restores our faith. He increases our endurance in trials. But we have to call out.

Who are you crying out to today? Is it the Lord God? Or are you crying out to someone else? It doesn't matter how skilled they are or how many degrees they have behind their name. No one can defend you or counsel you like Jesus.

O Jesus, You are the only one I can cry out to. Help me today to stand firm and strong against the enemy. Help me trust You to defend me against the accuser.

JUNE 13

CASTING THE RIGHT BAIT

Isaiah 55

BEST VERSE: 11

So will My word be which goes forth from My mouth; it will not return to Me empty, without accomplishing what I desire, and without succeeding in the matter for which I sent it.

Anyone who knows me knows I love to bass fish. There is just something about hooking a bass and landing it. My son says, "The tug's the drug." I guess that about sums it up.

But there is one key to catching bass—using the right bait. I have thrown everything imaginable in an attempt to get one to bite. I have used top water frogs and poppers, plastic worms rigged in several different ways, crankbaits, spinnerbaits and swimbaits. When I find the right bait, my casts seldom come back empty. But it is never a sure thing.

Our verse today is talking about the Word of God being cast out to the hearers. The Lord says through Isaiah, "It will not return to Me empty." The Lord will always reel in a lost soul. His Word is powerful. It is a tasty morsel to those who are hungry for peace. But it is our job, as believers, to cast it to them. We must share the Word of God in order for them to hear it and respond to it.

TEACHING MOMENT

What are you putting before your children each day? I bet you are very careful to educate them with the required subjects to finish school. I bet some of you are very careful to teach them a skill to help them repair something. I even bet some of you teach them how to do chores. But are you teaching them how to use the Word of God?

We won't always be around. We must teach our children how to handle the Word. We must teach them to cast the Word out so others can respond. We must show them the best times and places to cast the Word. We must teach them how to respond when someone "bites" the Word. You can have the most beautiful casts in the world, but unless you know how to retrieve lost souls (assist them in responding to the Word) you may only frustrate them.

Let's cast the Word to a lost a dying world. Let's be sure to teach our children the necessary "fishing" skills to "land" the ones who respond. The joy we receive by leading someone to Christ is only surpassed by the one who is making the decision to follow Him.

Help me, Father, to know where and when to cast Your Word for a strike! I want to reel in new believers that You have saved through Your Word.

FORGOTTEN BUT NOT GONE

Isaiah 17

BEST VERSE: 10A

For you have forgotten the God of your salvation and have not remembered the rock of your refuge.

You have probably heard the old adage, "Gone, but not forgotten." Let me promise you—God is not gone. He is still there. He hasn't gone anywhere! Yet, everywhere you look, it seems He has been forgotten. Our nation has kicked Him out of every place—schools, courthouses, and even some churches.

Why do we treat God that way and then call to Him in times of distress? Every hurricane season there seems to be the threat of a massive hurricane bearing down on the east coast of Florida. People ask for prayer. Many of them would not even think of prayer on most days, but bring in a storm, and they are on their knees. Don't misunderstand my words. We need to pray. I truly believe God allows these kinds of events to wake us up. But just praying doesn't cut it. God requires repentance and remorse. He demands holiness and surrender.

TEACHING MOMENT

This is a perfect lesson for our children. We need to teach them the importance of praying at all times. But we need to teach them that we first have to confess that we are sinners in need of salvation. We need to ask the Lord Jesus in our hearts. We need to surrender to His will. Then and only then can the God of all creation begin to work in our lives. If our children want the Lord to bless them, they must turn to Him in obedience. Through the river of obedience (surrender) flows blessings.

I am as guilty as the rest. I often pray habitually without truly confessing my filthiness and flesh. Will you pray the following prayer with me today? Oh, how He wants to hear from you.

Father, forgive me! Cleanse me! Purify me! Wash me whiter than snow! Then Father, let me be Your vessel to reach a lost and dying world.

IGNORANCE IS NO EXCUSE

2 Kings 22

BEST VERSE: 11
When the king heard the words of the book of the law, he tore his clothes.

Have you ever heard that saying, "Ignorance is no excuse"? Have you ever wondered what it means? Well, many people try to use the excuse that they just didn't know. If I had only known . . . Right!

Here in this passage Josiah discovers from hearing the Word of God that the nation had not been keeping the Lord's commands. He literally had not heard the words before. But he instantly repents and tears his clothes as a sign of remorse and repentance. He then begins a country-wide cleansing of all the pagan places of worship. He becomes totally sold out to God.

TEACHING MOMENT

Our children also cannot use ignorance of something as an excuse. They will be held accountable to a holy God, just like everyone else. It is our job to show them the Word and teach them how to walk in righteousness. Will they slip? Sure. Don't you? But we have to teach them how to live the Christ life and to honor Him in all they do.

Recently someone I know made the remark that there is just too much to understand in the Bible. Well, I agree to an extent. The Bible is exhaustive (and sometimes exhausting). The Lord does not expect us to memorize it all. He doesn't expect us to know every verse in Scripture. What He does expect, however, is that we spend time in it, striving to follow the truths it contains.

Take one verse a day and meditate on it. There are 31,102 verses in the Bible. It will take you over eighty-five years to do that. Or you could read one chapter a day. That would take less than five years to read through the Bible. Whatever you choose to do, not reading is not an option. Ignorance of God's Word when it comes to living is not an excuse. Read it! Live it!

I am thankful, Lord, that each day I discover new truths in Your Word. Show me deeper things. Reveal to me the exact message You have for me today.

NUMERO UNO

Isaiah 47

BEST VERSE: 10

You felt secure in your wickedness and said, "No one sees me." Your wisdom and your knowledge, they have deluded you; for you have said in your heart, "I am, and there is no one besides me."

Babylon had been used by God to discipline Israel, but it went to their heads. In this chapter, God is speaking through Isaiah to tell the people of Babylon they have gone too far. They had started believing there was no power larger than them. They were invincible—or so they thought.

No one is invincible. No one is dispensable. We can all be replaced. God wants to use us to accomplish His work here on earth. In fact, He desires that. But we can never begin to think that God will fail without us. He is the one in charge. He is the one who empowers and strengthens us to do the work.

TEACHING MOMENT

Two- and three-year-old children go through that stage when they want to do everything for themselves. "Me do it!" "No, me do it!" We want them to learn to do things on their own. But there are some things they just can't do yet. Letting them try and fail is hard. And it takes time. The best way for them to learn, however, is by doing.

God does the same thing with us. He will not stop us from trying to do it on our own. Just like two-year-olds, we are stubborn and rebellious. We are basically saying to God, "No, me do it!" The next time your little one says that, be reminded of this. We adults are doing the same thing.

Have you done that lately? Have you determined to do something on your own? Have you tried to open a door that God has either not opened yet or has closed? Be very careful. God may just let you open it to show you that He knows best. Let Him be God. He's had a lot of practice at it.

Father, I recognize Your deity. I know You are God and I'm not. Help me trust You and Your timing for my life.

PROMISES KEPT

Isaiah 54

BEST VERSE: 10

"For the mountains may be removed and the hills may shake, but My lovingkindness will not be removed from you, and My covenant of peace will not be shaken," says the Lord who has compassion on you.

If there is one thing that is for sure, the Lord keeps His word. If He says it, you can take it to the bank. And here in today's verse He says something. Basically, he says, "The world may be falling apart around you, but I will always love you and keep My covenant with you." Wow! What a promise.

If you look around the world today, things are crazy. There are floods, earthquakes, mudslides, volcano eruptions, tornadoes and hurricanes. There are mass shootings at schools and churches. There are attacks on police along with rampant gang violence. But this verse still holds true. God loves you. If you are in covenant with Him through His Son, Jesus, there is nothing that can touch you that He doesn't allow.

TEACHING MOMENT

This is a reassuring verse for children. They want to feel safe. The next time little Johnny or Susie is anxious about something, read this verse. It should calm their spirits. The very God of all creation loves them and always will. The God who knows every soul knows them personally and wants them to know Him.

These are the truths our children need to know and understand. There is no other person who can be totally trustworthy. People fail us. But God never will. When we trust His sovereignty in our lives, we can truly rest. Teach your children that.

More importantly, show them that. When you are up against a wall with no help in sight, trust Him. Let your children watch you trust. Let your children watch you praise Him in the valley. Let your children watch you turn to the only one you can trust.

O Father, I trust You. I know You will always be there for me. I thank You for loving me enough to make me Your own.

THE BEST-LAID PLANS

Isaiah 46

BEST VERSE: 11B

Truly I have spoken; truly I will bring it to pass. I have planned it, surely I will do it.

You may have heard the saying "the best-laid plans of mice and men." Do you know where that comes from? It comes from a line in the poem "To a Mouse" by the Scottish poet, Robert Burns. Here is a modern English translation of the line: "The best laid schemes o' Mice an' Men go oft awry." So, what does that mean? No matter how carefully a project is planned, something may still go wrong with it.

I am a planner. I like to know what I am doing long before I do it. I have a one-year planning calendar on my office wall that I use to map out my year. But sometimes, God gets in the way of that. Do you know what I mean? Our verse today is telling us that God's plans will always come to pass. We get in the way sometimes of God fulfilling His plan the way and time He sees as best, but He will fulfill His plans. Why would we think we could stop God?

TEACHING MOMENT

It is so important to teach our children to plan ahead. Most schools require students to have a planner as part of their schoolbooks. This gives them a place to mark down homework assignments, upcoming tests, and school events. But we need to make sure we don't teach them to over-plan.

Your children need to allow the Lord to direct them as He wants. But hang on, Mom and Dad. That may even mean He directs them in a way that is against your plans for your child. How dare He do that! Right? Remember, your child is on loan from God. They really belong to Him. He has given you temporary stewardship, but they are His. Let Him lead them.

Are you allowing God to direct your plans? You may have your next ten years all planned out. Be careful. The mouse in the poem had his home established too, but the next harvest destroyed it (Google "To a Mouse" and read the whole poem). We must be willing to flex our plans to follow the Lord. After all, He sees the whole picture. We can't.

Lord, it is so hard to give up my plans to follow Your plans. Help me hold my calendar loosely so I can let it go if necessary. Let me teach my children to do the same.

JUNE 19

GOOD COMPANY

2 Kings 3

BEST VERSE: 14

Elisha said, "As the Lord of hosts lives, before whom I stand, were it not that I regard the presence of Jehoshaphat the king of Judah, I would not look at you nor see you."

Jehoram, king of Israel, wasn't exactly a godly king. When he came, along with Jehoshaphat, to ask Elisha's counsel, Elisha said these words which we read in verse 14. Elisha would not have even talked to Jehoram, except for the presence of Jehoshaphat. Elisha was quick to exact punishment on others. Jehoram knew that. That is probably why he took Jehoshaphat with him.

Jehoshaphat was a king who was trying to please the Lord. God honored him for that. Elisha knew that about Jehoshaphat, so he, too, showed him honor. My point for today is this—show honor to those who seek the Lord. They will only bring you closer to the Lord and may be a source of blessing in your life.

TEACHING MOMENT

So, what's the lesson for our kids? We should guide them to choose friends like Jehoshaphat, people who love the Lord and strive to please Him. Those friends will not lead them into mischief and bad deeds. They will point them toward the Lord. They may be the very people God uses to bring your children to Christ or help strengthen their walk with Him.

Now, you can't choose your children's friends. I know that. But you can, at least while they are young, limit their exposure to people who aren't going to encourage them in their walk with Christ. You can keep them from spending time at the home of unbelievers. And you need to do that, at least until they are strong enough in their faith to stand for themselves.

Do you have godly friends who influence you? I have several "Jehoshaphats" in my life. I often turn to them for godly counsel, because

I have not achieved perfect knowledge yet. I still have much to learn about walking with Christ. These friends help me do that by holding me accountable and praying for me.

If you don't have a Jehoshaphat in your life, you need to find one. Good company breeds good morals, or so the saying goes. Bad company . . . well . . . you know.

Father of Glory, give me the kind of friends who will teach me to follow you. I want friends whose reputation for following you precedes them. I thank you for putting those saints in my life.

JUNE 20

DISAGREEMENTS

Acts 15

BEST VERSES: 39–40

And there occurred such a sharp disagreement that they separated from one another, and Barnabas took Mark with him and sailed away to Cyprus. But Paul chose Silas and left, being committed by the brethren to the grace of the Lord.

We don't talk about this a lot. Christians disagree. We don't all agree on everything. Different denominations have different traditions and practices. There are some things that we must all agree on, and there are others that really aren't doctrinally critical. Whatever we do, we must agree to disagree in unity.

Paul and Barnabas disagreed about Mark. Barnabas wanted to take him back (he had deserted them earlier), but Paul didn't trust Mark yet. Later on, however, toward the end of Paul's life, he actually asked Timothy to bring Mark to see him. So, they must have made up.

TEACHING MOMENT

As parents, we must teach our children how to disagree agreeably. The world is watching us, and we must not do anything to confuse them. When they see believers fighting over stuff, they are not drawn to the Lord. In fact, they are repulsed. Your children can learn at an early age how to get along with others, so they will not be a stumbling block to others.

That means you have to live that way, too. You can't be seen and heard by your children putting down or demeaning another person. You especially need to be observed building up other believers. Children will model what they see in their parents. When they see you being ugly to someone else at church, they will believe that is acceptable behavior. Don't be guilty of that.

Do you need to go to someone and make things right? Perhaps you had a falling out some years back and you still don't see eye to eye. That's okay, but you must learn to live in unity. Others, especially the lost, are watching.

Father, help me love others as You do. Help me put aside my petty differences for the sake of Your kingdom. Let me be the one to make things right.

JUNE 21

COVENANT EYES

Job 31

BEST VERSE: 1

I have made a covenant with my eyes; how then could I gaze at a virgin?

It is hard today to not see at least one commercial or advertisement that uses scantily clad men or women to sell a product. With internet access, it is even more "in our face." Even the most innocent searches on the web can open up portals to things our eyes shouldn't see.

Job was a righteous man. He had made a covenant with his eyes to not look on another woman with lust. He knew that was sin and had chosen to guard his spirit. There is actually an internet filter called "Covenant Eyes" which you can purchase to block some of those images I mentioned earlier. I wonder if the name came from this verse.

TEACHING MOMENT

We begin teaching our children when they are young to respect other people. We teach them to say, "Yes ma'am" and "No ma'am." We even teach young men to open the doors for ladies. But do we teach them to respect another person's image? Do we teach them to look at every person with respect and not as some object?

The next time you and your children have one of those images from a commercial or billboard flash before your eyes, take the time to talk about how it does not honor God. If we don't explain what's wrong with the images, they will accept it as okay. We certainly don't want that. We want them to make a covenant with their eyes, like Job did.

Parents, are you guilty of looking at things you shouldn't? Are you filling your mind with images that betray your walk with Christ? If so, put the images down. Pick up the Word. Make a covenant with your eyes.

Lord, forgive me for not seeing everyone as You see them. Help me teach others the importance of keeping their eyes focused on You. Help me protect innocent eyes.

JUNE 22

ON A LEASH

Job 31

BEST VERSE: 6

So the Lord said to Satan, "Behold, he is in your power, only spare his life."

So many people question the Lord allowing Satan to attack Job. Why would the Lord let that happen? But look closely at this verse. God gives Satan just so much rope—just enough to hang himself.

You may not know this, but Job is believed to be the earliest book written in the Bible. The exact date is unknown. I find it interesting that the very first book written in God's Word is a story about trials and God's providence. Satan may attack us, but only as much as God allows.

TEACHING MOMENT

It is so important for our children to learn this lesson. I truly believe that once they learn about the sovereignty of God, everything else will make sense. They will trust Him, knowing that if He allowed this in their lives, He means to make us better.

That concept alone will fuel our faith. The idea that God is aware of every struggle and trial in our lives should bring us comfort. Our children will watch how we respond to adversity. If we wring our hands and panic, they will too. If we trust Him through the storm, they will learn how too.

Are you going through a Job moment? Do you feel like Satan is personally attacking you? Rest in the fact that God is aware and is watching. He is watching how you choose to respond. Respond with grace. Respond with faith.

O Father of all, I trust that You are watching. You know my struggles. Help me rest in Your strength and power.

JUNE 23

VAINLESS

1 Corinthians 15

BEST VERSE: 10

But by the grace of God I am what I am, and His grace toward me did not prove vain; but I labored even more than all of them, yet not I, but the grace of God with me.

Do you remember the song "You're So Vain" by Carly Simon? If you do, you are telling your age. Ha! Being vain is not a good thing. You think too much of yourself and not enough of others. But that's not the meaning of this verse. What is Paul saying here?

Actually, the Greek word for "vain" means "hollow" or "empty." Isn't that great? God's grace toward us is not hollow or empty. God's grace is full and limitless. It is full and rewarding. It is anything but empty.

TEACHING MOMENT

Think of all the things you give your children. Think of all the things you do for them. Are any of those "in vain"? Of course not! All we do as parents for our children has a purpose, or at least they should. We have the opportunity every day to teach our kids why we are doing what we are doing for them. We should be always pointing them in the direction of Christ.

Now, do your kids always appreciate what you do or give? No! But let me ask you this—do you always appreciate the grace God has extended you? Probably not! We are ungrateful little kids sometimes. We don't realize that everything in our lives is simply due to the grace of God. The last part of the verse even says, "yet not I, but the grace of God with me."

Let the grace of God reign supremely in your life. Let nothing in your life be in vain. Let all your actions point to Him, not to yourself. That would be as the song goes, so vain!

I get too big for my britches sometimes, God. Please keep me forever humbled at the extent of Your mercy and grace. I want to show others how strong You are, not me.

JUNE 24

FOOLISH PEOPLE

Psalms 53–54

BEST VERSE: 53:1

The fool has said in his heart, "There is no God," They are corrupt, and have committed abominable injustice; There is no one who does good.

I bet you have banned the word "stupid" in your house. Most parents do. We don't want to hear our children call someone stupid. It is just not polite and definitely not Christ-like. "Dumb" and "stupid" are close in definition, but I have always heard "dumb" is not knowing something while "stupid" is knowing and still doing it wrong. That may well be.

But in this verse, we see another word, "fool." Have you ever known a fool? I have known a few. Fools also know better, but still they make poor choices. David says here in this psalm that a fool says, "There is no God." He didn't say they didn't believe there was a God. Many believe in God but do what they want anyway, thinking He won't intervene at any point. That is just plain foolish.

TEACHING MOMENT

Do you want foolish children? Of course not. You want to raise wise children. You want them to acknowledge the reality and the presence of God in their lives. You don't want them living their lives without purpose or hope. The wisest thing you can do, then, is teach them about the Lord. They need to know that without Him in their lives they are doomed to be like David says, "There is no one who does good."

And start early, because once a fool is established in his ways it is hard to "unfool" him. (Yeah, I just made that term up). The problem with fools is they actually believe they are right. They actually believe they are doing what matters to them. They have been blinded by the one who leads all astray. They start believing in themselves too much.

If I am going to be a fool, then let me be a fool for Jesus. I will abandon all else and rely on Him to guide me. Some say that is foolish. Then call me a fool, as I don't mind being called a fool for Christ's sake.

Lord Jesus, I will be a fool for You. I will willingly follow You even if no one else does. Let my foolishness be centered on You.

JUNE 25

PEACE

Isaiah 11

BEST VERSES: 6–9

And the wolf will dwell with the lamb, and the leopard will lie down with the young goat, and the calf and the young lion and the fatling together; and a little boy will lead them. Also the cow and the bear will graze, their young will lie down together, and the lion will eat straw like the ox. The nursing child will play by the hole of the cobra, and the weaned child will put his hand on the viper's den. They will not hurt or destroy in all My holy mountain, for the earth will be full of the knowledge of the LORD as the waters cover the sea.

This is a great passage to read to your children. Can you imagine this scene one day? Look at the cast of characters, especially the normally hostile and aggressive ones. We will see wolves, leopards, lions, bears, cobras, and vipers. Then the meek ones are the lamb, young goats (so appropriately named kids), a little boy, a cow, an ox, a nursing child, and a weaned child. Two very different groups. One group hostile and the other one meek and gentle.

TEACHING MOMENT

One day these groups will live together in perfect harmony without any desire to harm each other or flee in fear. Why can't we live that way now?

Because we live in the presence of sin which affects even the animals. This is a perfect passage to share with your kids (not the baby goats) the next time they get into a fight with their sibling or a friend. It's a great passage to share the next time they witness two dogs fighting or a dog/cat fight. These incidents will all cease one day.

But remember, that future day of peace can only be made possible due to the absence of sin. We live daily with the inherited sin nature, which is only conquerable through Jesus. Your children need to know that they can walk in peace with others through His power. That does not guarantee that others won't try to attack them, but we can determine our response if we surrender to His control daily.

Don't you want to live in peace? Wouldn't you like to live in perfect harmony with your spouse and children? It is possible, if all of you surrender. I know I can't do it on my own. I can't last one minute. I tell people all the time that the only thing good about me is Jesus. I am pretty sure that is true for you too. Am I right? So, let Him reign and let yourself drain. Hey, that rhymes!

Father, I want to diminish so You can be lifted up. I want the world, including my family, to only see You. I am thankful I am free from the power of sin, as I surrender to You.

JUNE 26

GOD IS WITH US

Isaiah 8

BEST VERSE: 10C
For God is with us.

There can be no doubt. God is with us. No matter our situation, God is with us. He will always be with us. We, on the other hand, may not always be with God. We can choose to walk in darkness. (1 John tells us that.) We can refuse to submit to His will, yet He will not abandon us.

But God being with us does not mean He will condone or ignore our behaviors or our sins. You see, once we cut covenant with God through the blood of His Son, Jesus Christ, He will stand with us forever. But that covenant demands us to follow His commands, not ours. So, don't assume just because you are His that you have license to do as you please.

TEACHING MOMENT

Ask your son or daughter what privileges they have by being in your family. Let them name a few. Ask them if the stranger down the street has the same privileges. Explain how the two of them are different in the rights they have versus the rights a stranger has.

Then ask them if the stranger has the same responsibilities as they do around your house. Does a stranger have to clean the house or take out the garbage? They may say, "Yeah, that's a great idea." Not so fast, Johnny! Of course, they don't. Family has privileges, but also obligations.

Are you fulfilling your responsibilities to the Father, or are you assuming you deserve blessings just because? Just because is never a good excuse or reason. Didn't you hate that answer when you were a child? God is with us, and He expects us to act like it.

O God, thank You for being with me. I feel Your presence and long to be near You. I will do what You ask today to be drawn even closer.

JUNE 27

STICKS AND STONES

Nehemiah 4

BEST VERSE: 3

Now Tobiah the Ammonite was near him and he said, "Even what they are building—if a fox should jump on it, he would break their stone wall down!"

Get the picture? Nehemiah had returned to Jerusalem from exile and was leading the people to rebuild the walls around the city. They had worked hard for days and were seeing progress. However, the enemies of God did not want to see this accomplished.

Tobiah mocks them by saying even a fox could knock down the wall. If I had been Nehemiah I may have said, "I'll show you what a fox can knock down!" But not Nehemiah. He was a humble servant, bent on doing what was right on behalf of his God. He was patient and deliberate. He simply prayed that God would take care of them.

TEACHING MOMENT

Our children are going to encounter people who will make fun of them. Kids can be cruel at times. They make fun of people's hair, nose, glasses, weight—you name it. Teaching our children to not take these insults personally is a skill every parent must have.

What do you say? Use the Word. God made each of us in His image. So, any remark against them is an insult to God's creativity. That is your child's comeback, if you want to call it that. They need to be reminded, time and time again, that they are perfect in the eyes of God. He made them just like He wanted them. God does not make junk.

Now, I realize that sounds awfully simplistic. But when the tears come after they have been ridiculed or insulted, you will want to "show them what a fox knock down." Don't! Instead, like Nehemiah, let God handle it for you. Pray for the other person. Better yet, lead your child to pray for them. Now that's power!

Jesus, my Savior, keep my flesh under Your Spirit. When others throw insults at me, let me respond in love, Your love. Let my response be so Christ-like that they are drawn to You.

JUNE 28

PROMISES KEPT

2 Kings 8

BEST VERSE: 19

However, the Lord was not willing to destroy Judah, for the sake of David His servant, since He had promised him to give a lamp to him through his sons always.

There is only one true Promise Keeper—The Lord Himself. Try as we may, we are likely to break a promise to someone along the way. Sometimes we make rash promises that we know we cannot keep. Other times the promises are made with the best of intentions, but things happen that bring change and can cause us to not keep that promise.

God had promised David that a king would always be on the throne from his lineage. He kept that promise and fulfilled it completely by inserting His

Son into that very lineage of David. Jesus is the eternal King of Glory and will forever reign on His throne.

TEACHING MOMENT

Children make promises all the time. Have you ever heard your child make a "pinky swear" vow to a friend or sibling? You know when you hear it that there is no way they will ever be able to keep that promise. What a perfect time to step in and teach them about promise keeping.

Making promises is part of life. We promise to love, honor, and cherish our spouses. We promise to pay for a car or home when we sign the loan papers. But we must be mindful that only God has the supreme power to keep His promises to us. Remind your children of those. He is the ultimate Promise Keeper.

Are you a promise keeper? Are you trustworthy to your family in keeping your promises? Or do you make promises all the time knowing you will never keep them? Stop doing that? Emulate our Lord. Be the one known as the promise keeper. People should know they can believe you when you make a promise.

Do you need to fix some broken promises? We hurt our children when we break our promises to them. Don't make a promise you can't keep. Even if it means disappointing them now, don't make it.

O Father God, thank You that You are the Master Promise Keeper. When You promise us grace and mercy we know it is coming. You are faithful and true. Help me to be more like You today.

JUNE 29

DESERVED

Isaiah 3

BEST VERSES: 10–11

Say to the righteous that it will go well with them, for they will eat the fruit of their actions. Woe to the wicked! It will go badly with him, for what he deserves will be done to him.

One thing I have learned is that God will take of everyone in His own time. I do not have to worry about someone getting what is coming to him. That is not my concern. Whether they "get away" with something is not up to me. God will judge the righteous and the wicked in due time.

But, man oh man, I want to see the wicked punished. Don't you? I hate it when I see good people suffer and those who have a blatant disregard for God seemingly prosper and flourish. Today's verses remind me to let God handle it. He knows. He always knows.

TEACHING MOMENT

There are few lessons that are more important than this one to teach our children. And we can preach and preach it until we are blue in the face. But our children will learn this best by observing us. They will listen to how we respond when we see an injustice. They will imitate us in how we treat someone who speaks unkindly about our Savior.

The bottom line to teach our children is this—sinners sin. Expect them to. When bad people do bad things, we should not be surprised. When lost people speak evil things, we should not gasp. Without the indwelling of the Holy Spirit, we would be doing the same. Our children need to know that.

For whom do you need to pray instead of judge today? What lost person do you need to approach today in love? How can you direct your children to pray for that lost friend? Whatever you choose to do today, do it to please your Master. Let Him be your guide in dealing with others.

Father of all, forgive me of my judgmental attitude towards others. Forgive me for not being more forgiving. Teach me, Lord, to rest in You and allow You to convict the lost.

JUNE 30

A BROKEN HEART

Psalms 51–52

BEST VERSE: 51:17

The sacrifices of God are a broken spirit; a broken and a contrite heart, O God, You will not despise.

When you hear that phrase "a broken heart" you probably immediately think of someone who has been hurt by someone else. A boy dumps a girl or vice versa, leaving them heartbroken. A child forsakes his family, thus breaking his parents' hearts. We automatically think of something bad.

But not in this verse. David has repented of his adultery and murder and now is begging God's forgiveness. He knows that only through having his heart broken in repentance is he truly repentant. Just saying "I'm sorry" doesn't cut it for David. God knows his motive. David knows that he must truly repent to receive the forgiveness he so desires.

TEACHING MOMENT

Can't you tell, as a parent, when your child is truly remorseful for something? You may catch your children fighting or arguing, so you tell them to stop and tell each other they are sorry. Little Susie wants to hug her brother and make up, but Johnny wants nothing of it. He mumbles an apology, but you can tell he has not forgiven anyone.

We have to take our children to scripture to explain true repentance. What better passage of scripture than Psalm 51. Without going into all the details about David's sin, you can show them how David came to the Father for forgiveness. You can explain to them that we must come to the same Father to confess our sins. Until we do, we are miserable and unusable.

How about you? Have you been to the altar lately? Have you gone there with a broken heart over your sins? Have you truly repented, or are you just sorry for getting caught? Will you bare your soul today to the Father? He wants full fellowship with you. Come to Him.

Father, You know I have sought a broken heart for others numerous times, but I am very slow about asking my own heart to be broken. I confess that as sin and ask You to forgive me. Thank You, Lord for breaking my heart.

NOTHING'S TOO SMALL

Job 36

BEST VERSE: 5

Behold, God is mighty but does not despise any; He is mighty in strength of understanding.

At this point in the book of Job, Elihu, the young man who had been watching and listening to the three friends of Job, begins his discourse, berating them all for not being able to put Job in his place. Whether Elihu's response was correct or not, he does speak some truth in the midst of his ramblings. This verse today is one of those. Look at it.

He is basically saying that no matter how big and mighty God is, He does not overlook anyone. Aren't you grateful God doesn't just look on the wealthy or the strong or the beautiful (I especially like that one) or the intelligent? He cares for each and every one. He cares for the lowest of the low and the smallest of the small.

TEACHING MOMENT

What a great lesson for our children! God loves them despite of who or what they are. He will always love them, even while He chastises them. He will always love them, even when they are disobedient and stray. He will always love them, even if they are perfect (or think they are).

How do you love your children? Is it conditional on the cleanliness of their room or the promptness of their obedience? Is it dependent upon their affection back to you? Do you love them more for the "A"s on their report card? Of course not! That's our God! He loves us so much stronger than deeper!

Our children must know that! We must tell them that all the time. God is mighty but does not despise any! Hallelujah!!

I can never be separated from Your love, O Lord. You love me with an everlasting love. You will love despite me.

PUT ME IN, COACH

Isaiah 6

BEST VERSE: 8

Then I heard the voice of the LORD, saying, "Whom shall I send, and who will go for Us?" Then I said, "Here am I. Send me!"

I have always loved this verse. I know what it means to me, but what does it mean to you? Does this verse scare you? Do you feel guilty because of a calling you received from the Lord that you have not fulfilled? Where does He want you to go? Are you willing to go?

Those are all good questions. The bottom line is God wants to use us to accomplish His will. He doesn't *need* us to do that, but He prefers useful vessels. He prefers willing servants. He prefers *you*! Will you say to the Lord, "Put me in, Coach!"?

TEACHING MOMENT

I will never forget watching my kids sitting on the sideline or on the bench during games. They were so anxious to get into the game to play. They had practiced for this and were ready. Are your children ready to respond when the Lord calls them to "play"? Our job as parents is to prepare them. We are their earthly coaches. When the head coach calls, we want them ready to respond.

Part of that "coaching" is looking for our children's areas of strengths. Every good coach uses his players according to their strengths. For instance, in football you don't put a 300-pound, 6'8" player as running back. You want him on the line protecting the quarterback. In the same way, your child is gifted for certain areas of service for the Lord. Recognize those and groom those.

So, the question has to be asked of you. What has the Lord gifted you to do? Are you doing it? Our gifts never wear out or get used up. God may shift us to another area of service, but we are part of the larger body of Christ that needs all its parts working.

Father, help me yield to Your coaching. I want to be of service to You today. Put me in, Coach!

EVERYTHING'S BACKWARDS

Isaiah 5

BEST VERSE: 20

Woe to those who call evil good, and good evil; who substitute darkness for light and light for darkness; who substitute bitter for sweet and sweet for bitter!

When I read this verse I thought, "Wow! This is exactly what is going on today all around us." Our society has everything backwards. The things that the Lord says are evil, the world says are okay. You are considered intolerant and wrong if you insist that marriage is between one man and one woman. You are told you are closed-minded if you insist that abortion is wrong. I could go and on, but you get the picture.

How do we combat this constant barrage on the truth of God's Word? Simple! We just keep preaching God's Word. His Word speaks for itself. We do not have to defend it. We just have to believe it. Even in Isaiah's day he fought this battle. He simply spoke God's Word and waited for God to move in His mighty power.

TEACHING MOMENT

It is our responsibility as parents to teach our children the difference between good and evil, not according to the world's view, but according to God's view. We have the upper hand since we have the playbook. Our children need to be taught that His Word is the only source of truth and that it contains the answers to all life's questions.

What has your child encountered lately from friends or school that runs contrary to the teachings of Christ? Don't use your wisdom to counter that. Use God's Word to show your child the answer. Constantly bring them back to His divine counsel. Help your child develop their own defense for the lies that are hurled at them. If your child hasn't faced that yet, just wait. It's coming. Be prepared.

How about you? Are you prepared? Are you able to recognize untruth when you see or hear it? Don't believe every preacher or teacher. Check them out with the Word of God. Can I give you one hint? If that preacher or teacher does not use the Word as his text, stop listening. Too many today are "referring" to the Scriptures, but not teaching them. They make a passing comment about a verse or a part of a verse to back up their main points. God's Word doesn't need help to convey truth. It *is* truth. Be mindful of the old bait and switch. Be on the alert!

Thank You Father, for the Truth of Your Word. Thank You that I can always rely on it. Give me the words to teach my children the real Truth from You.

JULY 4

GRAINS OF SAND

1 Kings 4

BEST VERSE: 29

Now God gave Solomon wisdom and very great discernment and breadth of mind, like the sand that is on the seashore.

What was the source of Solomon's wisdom? We know from Scripture that it was Jehovah God. Solomon prayed for it, and God blessed him with it. What a smart prayer! This verse says Solomon's wisdom was "like the sand that is on the seashore." That's a lot.

TEACHING MOMENT

Do you pray for your children to have wisdom? There have been times when I have prayed for my children to make wise decisions to honor God. Usually those were big decisions in their lives. But what about the everyday decisions? I have to admit that wisdom was not on my daily prayer list for my children. I have been too "selective" in asking for it.

But is that right? No, of course not. Our children need wisdom every day. Just think about the decisions they have to make every day. They have to decide how to treat their sibling every day. They have to decide whether to yield to temptation and cheat on that test or not. They have to decide if they should follow their friends in behavior that may not be good.

They need wisdom every day. The Word says that people came from all over to hear Solomon's wisdom. Wouldn't it be cool to see others coming to your child for advice? Wouldn't it please you to watch your child make the right, God honoring decisions each time they are faced with one? That cannot happen unless they rely on God as their source for wisdom.

So, where do they get it? There is one source from which they can find the answer to every one of life's questions. That's right—His Word. The next time your child comes to you with a situation that needs wisdom, take them to the Word. Show them that it too is "like the sand that is on the seashore."

God, You are the God of all wisdom! I pray You will give me the wisdom I need each day. Help me pass that on to others.

JULY 5

JOB'S SIN

Job 29

BEST VERSE: 14

I put on righteousness, and it clothed me; my justice was like a robe and a turban.

The book of Job has always been an interesting one. Satan gets a sucker punch at Job. God allows it. Job suffers. Others accuse him. He refuses to sin. But wait . . . did he? Look at today's verse. We may just discover something that happened to Job during this trial.

There is no doubt that, at the beginning of this trial, Job was simply serving the Lord and attempting to do the right thing for himself and his family. But during the trial itself, Job clings to his righteousness. And by doing that, he sins. Yes, I truly believe that. Others may disagree with me, and that's okay. But when anyone begins to tout their own righteousness, that becomes sin.

TEACHING MOMENT

Have your children ever said, "But Mom, I didn't do anything wrong!" While that might be true in regard to the immediate issue, that statement wouldn't hold water. I guarantee they have done something wrong in the past and will do something wrong in the future. They have no righteousness in themselves.

We must teach our children that our righteousness only comes through our surrender to Christ. It is His righteousness that clothes us. We have nothing to put on ourselves but guilt, shame and regret. But in Christ, we walk as sons of the King. That's a truth worth sharing with our children. We glory, not in ourselves, but in Christ.

Do you see yourself as righteous? Or do you see yourself as hopeless. I claim the righteousness of the Lord for my life because He died to make me righteous. I know the only thing good about me is Him and in that I boast.

Remind me, Lord, to glory only in You. When others praise my efforts let me be quick to point to You. Help me show others Your righteousness that is available to all who believe in Your name.

JULY 6

DAY AND NIGHT

Psalms 73-74

BEST VERSE: 74:16

Yours is the day, Yours also is the night; You have prepared the light and the sun.

Day or night, night or day—they both belong to God. He is the One who created them. He established the sun to rule by day and the moon to rule by night. He placed the sun in its orbit and gave the moon the power to affect the tides of the sea.

Don't you realize the power that is in that? If these two lights were not exactly placed where they are, the earth would either freeze or burn up. The seas would either flood the earth or they cease from rising. God's plan is perfect.

TEACHING MOMENT

Have your children ever been to an observatory? They are pretty fascinating. You sit in this dark room and they reveal the constellations and planets to you. Of course, they explain everything in terms of science. But we know better. We know who put them all in their places.

Explain to your children the importance of the placement of the stars, including the sun and moon. Explain to them how God knew EXACTLY where to put them to give life on earth. Explain how He had the exact same perfection when He placed them in your family. They were put there purposely. Pretty cool!

Do you struggle with accepting situations in your life? Do you realize that, as a believer, everything that touches your life goes through God's hands first? The very hands that placed the sun and moon touches your life daily. Won't you let Him place you in the perfect spot He has for you?

As I look at the sun and moon, Lord, I am reminded of Your perfect plan for me. Thank You for placing me perfectly. Thank You for allowing only those things that You touch to touch me.

JULY 7

LIKE FATHER, NOT LIKE SON

2 Kings 16

BEST VERSE: 2

Ahaz was twenty years old when he became king, and he reigned sixteen years in Jerusalem; and he did not do what was right in the sight of the LORD his God, as his father David had done.

You have probably heard both of the following expressions sometime in your life. "Like Father-Like Son" means to imply the same thing as, "The acorn doesn't fall far from the tree." But many times, that is not true. Just like the example we have today in Ahaz, the son of Jotham. Jotham was a good king and had followed his father's (Uzziah) legacy. Not Ahaz, he did not do that. He followed other gods and led the people astray.

Most Presidents or Heads of State in countries around the world want to leave a legacy. They want to be remembered for something. They want their years spent in their office to have some lasting results. But they have to choose if those legacies will honor God or themselves.

TEACHING MOMENT

Moms and Dads, you are instructed to train your children to follow in your footsteps spiritually. They need to be shown which steps to take and where. They need to be directed along the way. But you cannot make them follow you. Once they are adults, they will choose their own way.

Ask your children what they think is important to be taught by you. Hang on! They may just give you a challenge. But probably they will name some things that you just hadn't thought about. The things I learned from my dad have been passed down to my son. Hopefully, he will keep passing them down.

How are you doing with this assignment? It is not too late to start leaving a legacy. Let others remember you as someone who followed the Lord. Leave an impact on the world.

Lord God, I only want others to see You in me. I want to leave the imprint of Your seal on my life. Help me show others the way.

JULY 8

GOD'S HOUSE

Nehemiah 10

BEST VERSE: 39B

Thus we will not neglect the house of our God.

Nehemiah and the believers in Jerusalem made vows that they would take care of the rebuilt Temple. It had gone so long in ruins that many had forgotten their responsibility to provide for the Priests and for the basics such as wood for the sacrifices and oil for the lamps.

TEACHING MOMENT

Our children today normally do not get the opportunity to help clean or provide for the church in tangible ways. I remember earlier in my ministry when many church members would show up on Friday or Saturday at church to clean windows, sweep, vacuum, and other basic duties. We have lost some of that today. That's too bad. There are always things that need to be done.

In fact, why don't you, moms and dads, ask a pastor or the facilities director at your church what you as a family can do to help. I guarantee they have needs you can meet. Now, I must warn you. It may be cleaning toilets and mopping a floor. It may be setting a room for Sunday or cleaning out a closet. But these are all tasks around God's House that need tending to.

Teaching our children to give of their time and energy is just as important if not more important as teaching them to give of their resources. Both are expected and both are needed. Ask your children tonight if they could help at church what they would want to do. Then find a way to get them to the church to do it.

There is just something about watching kids serve. They do it without expectation or reward. They just like doing it. How about you?

My hands are Your hands, Lord. My feet are Your feet. Let me be used by You to honor Your people and Your church.

JULY 9

JUST A REMINDER

Song of Solomon 6

BEST VERSE: 3A

I am my beloved's and my beloved is mine.

How do we apply this verse to our relationship with God? Easy! We need to remind ourselves that we belong to God, once we have accepted His Son Jesus as our Savior. And, if we belong to Him, He belongs to us. Now, we don't own or control Him, but He is covenanted with us for eternity.

Can you believe that? Don't let anyone ever tell you anything different. Nothing can separate us from His love. But we feel sometimes that we have separated ourselves. We think our failures cause a breach between us. Your sins are forgiven although they are not condoned. Big difference.

TEACHING MOMENT

Children can easily feel defeated when they mess up. It is up to us as parents to remind them they are loved, by us and God. Let me encourage you every day to tell them that. They need to know there is nothing that stops His love from flowing to them. Although your love is strong, His is stronger. Although you forgive them, He forgives and then forgets their sins.

But how do you convince little Susie of God's love? You can hug her and kiss her to remind her. But God can't hug and kiss her. She needs a real touch. Then explain to her that God has given you to her as her parent to do that for Him. You are His instrument of physical love to her. He can love her through you. What a privilege!

Do you need a reminder today of God's covenant? Have you slipped out of His reach (or so you think)? Do you feel He has lost sight of you? He hasn't. He hasn't moved. He is still your beloved, and you are His.

Father, my Beloved, thank You for loving me every day. Thank You for always being there for me. You are forever mine.

JULY 10

PITY PARTY

1 Kings 21

BEST VERSE: 4

So Ahab came into his house sullen and vexed because of the word which Naboth the Jezreelite had spoken to him; for he said, "I will not give you the inheritance of my fathers." And he lay down on his bed and turned away his face and ate no food.

Here is the king of Israel pouting like a baby. Can you believe him? But wait, have you ever pouted about anything? *Not me, Carl.* Yea, right? We have a tendency to pout when we don't get our way. Ahab was no different.

He wanted a vineyard, and when Naboth would not sell it to him he had himself a pity party. The only thing wrong with pity parties is you are the only who comes. It is really somewhat sad. It doesn't help anything. Feeling sorry for yourself is really a waste of time and energy.

TEACHING MOMENT

Our children will naturally play the pity card unless we teach them it doesn't work. Your little Johnny will learn to pout and cry when he doesn't get his way if it works. Don't let it. Be firm. Be consistent. Love him like nobody's business, but don't let that love let you get pulled into the pity party ploy.

I'll be honest. It's hard when our children are crying to not go into the room and comfort them and give them whatever their little hearts desire. Stop right there. Don't do it. When we are teaching them this lesson, it may just hurt us more than it hurts them (I know you heard that from your parents). Bear up under them.

Are you struggling with feeling sorry for yourself? Do yourself a favor and stop it. Allow the Lord to satisfy you as no one else can. He will remind you of how special and complete you are. He will let you know what you can or can't do. Just go to Him.

Lord, You are amazing. You speak to me in my lowest times. You lift me when I am in need. You supply what I need when I need it. You are the only one who can.

JULY 11

BEST QUESTION EVER!

2 Chronicles 1

BEST VERSE: 7

In that night God appeared to Solomon and said to him, "Ask what I shall give you."

Okay, just imagine! You are in your prayer time. You are diligently asking the Lord to bless those in your family, the missionaries you know and support, our country, and so forth. All of a sudden you hear, "Ask what I shall give you." Man, I would probably freak out!

But then, does your mind go to that new Nitro bass boat or the condo on the beach or. . . ? You fill in the blank. Or does your mind automatically go to asking for wisdom to guide your family? Now, isn't that a humbling thought? Too many of us might jump at the chance to ask the "cosmic genie" for stuff we *think* we need. Yea, I said that. We do treat God that way sometimes. We just ask for stuff we think we need.

TEACHING MOMENT

So, how do we point our children to asking for godly things like wisdom, grace, mercy, tenderness, kindness, and love for our brothers and sisters? They have to hear us praying for the same things. Once again, Mom and Dad, we model the behavior.

Now there is nothing wrong with asking God to meet a need in our lives. He wants us to do that. He expects us to do that. I believe He is disappointed when we don't ask Him to meet our needs. He loves us so much that He wants us prepared to serve, and meeting our needs allows us to do just that.

Perhaps your kids can teach you to pray this way. They haven't learned how to pray wrong yet. They just pray and ask God to bless everyone, including your cat. Simple, pure prayers to someone they love. How about that? The child teaches the parent. Who would have thought?

Talking to You, Lord, is a sweet time. Help me lead my children in this lifelong pursuit to know You more. Thank You for hearing me each time I begin my prayers.

JULY 12

PREPARE FOR ABUNDANCE

2 Kings 4

BEST VERSE: 2 KINGS 4:3

Then he said, "Go, borrow vessels at large for yourself from all your neighbors, even empty vessels; do not get a few."

I just love this story. The woman told Elisha her problem. Her husband was dead, and the creditors were coming after her children to make them slaves to pay off her husband's debts. Now, that's quite a predicament. Elisha told her to take the *only thing* she had in her house and give it to the Lord for Him to use to solve her problem.

But look what Elisha told her. He said, "Go, borrow vessels at large for yourself from all your neighbors, even empty vessels; do not get a few." In other words, don't just borrow two or three. Get as many as you can. Expect God to bless beyond your imagination.

TEACHING MOMENT

What a great story for kids. I promise you they will love this story of God's provision. They may want to get all your pots and pans out and act out this story. But try as they may, they cannot fully act this out. They don't have the unlimited supply of oil to pour and keep pouring.

However, the lesson isn't about the amount of oil she got. Make sure your children understand that. It's about simply hearing God's Word and trusting it. That's the truth for today.

Are you trusting Him today? Are you believing Him for a miracle? He still does them. He still works through others to meet our needs in ways we cannot expect. Expect it! Believe it!

Lord, remind me that You know my need long before I even ask. I know You are not going to just give to me as I want. You will bless me according to my need. Thank You!

JULY 13

GLORY-FILLED

1 Kings 8

BEST VERSE: 10–11

It happened that when the priests came from the holy place, the cloud filled the house of the LORD, so that the priests could not stand to minister because of the cloud, for the glory of the LORD filled the house of the LORD.

I really love this passage. The ark has just been placed into the Holy of Holies in the temple for the first time. All of a sudden, the glory of the Lord fills the temple. The cloud of His presence is seen. It is such an awesome and powerful thing that the priests cannot stand before it.

No one here at the temple had ever seen this same cloud that led the people of Israel through the wilderness many years before. So, this was a new sight for them. The very presence of the Lord was among them. The priests were in awe. The people were in awe. The king was in awe.

TEACHING MOMENT

Let me ask you a question. Is the presence of the Lord so real in your life that people are in awe? Can they see the Lord's Spirit resting on you? Our children, of all people, need to see that. They need to be drawn to the very presence of God in your life. The first view of God they will see will be in you. Did you realize that?

So, how are you reflecting that presence? Would your children even be aware of it? I don't mean to imply that you need to walk around with a halo on your head, singing hymns all the time. But our children need to know that your life is governed and filled by the very Spirit of God. They need to know they can trust Jesus in you.

Have you experienced the presence of God like the priests did at the temple that day? When is the last time you were driven to your knees before a Holy God? You know, He is the same God. His presence is still awe-filled.

But now, through Jesus, we can stand boldly before His throne, knowing that right beside Him Jesus is interceding on our behalf.

Will you ask the Lord today to fill you with His presence so that others are drawn to Him? Don't seek His presence for your exaltation. Instead seek it for His. Let Him be exalted through your godly living and witness.

O Father, You are a holy and loving God. You say my body is Your temple here on earth if I believe in Your Son, Jesus. Will you fill me with your "cloud of presence" so much that others are in awe of You?

JULY 14

FOOLISH TALK

Isaiah 32

BEST VERSE: 6A

For a fool speaks nonsense, and his heart inclines toward wickedness.

In Chattanooga, Tennessee, there is a scenic attraction called the Incline Railway, the steepest passenger railway in the world. It has been in operation since 1895 and travels up Lookout Mountain about one mile. It is controlled by huge cables attached to two 100-horsepower winches. It is a steep and scary incline but is totally under control—unlike the fool's mouth.

Isaiah says in today's verse that not only does the fool speak nonsense, but that his heart inclines toward wickedness. A fool is a fool is a fool. And his foolishness is not limited to his speech. His actions speak louder than words. Speaking nonsense is bad enough, but doing wicked things just reveals how foolish he is.

TEACHING MOMENT

Kids love silly talk. There is nothing wrong with being silly. Heck, I am silly a lot of the time. Being silly and being foolish are not the same thing. Being silly may get you in trouble if you are doing it at the wrong time (like I did many times in school), but being foolish will lead to wickedness, according to Isaiah.

So, what is foolishness? What is wickedness? Anything that goes against God's Word. Any action, any speech, any deed that does not agree with the

Word of God can lead to wickedness and foolishness. That's what we guard our children against. We model the behavior that imitates God's Word so our children will learn how to live their lives.

Have you spoken foolishness lately? If so, confess. Have you been inclined towards wickedness in your thought life? Confess! We must stay clean in our hearts to hear from God. As believers, all our sins are forgiven, but we still need to confess them to our Lord and strive to live our lives pleasing to Him.

Cleanse my mind and heart today, Lord. Help me to guard my lips from foolish words. Use Your Spirit to control my tongue so I will not speak wicked or unkind things about others.

JULY 15

WHAT'S YOUR GIFT?

1 Corinthians 12

BEST VERSE: 11

All these are empowered by one and the same Spirit, who apportions to each one individually as he wills.

There is much discussion about the gifts of the Spirit in churches. Some churches value some gifts over others. Some people claim to have gifts that brings them recognition. Others exercise their gifts quietly and behind the scenes. The bottom line is that spiritual gifts are a critical and essential part of the church. The church cannot function unless the gifts are being used by the Lord's followers.

Take the gift of service for instance. Without volunteers to clean the church, who would want to come to church and wade through trash and use a dirty bathroom. How about the gift of teaching? What would worship look like if we did not have the Word taught to us?

TEACHING MOMENT

Your child will discover their gift(s) once they have surrendered their heart to the Lord and not before. Now don't get confused—talents aren't gifts. Those are two mutually exclusive things. Having the gift of gab doesn't mean you have the gift of preaching or teaching. Being organized does not mean you have the gift of administration.

God can use your talents in the exercise of your gift(s), but not necessarily the other way around. When your child comes to Christ, begin watching for the gift the Spirit wants to emphasize through them. It might just surprise you.

Are you using your gift(s) to honor the Lord? Maybe you think you have used your gift long enough. It is time for someone else to use theirs. Nope! God has given us our gift(s) to use until He calls us home. What better way to go than to know you were using your gift(s) up until the moment you see Jesus.

Lord, I want to be used by You. How would You use me?

JULY 16

WHERE DOES YOUR JOY COME FROM?

1 Chronicles 12

BEST VERSE: 40B

There was joy indeed in Israel.

After a long reign by Saul, the first king of Israel, David is now king. He had been anointed years earlier by Samuel (who is now dead), but he had to wait until the Lord allowed Saul to be removed from the throne. Now, Saul and his sons are dead. Long live the king (David)!

The last part of verse 40 says, "There was joy indeed in Israel." Why? Because they had a new king whom the people loved. They had total confidence in David, well at least those whom supported him. It took a few years for all the kingdom to come up under David.

Aren't you glad your joy doesn't depend on a new king? Every U.S. Presidential race raises the hopes of each candidate's supporters. They get out and campaign for their "man" or "woman," telling everyone who will listen why their candidate is the *only* choice for the nation. But in the end, only one will win. The winner's supporters will be happy, but the loser's supporters will be sad (no joy).

TEACHING MOMENT

How can we show our children the futility of circumstantial joy? Why is it important to point them to the true source of joy? When we teach our children that Jesus is the only source of joy they need, then that joy will stay with them through whatever they go through in life. When they have all the friends they need or when they have no friends, their joy rests in Jesus. When that boyfriend or girlfriend dumps them, their joy rests in Jesus. When they have to move to a new school and start all over, their joy rests in Jesus.

How do you, Mom and Dad, reflect the joy of Jesus to your children? Do they see you living joyously in your life circumstances? When you don't get that job you wanted, do they see joy? When someone cuts you off in traffic, do they see joy? When hard times come (and they will) do they see joy in your response?

Live joyously, not for yourselves alone, but for the sake of your children and for the sake of others who are watching you. In everything you face, point others to Jesus through joy.

Lord, remind my face each day of the joy that lives in my heart. Help my joy be expressed so others will know. Let my joy bubble over on others.

JULY 17

BEFORE BIRTH

Isaiah 49

BEST VERSE: 1

Listen to Me, O islands, and pay attention, you peoples from afar. The LORD called Me from the womb; from the body of My mother He named Me."

Even though our granddaughter didn't arrive until about a month and a half AFTER Christmas, my wife, Mimi, had already bought her clothes and had packages under the Christmas tree with her name on it. You see, my son, Christopher, and Kira had already named her. She was already named and loved by many. I couldn't wait to meet her.

Isaiah is saying here in this verse that the Lord called him from his mother's womb. He even named him. God knows us from the moment of conception. He calls our name, even in the womb. If that is not a Pro-Life verse, I have never seen one. How precious to think that God sees us even then? He doesn't need an ultrasound.

TEACHING MOMENT

I am sure your children have asked about their names. What did you tell them? When did you name them? Did you wait until they were born, or did you have them named long before? Tell them how you loved them even before they arrived. Tell them how you prayed for them while they were still inside their mommy. Tell them how much God loved them even then.

I have watched my other grandchildren feel their mommy's tummy when London moved. I have watched them as they saw my son talking to London. This sends a great message to them. London is REAL now. She is already known by her family. But more importantly, they need to know that she is known by her Lord. He already knows her fully.

Do you believe that the Lord knows you fully? He does, you know. He knows you more completely than anyone. There is nothing about you He doesn't know. He formed you in your mother's womb. And He has been calling your name since conception. Listen, is He calling now?

Father, I know You know me. Thank You for not forgetting my name, like I do so many times with others. Help me pass on Your love to others.

JULY 18

THE BOOK

Isaiah 34

BEST VERSE: 16A

Seek from the book of the LORD, and read.

Why do I harp so much about reading the Bible? Why spend time reading a book that is so old? I have actually heard people say that. They do not understand that every, single word of Scripture is inspired. It's God talking to us through men He chose and equipped to pen His Words to us. Incredible!

Isaiah is pointing the people to seek the Lord through the book of the Lord. He knew, as we know today, that the Word reveals God in ways we could never discover on our own. Have you heard the Lord talking to you lately through a verse?

TEACHING MOMENT

Take the time each day to read a verse or a passage to your children. It's not about creating a habit of reading. It's about showing them the importance of God's Word in your life. When they see you taking the time each to dive into the Bible, they will begin to see how it can be used in their own life.

I remember when I came to Christ as a sixteen-year-old. I had grown up in church but didn't have an appreciation for the Word. But when I got saved, I developed a hunger for the Bible. Now, I did not always maintain that hunger. But the desire to know more was there. Help your children get that taste for it also.

When you wake in the mornings, does your thoughts go to getting into the Word of God? Develop a daily time to do that. Whether it is morning or evening, find that time that works for you and stick to it. I promise you it will pay off. You will see the rewards in your life and hopefully in the lives of others you touch.

God, You are the Word. Give me a hunger to dig deeper. Help me be consistent in my study of Your precious truths.

JULY 19

DECEITFUL REMORSE

Isaiah 39

BEST VERSE: 8

Then Hezekiah said to Isaiah, "The word of the LORD which you have spoken is good." For he thought, "For there will be peace and truth in my days."

Have you ever caught your children red-handed doing something they shouldn't have? Instantly, they say "I'm sorry," but you know they didn't really mean they were sorry. They were just sorry they got caught. That is the story here in this verse. Hezekiah had just been caught by Isaiah showing all the kingdom's riches and defenses to the son of the king of Babylon. He had spilled the beans, so to speak.

Hezekiah agrees with Isaiah's words, but is thinking, "At least it won't happen while I'm alive." Wow! Isaiah had just told him that his sons would be carried off into exile. Thousands would probably be killed, and Hezekiah shrugged it off. Sounds cold-hearted to me. How about you?

TEACHING MOMENT

We have to teach our children what true remorse is. They need to learn that just saying "I'm sorry" doesn't cut it. There has to be a change of mind and heart. Words don't mean anything unless our actions change. How can you teach them that? How do you get your children to understand true repentance?

This is another one of those skills that is better caught than taught. We have to show them through our own lives what it means. The next time you do something or say something in their presence you shouldn't, make it right quickly. Tell them how sorry you are that you did that and that they had to witness it. Then ask them to help you. "What!? Me, ask my child to hold me accountable!?" Yep! And I promise you, they will.

We all need people in our lives to help us walk the path Christ has laid out before us. I have people right now in my life who will nail me to the wall if I get out of line. For that I am grateful. I need accountability. I need someone to point out my flesh when it raises its ugly head. It happened just the other day. And because of the Holy Spirit in me I was able to apologize and make it right. Mind you, it wasn't me. It was the Spirit of God in me that drove me to that. I *never* want to admit I'm wrong.

Will you live true repentance before your child today? They need to see it lived out!

Forgive me, Father, for my flesh. I have no excuse. It's just sin, and for that I am truly sorry. Let me be transparent with those around me, including my children, to encourage them to seek forgiveness themselves.

RIGHTEOUS WEEPING

Nehemiah 8

BEST VERSE: 9

Then Nehemiah, who was the governor, and Ezra the priest and scribe, and the Levites who taught the people said to all the people, 'This day is holy to the LORD your God; do not mourn or weep.' For all the people were weeping when they heard the words of the law.

Wow! Can you picture this scene? Ezra and Nehemiah are standing before the people reading the Word of God, which had long been forgotten. When the people heard the law, they wept, knowing they had been unfaithful. They were broken and contrite and weeping for their sin—crying over the way they had forsaken God and His Word.

When is the last time you saw people weeping over God's Word? I bet it has been a while. People hear the Word and just yawn. They don't see it for what it really is—God's words spoken through the Holy Spirit to men who authored those sixty-six books. He loves us enough to send us a written message.

TEACHING MOMENT

Please take the time to teach your children to honor and love God's Word. Teach them that it is not just some book we pick up and carry to church on Sundays. It is not just a cute story book with some inspiring stories. No! It is God speaking to us.

When your children grow up, you will not be around to read the Word to them. They need to know how to read it for themselves. They need to know how to study it. They need to know how to share it. They need ***. . . you*** fill in the blank. The point is they need God's Word in their life throughout their lifetime.

How about you? How much time are you spending each day in the Word? "Well Carl, I have so much to do every day. I don't have time to study the Bible." You don't have time to not study it. Make fifteen to twenty minutes available each day. Get up early or go to bed late. Just make the time. Maybe you will shed a tear as you read.

Word of Life, You are so faithful. You have given us Your very words to guide us. Help me make Your Word a priority in my daily schedule.

JULY 21

NOTHING TO SAY

Job 9

BEST VERSE: 2

In truth I know that this is so; But how can a man be in the right before God?

As a child were you ever caught red-handed by your mom or dad? You were doing something you knew you shouldn't do and got caught. They looked at you and said, "Young man (or woman), what do you have to say for yourself?" I hated that question. I wanted to say, "Well, if you hadn't caught me, everything would have been just fine." But I knew better than to say that.

Job is being confronted by his friends, who are begging him to repent and make things right with God. Job was innocent of doing anything against God, but he was guilty of his own self-righteousness. At this point in the book, he hasn't realized that. But this statement says a lot about his mindset.

TEACHING MOMENT

How do we teach our children to be proud, but not arrogant? How do we teach them to be righteous, but not self-righteous? How do we teach them to follow the Lord's commands, but not be legalistic? It is a fine line, isn't it? Humility is hard to teach. Meekness is better caught than taught.

The only way I know is to try to show them through me. I have to live humbly. I have to live righteous. I have to live surrendered to His will and not mine. *Even when I know I am right*! That is the worst! I want to be right *all the time*.

I am sure Job's friends meant well. They sat for days with him before they even said anything. They wanted his suffering to end. They wanted to see him restored to his position before all this happened. But God does not work on our schedule or on the best wishes of our friends. He works in us according to His perfect will.

Rest in that my friends. And teach your children to rest in it. The hymn says, "Trust and Obey, for there's no other way." That pretty much sums it up!

God, I do rest in You. I place all my trust in You. I deserve nothing, but You gave me everything. Give me the passion to share this wonderful gift with others.

JULY 22

IRREVOCABLE

Romans 11

BEST VERSE: 29
For the gifts and the calling of God are irrevocable.

I am not sure how many times I have read this verse (at least once every year since 1987), but I have just never noticed it. Look at the verse again: "for the gifts and the calling of God are irrevocable." Do you get that? That means there is no change of mind, no regrets.

Once God bestows His gifts, once God's calling is on your life it is irrevocable; it cannot be changed. You can't escape it, no matter how hard you try. Do you understand that? God has you, if you have surrendered to Him, no matter what. He has gifted you for a purpose, no matter what. He has called you to a purpose, no matter what. *Irrevocable*!

TEACHING MOMENT

Have you ever made a decision about something your child has asked you about which required an irrevocable decision? I am sure you have. "Mom, can I light a fire around my brother?" NO!!!! "Dad, can I have the keys to the car?" NEVER!! You get my drift? There are some decisions we make with our kids for their safety that cannot be changed. What a perfect time to share this verse.

Our children need to know that we have the authority over some things that no amount of begging or pleading will change. Other things are negotiable. They need to know that the same applies to God. Once they are His, they are His! No ifs, ands, or buts about it. They are secure in that. What peace that brings!

Are you secure in that? Do you have "no regrets" in your relationship with Christ? Do you have that irrevocable gift and calling on your life? I pray you do. If you don't, will you give Him your life today? Don't wait another minute.

I am so thankful that Your gifts are irrevocable. I am grateful for the security I have in You. Nothing can alter our relationship.

JULY 23

HIDE AND SEEK

Job 23

BEST VERSE: 3

Oh that I knew where I might find Him, that I might come to His seat!

Who doesn't like a good game of hide and seek? Kids have played it for generations. There is something exciting about hiding in a spot and hearing the "it" person try to find you. But for the "it" person, it can be quite frustrating, especially if you keep being "it." (Okay, that is enough "its.") When people hide so good you can't find them or run back to "home" before you can tag them, it can be very defeating.

Some people, like Job here in this verse, feel like God is hiding from them. When they go through hard times, they think God has taken a vacation or has turned off his ears to them. That is so not true. You see, Job's perception of God at this point in the book has been marred by his physical and emotional suffering. He has allowed the circumstances of life to blind him. God is still there. He is just waiting for Job to see Him.

TEACHING MOMENT

If there is one attribute of God that our children need to learn it is this—that God is always there. He is omnipresent. He can be every place all the time. I do not begin to understand that, but I believe it. Our children need to understand that when they go through hard times (and they will) God has not gone anywhere. More times than not, we have taken our eyes off Him. We are looking in the wrong direction.

As believers, we don't have to try to find the Lord. He dwells within us through His Holy Spirit. We only have to stop and get quiet. We have to allow Him to speak. Sometimes that means we need to find a place that is free from all the noise of life. Sometimes that means we get into the Word (which is always a good way to hear Him) and read. He will speak. He does to me every day through His written Word.

Are you listening today to the voice of your heavenly Father? Are you screaming at God, "Where are You? I can't find You?" Stop yelling! Listen! Let Him speak truth into your hearts today.

I know You are there, Lord. Open my eyes and heart to see You. And help me show others Your presence in my life.

JULY 24

SCARED OF THE WORD

Acts 24

BEST VERSES: 24–25

But some days later Felix arrived with Drusilla, his wife who was a Jewess, and sent for Paul and heard him speak about faith in Christ Jesus. But as he was discussing righteousness, self-control and the judgment to come, Felix became frightened and said, "Go away for the present, and when I find time I will summon you."

Felix thought he knew what Paul was all about. He liked listening to him until . . . When Paul started discussing righteousness, self-control and the judgment to come, he got scared. Was he convicted? Did the Word offend him? Did he think Paul was trying to convert him?

We need to be bold in our witness to others. There is no time to diddle daddle about the gospel. People are dying and going to hell. That's right. Right before our eyes a lost world is busting hell wide open. What can we do about?

TEACHING MOMENT

Teach your children to share the Good News by doing it yourselves. Look for every opportunity to witness. Witness at the ballpark. Witness in line at the grocery store. Witness when you are behind the wheel of your car. Witness! Witness! Witness!

Equip your children, once they are saved, with the basic truths of the gospel that they can share with their friends. Children love sharing good news. They love seeing their friends come to Christ. Why not help them prepare to share the best news ever?

If we will invest in the lives of our children by equipping them to be bold witnesses, they will be prepared to face the unknown. They will be prepared to take on the gates of hell with a water pistol if necessary. Encourage them to invite friends over to the house and make sure you plan some time to get to know them. Plant seeds in their friends' lives.

Be like Paul was when he was before Felix. He didn't care whether he lived or died. He only cared about sharing the news Christ had given him.

I seem to be asking for this a lot, Father. Help me spread the good news of Christ to everyone I meet. Help me teach my children to share too.

JULY 25

NOSE PIERCINGS

2 Chronicles 33

BEST VERSES: 10–13

The Lord spoke to Manasseh and his people, but they paid no attention. Therefore the Lord brought the commanders of the army of the king of Assyria against them, and they captured Manasseh with thongs (nose hooks), bound him with bronze chains and took him to Babylon. When he was in distress, he entreated the Lord his God and humbled himself greatly before the God of his fathers. When he prayed to Him, He was moved by his entreaty and heard his supplication, and brought him again to Jerusalem to his kingdom. Then Manasseh knew that the Lord was God."

I have seen a lot of people with nose piercings. I have asked several what they did when they need to blow their nose. I would be afraid I would blow mine out, if I had one. Well, Manasseh had a nose piercing too. But his was put in by the king of Assyria, attached to a chain or rope and used to lead him into captivity. I bet that hurt!

God had to humble Manasseh greatly to get his attention. He was an evil king who had led Judah into horrible idolatry, worse than even the people who lived in Canaan before Israel arrived. Finally, God had enough. Will God have to take you into "captivity" to get your attention?

TEACHING MOMENT

Often children think if they are not caught for doing wrong, they must have gotten away with it. Moms and dads, we need to make sure they understand that all sin will be dealt with. Unconfessed sin in a believer's life begins to build that wall between us and God. Sure, we are still saved, but we lose that fellowship. Sooner or later, we stop hearing God's voice and feeling His Spirit.

God will not let His children continue in unconfessed sin. He will get our attention, one way or another. We must teach our children to stay "confessed up" with God. It's really simple. And how beautiful it is to have restored fellowship with the Lord.

Father, will You help me today to lay out all my dirty laundry before you? You already know it's there. Its stench is before You. Cleanse me, Lord, so I can walk confidently once again in Your presence.

JULY 26

LAUGHABLE

2 Chronicles 30

BEST VERSE: 10

So the couriers passed from city to city through the country of Ephraim and Manasseh, and as far as Zebulun, but they laughed them to scorn and mocked them.

In the past when you invited someone to church or tried to share the gospel with them, they would either politely listen or at least pretend to. Not anymore. Today people will literally spit in your face and laugh at you. There seems to be no respect for the things of the Lord. He is just not revered now.

The same was true in the days of Hezekiah. He tried to invite all of Israel and Judah to come to Jerusalem to celebrate the Passover together. Even though they were divided nations, he sought to unite them through their faith in Jehovah. But many of them had gone so far from God that when Hezekiah's envoys went to them, they laughed, scorned, and mocked them.

TEACHING MOMENT

One lesson to teach our children from this verse is respect. We should always show respect to others, even those with whom we disagree. Take for instance being visited by a Jehovah's Witness or a Mormon. Instead of slamming the door in their face, why not invite them in and share the gospel with them? Now, you need to be grounded in the Word, but showing your children how to defend the faith with respect to the other people is a great lesson for them to learn.

Everyone has the right to believe what they want to believe. God gave us that choice. And we have the obligation to share with them the love of God through the shed blood of Christ. We need to reach out to our nation to invite them back to faith, regardless of how they respond. You never know who just might come if you invite them.

Will you take the step this week to invite a lost person to church? How about sharing the gospel with at least one person? The Passover was a great celebration, but we celebrate the Passover Lamb who was sacrificed for us on Calvary. One sacrifice for all time. What better message to share and to invite others to experience?

Father of all, thank You for sending Your Son to die for me. Give me the courage today to share the Good News with someone who is headed toward the pit of hell. Use me to point them in the right direction.

JULY 27

DON'T DO THAT!

Titus 1

BEST VERSE: 7

For the overseer must be above reproach as God's steward, not self-willed, not quick-tempered, not addicted to wine, not pugnacious, not fond of sordid gain.

I recently taught this verse to our kids at church. We're studying the book of Titus, and we are calling the series "Intentional." One word, one long word, one intentional word—to describe a short, three-chapter letter from Paul to Titus. I walked the children through this long list of dos and don'ts regarding the qualifications of an elder. But guess what? These qualities really apply to everyone who wants to walk with Christ.

One word really got their attention—pugnacious. I don't think I had ever used that word in my vocabulary before. The word means bully, striker, or someone who fights. Now who, besides a prize fighter, wants to be like that? What believer wants to be a bully? No one should. It goes totally against the character of Christ. But so many of us can't wait for a good fight. Of course, we rationalize every one of those fights.

TEACHING MOMENT

You probably think this is an easy trait to teach our kids. They fight, and we discipline. Simple as that! But what kind of fighting are we talking about? Is it really as simple as that? There are all kinds of fighting and bullying. Today, that can happen online. Thousands of kids a day are being bullied through social media. You can fight without saying a word. I've seen girls who bully other girls without saying a word.

Being pugnacious has nothing to do with Christ. That word should not describe us either. No one should see your child coming and think, "Here comes that bully." How horrible that would be! So how do you prevent it? You model being unpugnacious (not sure that is a word) yourself, and you hold them accountable if you see a glimmer of that in them. Easier said than done, I know. But that is why you are getting paid the big bucks as a parent. ☺

Father, give us the wisdom as parents to recognize and correct any ungodly character we see in our children. Help us to point them towards You, the most "unpugnacious" of all.

JULY 28

NEVER ASSUME

Esther 6

BEST VERSE: 6B

And Haman said to himself, "Whom would the king desire to honor more than me?"

Talking about getting "egg on your face"! Haman was just sure the king was wanting to honor him. After all, he was somebody, or so he thought. He could have never guessed in a million years that the king was talking about Mordecai, whom Haman hated.

So, Haman rattles off what *he* would have wanted the king to do for *him*. His own words lead to his humiliation. I am sure many in the city knew of Haman's disgust for Mordecai. And now they are watching him lead Mordecai through the streets shouting, "Thus it shall be done to the man whom the king desires to honor."

TEACHING MOMENT

What a great life lesson! Teach your children to not assume what someone else is thinking or saying. Teach them to ask lots of questions to clarify the subject before they launch off into some activity. Have you ever had one of those tests that begins with the statement, "Read this entire page before answering any question"? You busily answer all the questions before reading the whole page and then the last statement says, "Do not answer any of these questions. Sign your name here and turn in to the teacher."

We need to teach our children to avoid such misunderstandings, to not jump to conclusions, and to listen before talking. They should always be careful to hear someone out before they make up their minds about something. And they should never think too highly of themselves (like Haman did).

That's a lot to think about today. Are you guilty of making assumptions about people? Determine today to stop that. Look at others through the eyes of the Spirit. See them how God sees them. Then make up your mind. I bet you will have a different viewpoint.

Father of all, reveal to me the real motives behind others' actions. Help me to not assume anything about anyone. Let me see them as You do.

JULY 29

IMMEDIATELY

Acts 22

BEST VERSE: 10

And I said, "What shall I do, Lord?" And the Lord said to me, "Get up and go on into Damascus, and there you will be told of all that has been appointed for you to do."

I love this story of Paul's conversion. He is on the way to Damascus to arrest and possibly kill more Christians and is struck blind by the Lord. He quickly asks, "What shall I do, Lord?" No hesitation. He was ready to do whatever the Lord asked. Maybe he wanted his sight back, so he was willing to do anything. After all, Paul was human. I am sure he didn't want to remain blind. But it took losing his sight for him to clearly see.

That was the beginning of Paul's illustrious missionary journey. From there he started preaching the good news of Jesus to the Gentile world. God gave him his sight back and set him up for a lifetime of service to those he had previously spat upon.

TEACHING MOMENT

Wouldn't you love for your children to offer immediate obedience to you? What parent wouldn't want that? No more punishing for not cleaning their room. No more nagging about taking the trash out or mowing the lawn. Wouldn't that be heavenly?

But wouldn't you rather them offer immediate obedience to God? If that happened, they would naturally obey you, right? We teach and teach them to obey us when we should spend more time teaching them to obey God. Unquestioned obedience is hard to teach. But when they experience the joy and sometimes immediate blessing, they will learn to do just that.

The next time your child obeys you without question, share this verse. Show them how God desires us to obey Him in the same way. He wants us to experience the joy He gives.

Today, will you obey without hesitation? Will you just do what He says when He says in whatever way He says to do it? Just do it!

O, that I would obey You, Father, without delay. Often, I know what You are asking me to do, but I put if off because I desire my will over Yours. Forgive me, Lord.

JULY 30

HALF-HEARTED

2 Chronicles 25

BEST VERSE: 2

He did right in the sight of the Lord, yet not with a whole heart.

Have you ever seen a ball team that played halfhearted? You could just tell they were not into the game. They didn't execute plays well. They stopped before the whistle blew. They walked when they should have been running. Amaziah is described this way. He was halfhearted.

God expects us to be all in, not halfhearted. When our heart is divided, we cannot receive all He wants to do through us. Amaziah did a lot of good things, but he also did not fully rely on the Lord, thus ending his reign as king of Judah.

TEACHING MOMENT

Your children may suffer from this "ailment" from time to time. They may halfheartedly do a chore, which means they have to do it again. They may halfheartedly study for an exam, which may result in doing poorly. As parents, our job involves preparing them for life. We have to teach them to give everything they have to the tasks they have.

Whether they are playing a sport or studying, our children need to learn to give it their all. Doing something halfway almost always ends in disappointment. This applies to their walk with Christ as well. They can't have one foot in Christ and one foot in the world.

Do you struggle with divided loyalties? I have to admit there are times when I don't give my all. I get lazy. But thank God His Holy Spirit convicts me of that. I know my half-heartedness is not pleasing to Him. I have to confess that as sin and move ahead fully devoted. How about you?

O Lord, You remind me daily to do my best for You. Help me to persevere when things get hard. Remind me to give all I have to please You.

JULY 31

WHERE IS YOUR HOPE?

Job 13

BEST VERSE: 15A

Though He slay me, I will hope in Him.

If you have ever read the entire book of Job, you know that Job and his friends are arguing back and forth. The friends are begging him to repent, and Job keeps arguing his innocence. This goes on for chapters and chapters.

But even in the midst of these "discussions," we find nuggets of truth. Look at today's verse. "Though He slay me, I will hope in Him." Job still wants to hear from God and argue his innocence, but he also still holds hope. He still accepts that God is God.

TEACHING MOMENT

As we are raising our children and teaching them the deep truths of the Lord, we need to teach them that God does allow hard times in our lives sometimes. But as we believe in the perfect sovereignty of God, we know that everything that touches us has been allowed by Him to make us more like Christ. That is hard to teach. It has to be lived.

The next time your child suffers one of those hard times, search with them to see what the Lord is trying to teach them. Often, we have to wait for a while to see that. Other times we know almost immediately. That too is a lesson to be learned. But it is still important that we pray with our children to that end. We ask the Lord to reveal to us what He wants to teach us.

As I write this thought today, I have been a believer for over forty years. I am still learning to "hope in Him." There are still times when I too question why. I want to learn the lesson quickly, so I won't repeat it. Sometimes the Lord tells me, and other times I have to wait a while. I truly want to be able to say in each trial, "Though He slay me, I will hope in Him." How about you?

Lord, I know it all comes down to trusting You. I know You know what is best for me and how far I can be tested. Thank You for counting me worthy of trials.

AUGUST 1

HOW TO TRAIN A MULE

Proverbs 15–16

BEST VERSE: 15:1

A gentle answer turns away wrath, but a harsh word stirs up anger.

You are probably wondering about the title today. I bet. Well, there is a saying that goes, "If you train a mule with yells, it won't respond to a whisper." Have you ever heard it? It's an old saying, I'll admit. But boy is that true.

Think about it. If all you ever do is yell at your mule, they are accustomed to hearing a soft voice. But if you talk calmly and even softly, when and if you ever have to raise your voice, they will hear you immediately. It's all about training their ears.

TEACHING MOMENT

The verse today hints at the same idea. When we respond in anger toward someone, it seldom produces a calm response. Anger provokes anger. You had might as well expect it. But if we can stay calm and speak softly, perhaps we can deescalate the moment.

Your children will definitely respond quicker to a calm mom or dad than to an outraged one. I had the opportunity countless times to engage an out-of-control child when I ministered in children's homes. I never could out-yell or out-scream a child in a temper tantrum. But when I sat there calmly and kept them safe, they would eventually respond to my words.

What is your technique? Do you speak softly or harshly? Do you try to have the last angry word, or are you willing to allow things to subside? Follow the Lord's advice. A gentle answer works wonders. Let it.

O God, I am guilty far too often of speaking too quickly or harshly. Forgive me. Help me to control my tongue and allow You to give me those gentle words.

AUGUST 2

ONE MAN

Esther 10

BEST VERSE: 3

For Mordecai the Jew was second only to King Ahasuerus, and great among the Jews and in favor with his many kinsmen, one who sought the good of his people and one who spoke for the welfare of his whole nation.

What a great story! In today's passage from Esther, we read that at the end of the whole story, Mordecai became great among the nation. He looked past his own self-interests and to the good of everyone.

TEACHING MOMENT

Don't we want our children to have the same compassion for others, not just for those closest to them? How do we teach them to love all people? We have to look to Jesus, the Author and Finisher of our Faith, who came for all men.

Do you reach out to others who don't quite fit into your social circle? Unfortunately, many of us don't. How will our kids ever learn to reach others if we aren't doing it ourselves? We are commanded to reach the world for Christ. He has given us a mandate to go and make disciples. Won't you do that? Won't you take your children with you?

Mordecai saved an entire nation of people from extinction at the risk of his own life and the life of his niece, the Queen. One man risked it all! He knew he had to do it. *We have to do it*!

Make a difference! Teach your children to make a difference! You can with the help of Christ! He will give you the strength to do all He asks you to do.

O God, I know I can't save anyone, but I can bring them to You. Give me the passion to reach out to others, to offer them eternal life through Jesus. Help me teach my children the joy of leading someone to Christ.

AUGUST 3

SCATTERED ABOUT

Acts 11

BEST VERSE: 19A

So then those who were scattered because of the persecution that occurred in connection with Stephen made their way to Phoenicia and Cyprus and Antioch.

Why does a loving God allow persecution of believers around the world? Well, we have one answer right here in this verse. We read earlier about Stephen's death because of his testimony and preaching. Obviously, that persecution continued. We know that Saul (later named Paul) was one of the chief antagonists. So, the people fled the persecution, thus taking the Word of God with them.

God allowed persecution to push the believers out in order to spread the Word. There was no internet back then. There was no television nor radio.

People spread news by word of mouth. And what better news than the good news of Jesus Christ?!

TEACHING MOMENT

But how in the world do you explain persecution to your children? How do you explain that it can be "allowed" by God to further His kingdom? The best way I know is to find some testimonies of believers who have suffered persecution. They are our modern-day New Testament believers who, just like these mentioned in Acts 11, suffered persecution that forced them to leave their homes and perhaps their homelands. But through their persecution God has given them a pulpit to share His love.

Here is a web address to a great article *Christian Today* published recently that you could share with your children:

https://www.christiantoday.com/article/we-are-living-in-the-midst-of-the-greatest-turning-of-muslims-to-christ-in-history/56393.htm

God is moving among Muslims who, due to ISIS, have fled through countries.

Sometimes God allows events in our lives to "push" us in another direction. I have experienced God's shoves at times in my ministry. Sometimes that is a gentle nudge, and other times, well, let's just say I knew I had been pushed. Don't wait on that. Seek ways for God to use you right where you are. Let Him lead you in areas that you would *never* go on your own. You can trust His hand to guide you.

God, I don't want to be pushed into following You. I want to step forward willingly and be led by You. Help me lead others to a place where they can submit to You also.

AUGUST 4

THE PROTECTION OF HIS WILL

2 Kings 6

BEST VERSE: 16

So he answered, "Do not fear, for those who are with us are more than those who are with them."

When the king of Aram learned it was Elisha who was disclosing all his plans against Israel, he sent his army to capture him. I just love

Elisha's servant's response. He was alarmed and scared when he woke the next morning to see them surrounded. But when he tells Elisha, Elisha just keeps on eating his eggs and bacon and drinking his coffee (just kidding about the bacon).

What does Elisha say to his servant? "God's got this!" Then he prayed for the Lord to open his servant's eyes so he could also see the army of God that was protecting them. God still has that army. None of them have retired. None of them have refused to serve.

TEACHING MOMENT

When your children are scared at night of the "boogie man" read them this story. Reassure them that the same God who protected Elisha protects them. In fact, as believers, we have it better than Elisha because we have the very presence of God living within us through the Holy Spirit. Wow!

Now, we should never pick a fight with the devil or those who desire to do us harm. But we can be reassured that the Lord is with us. God will always defend His children. Our children can best learn to trust God's protection as we show them we trust that. We can't be wringing our hands and pacing the floor. We have to "open their eyes" to see God's chariots.

Are you blinded today? Can you not see the army of heaven defending you? Do you not believe He is more powerful than any other power on earth or heaven? He is. Stay in His will and watch Him work. It is pretty amazing.

Father in heaven, open my eyes today to see Your army surrounding me. Open my eyes of faith. Help me show others how powerful You are.

AUGUST 5

ZIP YOUR LIPS

Job 27

BEST VERSES: 3–4

As long as my breath is in me, and the spirit of God is in my nostrils, my lips will not speak falsehood, and my tongue will not utter deceit.

Most men would have uttered some bad words by now. Not Job. He was determined to hold to his faith. Was it tested? You had better believe it. Was he tempted? I am sure he was. But even when his own wife said, "Curse God and die," he refused.

We should all take a lesson from Job here. He guarded his mouth. I am so quick to speak out. I know I need to buy a muzzle. Oh, but I have one. It is called the Holy Spirit. If I will just listen to Him, He will muzzle me.

TEACHING MOMENT

Some kids have no filter between their brain and their tongue. They blurt out things before they think about it. We have to teach them to take a breath and think before speaking. Once the words are out, good or bad, they are out.

It probably won't be long until your little Susie lets something fly off the tip of her tongue. Take that moment and teach her this truth. Show her the patience of Job in this passage. Let her learn from the Master.

And you? You do it too. Don't spread rumors about someone. Don't speak out until you know what the issue is about. Make sure you know before you move your lips. Let the Lord be your mouthpiece.

Word Master, give me the self-control to bridle my tongue. Let me hold my words when needed to allow You to reveal real truth. I praise You for making my speech. Let me honor You with it.

AUGUST 6

HOLD YOUR TEMPER

1 Kings 12

BEST VERSE: 24

Thus says the LORD, "You must not go up and fight against your relatives the sons of Israel; return every man to his house, for this thing has come from Me." So they listened to the word of the LORD, and returned and went their way according to the word of the LORD.

Here we are! The kingdom of Solomon has been passed down to Rehoboam, but because of Solomon's sins God had told him his kingdom would be divided. Jeroboam rises up against the new king, and ten tribes follow him. Rehoboam, after taking the bad advice of the young men, wants to go to war to get back his kingdom. But God stops him.

Have you ever rushed to judgment and gotten angry before you knew all the facts? Of course not. You are more spiritual than I! Boy, I have. I have started to "retaliate" against someone for a wrong committed, only to find out it wasn't true. How embarrassing. We need to be sure before we act.

TEACHING MOMENT

Boy, oh boy! This is something that we have to be so careful to not teach our kids. They will respond the same way we do, if we are hot-headed. Teaching restraint and patience is hard. It's practically impossible. It requires that we practice it ourselves in front of our kids. Count to ten (or maybe one thousand) before reacting. Don't start plotting your response before you have sought the Lord.

If you will go back and read all of chapter 12 in 1 Kings, you will notice that Rehoboam never sought the Lord's counsel. Do you think that's because the wisest man in the world, his father Solomon, had stopped seeking the Lord and had begun to follow false gods? Solomon had *not* set the example for his son to follow.

Stop right now if you are contemplating some type of revenge. Make sure you have really been offended and then let the Lord handle it. Forgive! Extend grace. After all, think of all the wrong you have done against the Lord. He still loves you and extends you fresh grace every day.

O God my Father, forgive me for rushing to judgment of others. Forgive me for getting angry about things that really have no eternal significance. Forgive me for not setting the example for my children that You require.

AUGUST 7

THE APPOINTED DAY

2 Chronicles 9

BEST VERSE: 31

And Solomon slept with his fathers and was buried in the city of his father David; and his son Rehoboam reigned in his place.

Now, I don't want to sound morbid, but we will all die one day. Look at today's verse. As great as Solomon was, as rich as Solomon was, as wise as Solomon was—he still died and left all he had to his son. Nothing he accrued here on earth went with him.

The same is true for us. Whether you are a beggar on the street or the President of the United States, you will meet your Maker one day. Nothing can prevent that. So, the question begs to be asked, "Are you ready?" That is the most important question I may have asked in this devotional book. Are you ready for eternity?

TEACHING MOMENT

Your children are your children for a season. God has entrusted them into your care for one reason—to lead them to Him. That's your job. It's not the pastor's job. It's not the Sunday school or small group leader's job. It's yours. If you spend all the time and money you have educating, feeding, and clothing them, and they die and go to hell, you have not achieved your purpose in child-rearing.

That's kind of heavy, huh? Now, I know the decision is theirs. They must make that personal decision to follow Christ as their Savior and Lord. You can't make them come to Christ. God knows that. He won't hold you accountable for their decision. However, He expects you to do all you can to lead them to that moment. What they do with it is up to them.

Death is certain. For some it comes early. For others it comes later. But it will come to all (unless the Lord returns before that day). Live your life as if it is your last day. Share Christ with others. Live Christ in front of others. And know that you are ready any day to see Him face to face.

O God, My Savior, I am ready. I long to see Your face. But Lord, there are many in my life who don't know You. Help me lead them to You.

AUGUST 8

BE A NOBODY

1 Corinthians 9

BEST VERSE: 22B

I have become all things to all people, that by all means I may save some.

I love these verses in 1 Corinthians 9:19–23. Paul had all the reasons to boast of his pedigree. He could have proudly stated his qualifications as a Pharisee and his learning under Gamaliel. He could have lorded over any new believer and demanded special treatment. But a funny thing happened on that road to Damascus. The Lord Jesus stripped him of all that pride.

After that, he just wanted to reach people with the gospel, no matter what he had to do to accomplish his goal. He would eat with the Jews or the Gentiles. He would sacrifice doing things he knew was perfectly legal if he thought it might cause a brother to stumble. We could learn a lot from this passage, if we would. I have known Christians who were so proud they could strut sitting down.

TEACHING MOMENT

We can't teach our children this. It must be learned firsthand. We can model it, though. They can watch us give up things for others. They can see us get down and dirty to pull someone else up. They can stand next to us as we explain the total inclusiveness of the gospel to a lost and dying world.

Are there restrictions on how far we can go? Sure, there are. There are some groups I can't or shouldn't try to reach. But if the Lord directs me to share with someone, my job is to figure out how best to do that. That may mean getting to know them first and developing that relationship. You have heard the expression, "People don't care how much you know until they know how much you care."

So, are you modeling behavior for your children that they can emulate? Are you coaching them in the skills they will need to reach that lost friend? When is the last time you actually shared the gospel with someone? Weeks, months, years?

Father, allow Your Holy Spirit to simply cut loose and speak through me. He will give me the words, just as He gives me the power.

AUGUST 9

OUR DISOBEDIENCE AND OTHERS

1 Chronicles 21

BEST VERSE: 14

So the Lord sent a pestilence on Israel; 70,000 men of Israel fell.

What was the big deal about David taking a census? I mean, come on, he was just trying to get an accurate count of the people. Well, if that was all, then why would the Lord be angered? Certainly, there was another motive in David's heart. We don't have a clear picture of that in Scripture, and to speculate the motive we would have to read into it things we just don't know. That is always dangerous.

Regardless, David sinned, and God was angered. So, consequences had to come. David is given three options, and he chooses to fall into God's hands. As a result, seventy thousand died of a plague administered by one of God's angels. Wow! seventy thousand! That's a lot of people. I am sure that number included men, women, and children.

The point is this—our sins can affect others. Moms and Dads, your sins can have a profound effect on your children. They can suffer because of your disobedience. I have known of many children who suffered because of their parent's incarceration. Others suffered due to their parent's substance abuse. What are you doing right now that is causing your children to suffer?

TEACHING MOMENT

And how do we teach our children this biblical truth? How do we show them that their choices in life can have lasting effects on their family? The best way I know is by reading them passages like this and explaining to them how David's sin led to this plague. There are other passages in Scripture with similar endings.

We are responsible to live our lives in such a way that are always leading others toward Christ, not away. We must choose to live our lives to bring honor to Him. By doing so, we are allowing God's blessings to come into the lives of our children. By doing so, we are protecting them from suffering for our bad choices. Be the one to obey, and by doing so, lead your children to follow in His footsteps.

Father, may my sin always be accidental and when I sin, please protect those around me. Guard my heart and mind to keep focused on Your truths and Your Word. Put a hedge about me.

AUGUST 10

JUST THE FACTS, MA'AM

2 Chronicles 18

BEST VERSE: 13

But Micaiah said, "As the LORD lives, what my God says, that I will speak."

Many of us remember the 1960's TV show, *Dragnet*. One of the phrases you heard practically every week on the show from Joe Friday while he questioned a witness was "Just the facts, ma'am." In other words, I only want to hear what you actually know.

The men who came to retrieve Micaiah to face Ahab and Jehoshaphat told him to agree with the other prophets. But Micaiah could only stick to the facts that God had told him. He could only speak God's words, which were in fact the truth.

TEACHING MOMENT

I think the lesson for our children here is plain. Speak the truth and only the truth. Stick to God's Word. Trust the Lord to give you the words to say when you are faced by your enemies. Just like Micaiah, God will give your children the words to say. But they must turn to Him for those words.

Are you speaking God's Word into your children daily? Are you showing your reliance on His Word in the way you speak to your "enemies"? Your children will learn how to speak God's Word best by observing you speaking them.

When is the last time you relied on the Lord to speak through you? We tend to want to defend ourselves very quickly. Don't you think the Lord is capable of defending you? In order to speak God's Word, however, you have to know God's Word. Get into it daily. Ask Him to show you how to use it.

Lord, guide my mouth. Speak through me. Use me to be Your mouthpiece to a lost and dying world.

AUGUST 11

VALOR

1 Chronicles 7

BEST VERSE: 2B

The sons of Tola were mighty men of valor in their generations."

You don't hear that word anymore—*valor*. It seems in our generation that if someone is known for valor, they are called a warmonger or murderer. Nothing could be further from the truth. Do you even know what the word really means? The Hebrew word *chayil* means strength, might, and power. Now what is wrong with that?

Don't you want to be like that? Don't you want to be strong and powerful. It's interesting that whenever this word is used in the Old Testament, it refers to those who are fighting for the Lord. They were fearless men who would endure to the end. The sons of Tola weren't the only men of valor in the Bible, but they are an example of it.

TEACHING MOMENT

Wouldn't it be great if your little Johnny or Susie was known for valor? They don't have to be warriors to show valor. That can be shown in their daily lives by standing up for what is right. In this day and age, that takes valor. The world does not want us to represent Christ and to oppose evil. That is seen as intolerant. No! That shows valor!

Do you know how you can help your children have valor? By teaching them to be brave, fearless, bold, gallant, and steadfast. Those are all words which describe valor. And the only way your children can do any of those things is through the strength of the Lord. If valor is present in their lives, it is only because the Lord gives it.

Will you be known for your valor? Or will you be known for your cowardice? No one wants to be known as a coward. No one who stands up for the Lord and for what is good and righteous in this life can be a coward. Will you decide today to show valor in your daily walk? He will give you all you need to do just that.

Father, You are the giver of valor. Let me be known as a son of valor. Let me be known as one who stands for You, no matter what.

AUGUST 12

SPARE THE ROD

Proverbs 13–14

BEST VERSE: 13:24

Whoever spares the rod hates his son, but he who loves him is diligent to discipline him.

Don't get me started about discipline! Wow! In my years of ministry, I have witnessed first every conceivable method of child-raising. You have both extremes in the church. You have those parents who don't want to hurt the child's feelings, so they let the child dictate their behavior. Then you have the "slap and shout" method where the child resembles a gun-shy dog afraid to even raise their head.

God's Word is plain. We must discipline our children. To not do so is *not* loving. I am asked all the time what that means. There is no easy answer as it depends on the child. But one thing is always true. We must discipline in love. We discipline because we love. We discipline to show them love. We discipline because God in His love for us disciplines us.

TEACHING MOMENT

You may have the most compliant child in history living in your home or the strongest-willed child ever born. Be Jesus to them. I often wonder what kind of dad Jesus would have been. I mean, He was perfect, so He would have been the perfect dad, but what does that look like?

I believe child-rearing is more about us, the parents, learning to die to self than us teaching our children anything. As we die to self and become more Christ-like, our children are drawn to us. Well, they aren't drawn to *us*. They are drawn to Jesus in us. Isn't that what it is all about anyway?

What truth about discipline do you need to learn? What is it about being disciplined that you do not like? Give that to the Father. Let Him show you how to live today that honors Him. He will be glad to do it.

Father God, I am grateful for the way you correct me. Your Spirit in me reminds me when I err. Your Spirit in me corrects my path. Keep me compliant. Help me listen the first time.

AUGUST 13

JUST DIRT

Job 10

BEST VERSE: 9

Remember now, that You have made me as clay; And would You turn me into dust again?

You could say Job was having a bad day. Now his "friends" are giving him spiritual advice, and he is feeling like a complete failure. This is all new for him. He had been living at peace with the Lord and men. He had not experienced these kinds of trials before, as far as we know.

He looks up to the Lord and asks, "Are you just going to grind me into dust here?" He is feeling worthless. He is feeling hopeless. He is feeling beat down and thrown away. Have you ever felt that way? Have you asked the same question?

TEACHING MOMENT

These are the moments when our faith grows most. These are the moments when our kids' faith is built. When they are struggling with the pressures of life, struggle along with them. Lean on Jesus. He can take it. Your children need to learn that at an early age. There is nothing He can't handle!

Now, I have to admit that most of the "major" issues our children face aren't really major issues. But they are to them. And as they learn to trust the Lord in these struggles, they are building the faith necessary to trust the Lord later in life when they are facing those real-life struggles like the loss of a child or the loss of a job or the loss of a home. The struggle of faith is not for the now as much as it is for the future.

Are you there right now? Are you facing a day in which you feel like dust? Shake off that dust. Fall on your face before a holy God and say, "Through it all, Lord, I trust You."

Father, I don't understand all the trials that come my way. I don't like them either. But I trust You. I know You know me best and will allow only those things that will make me better to touch me.

AUGUST 14

JUST ONE ANGEL

Isaiah 37

BEST VERSE: 36

Then the angel of the Lord went out and struck 185,000 in the camp of the Assyrians; and when men arose early in the morning, behold, all of these were dead.

Pretty amazing, huh? The entire Assyrian army is laying siege to Jerusalem, so what does God do? He sends one angel, not two, not three, not a legion of angels. One lonely angel. What was He thinking? You see, when it's the angel of the Lord, that's all it takes.

Now, how did this "angel" do that? Well, we aren't told, and it really doesn't matter. It was done. The Assyrians were threatening God's people. They even questioned His power. He had to show them who was powerful. So, He sent just one angel who was empowered by God. That's all it took.

TEACHING MOMENT

What a great story to read your child! This is "made for TV" type stuff. They will love hearing how God defended Jerusalem. Let them speculate how He did it. Since we don't know, they can just dream. But don't lose sight of the truth of this story. What is that?

God is still defending His people. He still hears us when we cry out to Him. He still comes to our aid to defeat the enemy. Satan is no match for God, and he knows that. Your children need to know that. Knowing God is always there is comforting. It does not matter who is battering the gates, He is there.

Are you looking for the angel of the LORD? I am! I am always looking for His Son to appear. He is coming back. He will take us home. He will defeat Satan permanently. He will rule and reign forever. Won't you just believe that?

O Lord, You are my rescuer! You are the one who stands for me against those who want to harm me. I trust You to defend me and my children.

AUGUST 15

GOD'S ONE LIMITATION

Job 34

BEST VERSE: 12

Surely, God will not act wickedly, and the Almighty will not pervert justice.

In chapter 34 of Job, Elihu is still at it. He is seeking to school Job and his friends on what he knows about God. Although he is completely wrong about Job, he does spout off a few true things about God that are worth repeating. Today's verse is one of them.

God only has one limitation. He is incapable of doing evil. It is a limitation He imposes upon Himself. He is pure and holy. He is righteous and good. There is nothing in Him that can be considered bad. Everything He does is for our good. He will remain just and right throughout eternity. Wouldn't it be great if we followed Him in this attribute?

TEACHING MOMENT

Our children are born sinners. I know you don't want to hear that. When I held my granddaughter for the first time and looked into her little face, I knew that was true. It was hard to imagine that she was a sinner by flesh. It doesn't take long, however, for us to see the flesh come out. Sin is present in this world.

Our job as parents is to teach our children to draw near to God. We are to lay the foundation in their lives for them to be able to hear and respond to God's calling. And with that calling, they are to choose to do what is right and holy, just like our Lord. Unlike God, they are very capable of evil. For them (and us) doing the right thing is a choice. But it is a choice we must make.

What are you choosing today? Have you chosen evil or good? I promise you today you will have that choice once again. Something or someone will cross your path to allow you to make that choice. Choose good! Choose to honor and please your Lord today.

Father, I am incapable of doing what is holy without You in my life. My flesh is strong. My will power is weak. But I can do all things through Christ who strengthens me.

AUGUST 16

I DON'T WANT TO HEAR THAT

Isaiah 30

BEST VERSES: 10–11

Who say to the seers, "You must not see visions"; and to the prophets, "You must not prophesy to us what is right, speak to us pleasant words, prophesy illusions. Get out of the way, turn aside from the path, Let us hear no more about the Holy One of Israel."

Remember as a child (or maybe you still do it) when you would cover your ears with your hands and say, "la, la, la, la, la" when you didn't want to hear something? Perhaps your brother or sister was giving you some kind of instruction from your mom or dad. You just didn't want to hear what they had to say.

The people of Israel did not want to hear the truth. They wanted to hear pleasant things. They did not want to hear from the Lord. Before you gasp in disbelief, we are no different. We do not want to be told we are in sin. We do not want to be told that our choices aren't in line with God's Word. Right?

TEACHING MOMENT

Your children may do the same thing to you. They don't want to hear the truth. They don't want to obey. Just remember, you are no different. The best way to teach the truth is to live the truth. Live in front of your kids in such a way that they are drawn to it. Instruct them in such a way that they want to obey.

Okay, that might be a stretch. But I truly believe and have seen that when children see truth lived out, they seek it. They had much rather live in truth than in lies. Lies destroy. Telling your children what *they* want to hear will not lead them to the truth.

You may be thinking, *But Carl, I have never asked anyone to tell me what I want to hear.* I bet you have said it without saying it. Your actions speak louder than words. Let me encourage you today to go to the Lord and ask Him to reveal His truth to you today, no matter how hard it is to hear it. Listen and learn.

God, You are the truth teller. I don't always like what I hear, but I know if You say it, it is true. Teach me to follow You.

AUGUST 17

TIME CHANGE

2 Kings 20

BEST VERSE:

Isaiah the prophet cried to the Lord, and He brought the shadow on the stairway back ten steps by which it had gone down on the stairway of Ahaz.

I don't know about you, but I hate time change. Here in the U.S., we have Standard time and Daylight Savings time. We "fall back" an hour in the Fall and we "spring forward" an hour in the Spring. I would prefer if we just left it alone. But that's just my opinion.

Hezekiah wanted a sign he would be healed, so he was given a choice. The sun's shadow would be moved forward or backwards on the steps based on his wish. He chose to get ten minutes back, so it went backwards. Ten extra minutes in time—forever.

TEACHING MOMENT

Our children have to learn the concept of time. When they are young, they don't have to worry about it a lot. Everything they do and everywhere they go are determined by parents. But sooner or later they have to learn about time. Being on time is a courtesy and a great trait. As parents we teach them this.

But the more important concept of time is eternity. Little Johnny or Susie must be taught about eternity. We will all spend eternity somewhere. God's eternal clock is ticking. Christ is one day closer to His return each day. Mom and Dad, make sure your kids understand the finality of eternity. Time matters. Spend it wisely on your children.

Are you "wasting time"? Are you so busy with frivolous things that you forget how precious little time you have in the eyes of eternity? Make every day count. Make every hour count. God may prolong your days, as He did for Hezekiah. Or He could call you home today. Be ready. Be on time!

God, You are the maker of time. I know you see all of eternity at once, and You know my end day. Give me the ability to see each day as You see it—precious and important.

AUGUST 18

DOING THE RIGHT THING

1 Kings 15

BEST VERSE: 11, 14B

Asa did what was right in the sight of the Lord, like David his father. . . . nevertheless the heart of Asa was wholly devoted to the Lord all his days."

Asa was the great, great grandson of David. He was he first king of Judah, since David, who held true to the things of the Lord. That took courage. He had to shift the nation in a different direction. But he did. He stood for the right things and put away the wrong things.

Why did Asa do that? Who taught him the way of the Lord? Perhaps he visited that magnificent temple his great grandfather had built. Perhaps he spent more time reading the law of God. Perhaps he saw the wickedness of his father and decided to turn course. We don't know exactly what caused him to be the loyal king to God. But he was.

TEACHING MOMENT

It is our responsibility as parents to "set the table" for our children. We can't make little Susie or Johnny eat "of the Lord," but we can sure make the "food" is available. We will be held accountable for the way the way we raise our children. We won't be for the way they choose to live. That is their choice.

Perhaps you have an "Asa" who longs to please the Lord. That is awesome. Your job is much easier. You may have an "Abijam" (Asa's father) who was wicked and did what was evil in the sight of God. Then you have your work cut out for you. The only position to take with "Abijams" is on your knees. Give them to the Lord and live your life in honor of Him.

Which king are you? Are you David, who sought after the Lord? Are you a Solomon, who, although he was wise, was foolish? Are you Rehoboam, who lost the kingdom due to following unwise counsel? Are you Abijam, who refused to bow to the Lord? Or are you Asa, who sought to follow the Lord and please Him in all he did? It's your choice. But every choice has consequences.

O Lord, give me the heart of David and Asa. Help me to seek after You and to please you in all I do. Give me the wisdom to teach my children to follow, not in my footsteps, but yours.

AUGUST 19

WHAT DO YOU KNOW?

Job 32

BEST VERSE: 8B

And the breath of the Almighty gives them understanding.

It seems many of us think we know more than we really know. Have you ever known any one you could call a "know it all"? Boy, I have. But I have also been called that myself. My momma would have said I was "too big for my britches."

Elihu, the youngest man to confront Job and his friends, rightly said that it is God who gives us understanding. And where does that come from? From His Word. His Word is like an artesian well that never stops flowing. It keeps giving us wisdom and knowledge. But we must spend time in it.

TEACHING MOMENT

Have you ever had to help your child study for a test? If so, you know how hard it can be to instill knowledge. Memorizing spelling words or algebra formulas can be a daunting task. But learning God's Word is taught through the Spirit. As your child (and you) surrender to His will, the Spirit gives you the understanding.

The next time you find yourself drilling your child on vocabulary or math, remind them how the Spirit comes to our aid as we turn to His Word. In fact, why don't you both start memorizing a verse a week. You just might learn something new.

Are you still a learner? Do you seek God's mind on things or push through with your own wisdom? Let Him teach you great and mighty things. Let Him fill your mind with His knowledge and understanding. I promise He won't disappoint.

O Great Teacher, fill my mind with godly things. Fill my thoughts with You. Teach me today the truths You would have me know.

AUGUST 20

NOT ASHAMED

Romans 1

BEST VERSE: 16

For I am not ashamed of the gospel, for it is the power of God for salvation to everyone who believes, to the Jew first and also to the Greek.

Most of us would never admit that we are "ashamed" of the gospel, but we just never share it. We love to tell others at church how we *love* the

Word, but we never tell an unbeliever about it. So, if you never share something that you have, isn't that either being selfish or ashamed?

Paul is telling the Romans here that he knows the power of God for salvation. He cannot contain it. He has to spill it. He wants everyone to experience what he experienced on the road to Damascus (except for the blinding part). Do you want the same?

TEACHING MOMENT

While your children are young, teach them to love God's Word and to share it with others. There will come a day when they are outside your direct influence. It will be then that they have to decide how bold they will be in their witness. It will be then that they have to decide if they are ashamed or proud of their Lord.

The only way they will learn to be bold and unashamed is to watch you proclaim the gospel. If they *never* see you sharing the Word with others, they may presume that it is just something to keep to yourself. Show them how to share it. Show them when to share it. Show them.

You have to make this decision. God won't force you to share. But if you have the greatest news the world has ever heard, wouldn't you want to share it? If you possessed the cure for cancer, wouldn't you tell everyone? If you are a believer, you have the cure for everything—Jesus. Tell someone.

Father, forgive me for not sharing my love for Your Son more. Give me the opportunity today to be a witness. I am not ashamed of the gospel of Jesus Christ.

AUGUST 21

MIXED EMOTIONS

Nehemiah 3

BEST VERSE: 13

So that the people could not distinguish the sound of the shout of joy from the sound of the weeping of the people, for the people shouted with a loud shout, and the sound was heard far away.

When you read this verse, you may think of a national championship ballgame. One side is going to be shouting for joy at the end of the game. The other will probably be weeping because they lost. Either way, great emotions are going to be seen. The same thing was seen and heard when the foundation was laid for the new temple. Those who had seen the old one cried, but those who had not seen it shouted for joy.

Isn't that the way we are today? When a new direction is presented at church or at school or at work, we either shout for joy or cry from despair. There really is no way to make everyone happy. However, the key question to ask is: *is this the Lord's leading*? If it is, then we should all submit and rejoice.

TEACHING MOMENT

The same thing goes for our families. If you have more than one child, there will come a time when a family decision will make one child happy and the other sad. Even a small thing like where to go eat can cause mixed emotions. While one child is sitting at the restaurant all smiles, the other one sits with their arms crossed with a scowl on their face. Life lesson! Submission!

As God directs us in our surrender to Him, we will be faced with opportunities that will either thrill us or scare us. We will either be excited or sad. Our children will watch how we respond to those less-than-desirable situations. They will watch how we rejoice in the incredible situations.

When is the last time the Lord asked you to do something that you didn't really want to do? Did you shout for joy or cry? God gave us emotions on purpose. He doesn't expect us to squelch them. But He does expect us to surrender to His will and do what He asks anyway.

Father, I thank You that You love me enough to challenge me. You give me opportunities to serve You and others. Sometimes they are enjoyable and sometimes they aren't. But I will serve You regardless.

AUGUST 22

SHAKEN TO SALVATION

Acts 16

BEST VERSES: 29–31

And he called for lights and rushed in, and trembling with fear he fell down before Paul and Silas, and after he brought them out, he said, "Sirs, what must I do to be saved?" They said, "Believe in the Lord Jesus, and you will be saved, you and your household."

I have watched a lot of movies in which the prisoners escape from jail or prison. I love the old film The Great Escape. Those guys tunneled out of a German POW camp right under the noses of their captors. It took them months and a lot of digging to do that.

But here in Acts 16, Paul and Silas were not digging or trying to overcome the guards. Nope, they were just singing when an earthquake hit and all the doors opened, and all the chains fell off of all the prisoners, not just Paul and Silas. The jailer, thinking that all had escaped, was going to kill himself, but was stopped by Paul. He was literally shaken to salvation.

TEACHING MOMENT

Now, I am not advocating shaking your children until they repent. That would not be very Christ-like, would it? But how can we make sure our children know the importance of surrendering their life to Christ? I am sure there is not a parent reading this right now who wants to see their children face eternity without Christ. But sometimes we are too sensitive about telling them the enormous consequences of not coming to Christ.

The best and only way to point your children to Christ is to show them in Scripture. God's Word is so clear on this subject. If you have been reading them the Word and teaching them the truths of God, then don't shy away from those passages that clearly show that the weight of their sins without Christ will drag them straight to eternal damnation.

This is probably one of the "heaviest" devotions I have written so far. But I am convinced that we need to be begging God for the salvation of our children. We need to be straightforward with them, once they are able to comprehend, about the consequences of spiritual inaction. There is no greater joy than seeing your child surrender their life to Christ. Let's rejoice in that and covenant together to do our part in this ongoing battle against the Evil One.

Sweet Jesus, use Your Spirit to draw my children to You. Let them feel the tug in the heart to respond. May we all rejoice when we hear them admit they are sinners in need of grace!

JUST A COOL VERSE

Psalms 85—86

BEST VERSE: 85:10

Lovingkindness and truth have met together; Righteousness and peace have kissed each other.

I have read through the Bible 30 times, and now I am working on my 31st, but have just never noticed this verse till now. Funny how that happens every year! But seriously, this verse is just cool! Look at it.

"Lovingkindness and truth have met together; Righteousness and peace have kissed each other."

What was the psalmist thinking when he wrote this? My Bible says it was written by the sons of Korah who were servants of the temple. The first phrase is great, but the second blows me away. "Righteousness and peace have kissed each other." Think about that. You only kiss things you care about. Or at least, you should only do that.

When you are striving for righteousness you do receive the peace of God. He is pleased as you pursue His righteousness. And in return He gives you His peace. So, righteousness and peace kiss each other.

TEACHING MOMENT

The next time you kiss your child goodnight, read them this verse. I bet they have never heard it either. Kiss them with righteousness. Kiss them with peace. Let them know that God's lovingkindness and truth is at their fingertips. He wants to bestow all of that on them.

As you go through your next few days, meditate on this verse. I bet you it will bring a smile to your face. Just the thought of righteousness and peace kissing humors me. And who doesn't want to smile or giggle? If you see me giggling the next few days, I will be thinking of this verse.

Dear Lord, You kiss me with righteousness and peace through Your Son Jesus. He is the one who is "up close and personal" to me. Thank You for sending him to me.

AUGUST 24

THE END IS NEAR

Isaiah 13

BEST VERSE: 11

Thus I will punish the world for its evil and the wicked for their iniquity; I will also put an end to the arrogance of the proud and abase the haughtiness of the ruthless.

I know what you are thinking. *Carl, Isaiah was talking to people way back then, not us.* There is no doubt he was addressing his nation and the pagan nations around them, but these words apply to us, as well. One day, God the Father is going to send His Son Jesus back. Only this time He won't come back as a baby in a manger. He will come back to rule and to reign. All knees will bow.

Heavy stuff, right? Yep! But it's stuff that has to be understood. We have an obligation to the lost to warn them. We have a responsibility to share the message of salvation to as many as we can before He returns. Aren't you concerned? Aren't you burdened for your lost friends and family?

TEACHING MOMENT

There really is no need to "scare" your children with the impending doom of God's judgment on the earth. But we do have to be upfront and share with them the importance of His return and their need to be prepared. The urgency of the times demands it. As I have written about many times in my three devotional books, explain to little Johnny and Susie about the Lord coming to take all of us who are believers home one day.

They need to understand, though, that not everyone will go. Only those who have accepted Christ Jesus as their personal Lord and Savior will enter heaven. That will undoubtedly burden them to share with everyone. I have seen children approach total strangers and witness to them with absolutely no fear. We need to be as bold.

What are you doing about preparing your family for His return? Are you busy sharing with others? Are you teaching your children about the joys of heaven? There are so many things to teach. We need to get excited. He's coming back! And soon!

Lord Jesus, we anxiously await Your return. Thank You for promising to come back and take us all home. I know where I am going. Help me to bring as many as I can with me.

AUGUST 25

GENERATIONAL STUPIDITY

2 Kings 24

BEST VERSES: 19–20:
He did evil in the sight of the LORD, according to all that Jehoiakim had done. For through the anger of the LORD this came about in Jerusalem and Judah until He cast them out from His presence. And Zedekiah rebelled against the king of Babylon.

Zedekiah just wouldn't learn from the past. His brother Jehoiakim rebelled against Nebuchadnezzar, and then his nephew, Jehoiachin (the son of Jehoiakim), was taken into exile by Nebuchadnezzar. So, what does he do? He rebels too. He couldn't see that this was God's judgment on Judah (for his grandfather Manasseh's sin). His heart was turned against God, and he just wanted his way.

How often do we not see the mistakes of the past? Instead of breaking that cycle of abuse or addiction, we repeat them. The sense of hopelessness is strong. No matter how stupid it sounds, we just do the same things our parents or grandparents did and stay in that bondage of sin.

TEACHING MOMENT

Does your family have a secret family sin? Are you struggling with a generational curse of which no one in the past has confessed and repented? Stop it now! You must break this chain. Your children need to be free of this. Don't pass on the scourge of past mistakes and sins to your children.

It's hard to say to your parents or grandparents, "We will *not* continue in your ways." They probably do not see what they are doing. They may even see it as their birthright. Satan can confuse and entice us to do evil. Who do you think led these three kings I mentioned above to do evil? It certainly wasn't the Lord.

Will you agree today to examine your family tree? Look closely and make sure you aren't passing down some family "heritage" that goes against the things of the Lord. These things can be so subtle. Everything we pass down to our children should be centered on the Word of God and the Will of God.

O Father, search me and show me the evils I have harbored from generations past. Show me how to break this chain of guilt and rebellion. Free me of the "obligation" to continue whatever that is.

AUGUST 26

BUT I'M KING

2 Chronicles 16

BEST VERSE: 10A

Then Asa was angry with the seer and put him in prison, for he was enraged at him for this.

Asa was a good king for most of his reign, but toward the end he stopped relying solely on the Lord for deliverance and healing. Because the Lord loved Asa, He sent Hanani to rebuke him. I can just hear Asa now. "You, Hanani, come to me and tell me I'm wrong? I'm the king." So, he threw Hanani in prison.

We may not throw people in prison for confronting our sins, but we act the same way. "But I'm king of my castle. I don't need your approval." Have you ever felt that way when someone came to you as a brother or sister in Christ? It's hard to take criticism. None of us like it. But God may just be using them, like He did Hanani, to correct your path.

TEACHING MOMENT

When children learn to accept criticism, wanted or unwanted, as a message from the Lord, they will live more humble, obedient lives. It is hard for our children to hear they aren't doing something right. One of our jobs as parents is to show them how to hear criticism and measure it against God's Word. If the correction is from the Lord, it will not conflict with the Bible.

I have tried to always give my children advice through the lens of His Word. I haven't always been successful in that, but it is my goal. When I did that, and they didn't receive the advice, I knew it wasn't me they were rejecting. It was the Lord. I had done my job. The rest was up to the Lord and them.

Today, if someone critiques you, before you react, ask the Lord if this is from Him. The answer may just surprise you. I have always struggled with unwanted criticism. It just goes to show that you are never too old to learn a new biblical truth.

Lord God, thank You for using others to point out the error of my ways. I know I get blinded sometimes by my own agenda. You are faithful to lead me.

AUGUST 27

BRIGHTNESS

Psalms 75–76

BEST VERSE: 76:4

You are resplendent, more majestic than the mountains of prey.

To be honest, I had to look up the word "resplendent." Actually, I looked up the Hebrew word that is translated "resplendent." The word actually means "to be or become light." That's pretty cool. So, the psalmist is saying, "You are light."

We can't look directly at light with our eyes. It's blinding. And we have never seen true, pure light, which is God. That would certainly blind us. But one day, we will see Him. One day we will be able to look directly at Him with glorified eyes. His light will not only be bright, but it will also be inviting.

TEACHING MOMENT

Let's perform an experiment with light. Get a flashlight with your children and go in a dark room. Shine it toward them. Do it just for a second. Don't blind them. But ask them to look directly at the light. Then turn off the light and ask them if they still saw it briefly. Normally, we can still see the light in our vision for a couple of seconds after the light is out.

Now think about that. Your retina stores that image in your brain. The light is gone, but you still see it briefly. That's how it should be with us and God. If we are always looking at Him, at the brightness of His light in our life, then we should be able to maintain that light in the dark places. The key though is to keep looking at the light. Never take your eye off Him.

Have you lost the bright light? Have you turned your attention to something else? Turn your sight back to Jesus. Let Him shine in You. Let others see His brightness in the way you talk and act. In that way, others will get a glimpse of His glory at work in you. Wouldn't that be marvelous?

Lord, You truly light up my life. Let Your light shine in me. Help me keep my eyes on You.

AUGUST 28

IF . . . THEN

2 Chronicles 7

BEST VERSE: 14

And My people who are called by My name humble themselves and pray and seek My face and turn from their wicked ways, then I will hear from heaven, will forgive their sin and will heal their land.

This verse is quoted so very often by people who don't really look at the whole context. That seems to be the case with a lot of God's promises in the Bible. People want the promise without understanding what God expects.

Solomon had just delivered his awesome prayer to God at the dedication of the temple. The nation had celebrated for seven days and had made thousands of sacrifices to Jehovah God. The aroma of the burnt sacrifices probably still filled the air around Jerusalem. And God speaks to Solomon at night and tells him, "Yes, I will dwell here, and I will do all you ask if . . ."

TEACHING MOMENT

How often do you tell your children, "If you clean your room, then . . ."? Or you say, "If you want to go the park, then you need to . . ." *If . . . then.* The next time you catch yourself saying that, pull out this verse and talk to them how the Lord told Solomon the same thing. If he stayed true to the Lord, then the Lord would bless him. If the Lord's people would "humble themselves and pray and seek My face and turn from their wicked ways, then I will hear from heaven, will forgive their sin and will heal their land."

If . . . then. This promise still holds true today. I truly believe the reason America is going through the times we are right now is because we have *not* done these four things. As Christians, our salvation does not rest on us *doing* anything. But we need to help our children understand that God's blessings will be missed if we aren't true to Him.

Let me ask you a question. Are you humbling yourself, praying, seeking His face and turning from your wicked ways? If not, then it is no wonder you are not "feeling" God in your life. God cannot dwell in the midst of sin. He is holy. He is righteous. God is waiting to respond to you, if you will do these four things.

I don't know about you, but I want God's blessings on me. I want to be healed. I want to be full of Him. But I know that is only possible to the extent that I yield all of me to Him.

Dear Lord, dweller among men, forgive me of my sin. Cleanse me and make me whole. Hear my prayer. I pray for our nation and our world. I pray You will move and make Your presence known among the people.

AUGUST 29

DROUGHT RESISTANT

Isaiah 40

BEST VERSE: 8

The grass withers, the flower fades, but the word of our God stands forever.

Did you know you can actually buy drought-resistant plants? I didn't, until a few years ago. I grew up in the South where it rains a good bit every year. Sure, every few years we would have a dry year, but I never thought about buying drought-resistant plants. I always depended on the rain to take care of things.

This verse is a reminder to us that the Word of God will never dry up, wither, and blow away. It is always fresh and growing. It is always giving new life. It doesn't depend on anything to flourish. In fact, it's just the opposite. If we want to flourish, we must come to it and partake of it.

TEACHING MOMENT

What part do you play in your child's growth? Do you do anything to help them grow physically? Sure, you do. You provide a safe, warm environment called a home. It doesn't take a huge home, just one in which they can get out of the elements. You provide food and water. You actually feed them on a regular basis and make sure they get enough to drink. Depending on where you live in the world, the food can vary, but it is still necessary.

You treat any cut or wound they may get to prevent infection. You make sure they get their immunizations to ward off any diseases. I think you get the picture. You do a lot to help your child grow physically. But all that is for naught unless you also feed them the Word of God. If they are the most perfect physical specimen on earth, yet die and go to hell, what good have you done?

Will you spend time today with your child in the Word? It doesn't have to be a lot. God's Word can enrich their life and your life in ways you cannot imagine. But you must take the time to dig into it. Let the Word indwell you so that you too may not wither.

I am so thankful, God, that Your Word never fades. I can depend on it no matter what season of life I am in. Help me to share that precious Word with others.

AUGUST 30

IS GOD DEAF?

Isaiah 59

BEST VERSE: 2

But your iniquities have made a separation between you and your God, and your sins have hidden His face from you so that He does not hear.

Have you ever prayed to God and felt He was deaf? You pray and pray about something, and all you hear is crickets. Silence! Nothing but the wind! Perhaps this verse is the answer. It says very clearly here that our iniquities, our sins, cause a separation between us and God. That separation is so severe that He hides His face from us and does not hear our cries for help. Until . . .

When we confess our sins and repent of our iniquities, God responds. He has to. He wants to. He is a holy, just God and promises that. And once that wall is knocked down, He turns His face toward us and hears us. No, God is not deaf. He is just holy.

TEACHING MOMENT

This should be an easy truth to teach our children. I am sure your little daughter does not hesitate to ask you for things. Am I right? But there are times when you just can't give her what she asks. Why? Because she has not earned it, or she doesn't deserve it. Her behavior has been abhorrent. She has disrespected you or someone else. She has to learn to obey.

When that next time occurs with your child, read them this verse and make the application to their spiritual life. Now, listen. We don't obey God to get stuff. We obey God because we love Him and want to please Him. That's why your children should obey you—not out of fear or to try to gain favor. We want our children to obey us out of love. It's the same with our Lord.

Are you tired of banging your head against the wall in prayer? Is your forehead bloody from that, and you are wondering where God is? Look inward. Confess. Repent. And once that is done, rest in the knowledge that God will hear and will respond in His time.

Forgive me, Lord, of not trusting You. Forgive me of demanding answers when I don't deserve them. Forgive me and hear my cry for help.

AUGUST 31

TOO MANY GIANTS

1 Chronicles 20

BEST VERSE: 8

These were descended from the giants in Gath, and they fell by the hand of David and by the hand of his servants.

Go back and read verses 4–8 of 1 Chronicles 20. This passage lists three other giants. Other passages list four. Whether it was three or four, it doesn't matter. Whether they were Goliath's (the giant David killed) brothers, sons, or a combination of the two, doesn't matter. The fact is there were other giants in David's life.

How did he handle them? Well, in the beginning when he killed Goliath, he had chosen five smooth stones. Hmmm, do you think he had seen the other giants in the crowd? Later, when he was king, he had mighty men in his army who were able to take enemies down. Regardless how they fell, David trusted the Lord to defend His name. God will always do that.

TEACHING MOMENT

That's my point. Teach your children that the "giants" they will face in their Christian walk aren't concerned so much about tearing them down. They want to nullify and disprove God's faithfulness to His children. God will not stand for that. He will rise up and defend those who proclaim Him. But He may ask them to pick up some stones too.

"Hold it, Carl. Are you saying God tells us to sling stones?" No! I am saying He wants us to be prepared for battle, just like David and his mighty men were. Our sword is the Word of God. Our shield is faith. When we clothe ourselves with the breastplate of righteousness, helmet of salvation, and put the gospel on our feet, we are able to withstand any enemy's attacks.

That's the lesson to teach your children. Children are fascinated with giants. When you read them this story, don't focus on the twenty-four fingers and toes on the giant. Focus on their defeat at the hand of God. Giants hold no power of fear over us.

God of all creation, I look forward to hearing about all your creation, even giants, when I get to heaven. But I look forward more to thanking You for the victories You gave me over those giants in my life who wanted to bring me down.

SEPTEMBER 1

JUST FOLLOW THE LORD'S DIRECTIONS

Isaiah 20

BEST VERSE: 2

At that time the Lord spoke through Isaiah the son of Amoz, saying, "Go and loosen the sackcloth from your hips and take your shoes off your feet." And he did so, going naked and barefoot.

Naked! Did the Lord say, "Take off your clothes"? I don't know about you, but if the Lord had told me to walk around naked and barefoot *for three years*, I might have questioned His wisdom. Not Isaiah! He just did it. He obeyed. I am sure he must have been a little embarrassed. He had to be. I am sure he got cold. I am sure people pointed and laughed. But he stayed true to the Lord's command.

Now, hopefully, the Lord won't ask you to strip down and walk around. You would get arrested today if you did. But what else has He asked you to do that you think sounds crazy? What command is He directing you to obey that you have thoroughly ignored?

TEACHING MOMENT

I am sure you give your children directives each day. They probably think your commands are just as stupid. They may have even said so. But does that change the fact that you asked them to do it? No! The next time this occurs in your household, use this verse to explain to them the necessity to follow the commands of God no matter how ridiculous they may sound. God has a purpose in everything He asks us to do.

In the day we are living most of the Lord's commands sound stupid in comparison to the world's outlook on life. Most of what the world is doing is in direct contrast to the Lord's commands. We may appear to them to be "walking around naked and barefoot." But we are supposed to be just like Isaiah here. He obeyed to send a message to the nation. The message was "if you don't repent, you are going to end up looking just like me, being led into exile."

We have a message for the world. It's the same message. If the world does not repent and begin following the Lord's commands, as we are trying to do ourselves, they too will end up in exile. But their exile will be eternal. So, keep preaching the message. Do whatever the Lord commands so you can be used, like Isaiah, to reach an unrepentant nation.

Give me boldness and courage to deliver Your message, O God. Let them hear Your words and not mine. May I inspire my children to do the same.

CHANCE AFTER CHANCE

2 Chronicles

BEST VERSES: 15–16

The LORD, the God of their fathers, sent word to them again and again by His messengers, because He had compassion on His people and on His dwelling place; but they continually mocked the messengers of God, despised His words and scoffed at His prophets, until the wrath of the LORD arose against His people, until there was no remedy.

How often do you read these stories in the Old Testament and say, "Boy, those Israelites were dumb. . . . God gave them so many chances"? Oh really? Aren't we the same? God sends people in our lives time and time again, but we ignore them. We hear our pastor preach the Word to us over and over, but we choose to do things our way instead. We are no different than the Israelites.

And, unfortunately, if we don't repent and turn back to Him, we will suffer the same wrath from the same God. Our only hope is Jesus. It says it here, and it is still true—"there is no remedy." I don't care how hard you try to "fix it," it can't be done. God gives us chance after chance. But He will not ignore our lack of change, our lack of repentance, or our lack of return to Him.

TEACHING MOMENT

Children must be taught early that their disobedience will result in discipline. We teach our children to obey, not to just have them comply to our rules. No! We are modeling what they must do to obey God. They learn to obey us so they will learn to obey God. That's why it is SO important that you model your child rearing after God's parenting style.

God has a parenting style? You had better believe it. He loves unconditionally. He sets guidelines and borders to keep us safe. He corrects us when we stray. He gives us free choice but holds us accountable for our choices. He takes us back time after time when we repent and ask for forgiveness. What better parenting style can you get?

Are you the rebellious one? Do you ignore God's prodding time and time again? Today, stop and return. Ask forgiveness. Seek mercy and receive grace. He is waiting.

O merciful God, forgive me for all the times I ignore Your messengers. Help me hear You through all the noise around me. Thank You for always loving me.

SEPTEMBER 3

THE EASIEST QUESTION

Job 7

BEST VERSE: 20A

Have I sinned? What have I done to You, O watcher of men?

Job was befuddled. He was living for God. He was doing all the right things. Why was he being punished by God, or so he thought? And then he asks this question. "Have I sinned?" At first glance we might say, "What a stupid question!" But Job was seeking to isolate a particular sin.

We are all sinners. The Bible tells us so. We don't need to ask if we have sinned or not. That's a question to which we know the answer—YES! But sometimes we may sin without intention. We still need to ask God to forgive us. As believers, all our sins are forgiven. Hallelujah! We still need to confess.

TEACHING MOMENT

Teaching our children to confess sin is best done at a very early age. When they are just learning to pray, their confessions can be so sweet. As they get older, pride can enter the picture and cloud their need to confess.

They learn best by hearing us confess. Now I don't mean we should air our dirty laundry in front of our kids. That is not appropriate. But we should confess those things they are aware of. When we speak harshly to them, confess that to the Lord in front of them. They need to hear that Mom and Dad aren't perfect and that they sin too.

What do you need to confess today? Are you aware of the sin(s) in your life that are preventing you from approaching the throne because of guilt? Go to Him now. Let Him hear you pour out your heart and ask for forgiveness. He eagerly awaits that.

Lord, You forgive me when I don't deserve it. I am thankful for Your grace and mercy. Help me be an example of humility and brokenness to others.

BOLD BUT NOT BRASH

Acts 4

BEST VERSES: 19–20

But Peter and John answered and said to them, "Whether it is right in the sight of God to give heed to you rather than to God, you be the judge; for we cannot stop speaking about what we have seen and heard."

Don't you just love the boldness of Peter and John in the face of threats and accusations? They were arrested, questioned, and warned to stop preaching about Jesus. But they just said, "Sorry, we can't do that."

How many times have we (and I am including myself) hesitated in standing up for Jesus? Most of the time we don't face an inquisition. We are just confronted by someone who doesn't believe or someone who believes differently. We are not faced with the threat of death very often, are we?

So how can we teach our children to be bold witnesses for Christ if we aren't being bold ourselves? Well, we can't. They have to see us being unashamed of the gospel of Jesus Christ. They need to see us taking a righteous stand for Jesus.

TEACHING MOMENT

Now, I don't mean we should be rude or arrogant. That never wins anyone to Christ. We can be bold without being brash. We can stand out without being the one they notice. Everything we do needs to be pointing others to Christ. Even when we are disagreeing with someone over the gospel, we need to do it in such a way that we are drawing them to salvation, not pushing them away by being a "holy roller."

Won't you take a stand today? Won't you show your children how to be that bold witness? Won't you show them just how much you love Jesus by laying it all on the line for Him today?

Lord God, give me the boldness of Peter. Give me the courage of Paul. Let me stand unashamed today for my Savior.

LIGHTS, CAMERA, ACTION!!!

Esther 3

BEST VERSES: 5–6

When Haman saw that Mordecai neither bowed down nor paid homage to him, Haman was filled with rage. But he disdained to lay hands on Mordecai alone, for they had told him who the people of Mordecai were; therefore Haman sought to destroy all the Jews, the people of Mordecai, who were throughout the whole kingdom of Ahasuerus.

Don't you just love the story of Esther? It would really be a good movie, don't you think? There's intrigue, love, jealousy, revenge, danger, and rescue. And of course, we have the villain, Haman. He hated the Jews. Why? Because of one Jew—Mordecai. Mordecai refused to pay homage to Haman, and that burned Haman up.

Haman was a proud man who thought he deserved unquestioned admiration. Obviously, Mordecai recognized something in this scoundrel that did not deserve respect. So, he took a stand which could have cost him his life. Mordecai would bow to no man, only God. Haman would have none of that.

TEACHING MOMENT

Okay, so how do we apply this passage to our kids? Our children need to learn to respect those in authority. There is no doubt about that. But there may come a time in their lives when they are faced with a tyrant whom they must stand up against. Taking a stand could cost them their job. It is doubtful their lives would be in danger, but the way this world is going, that could happen too.

Taking a stand and being true to your beliefs is never risky in the eyes of God. Mordecai knew, as do we, that God had his back. He trusted that God would handle his enemies. Our children must learn that too. God will deliver His children, sometimes in very creative ways.

What are you facing today that threatens you? Are you facing a Haman in your life? Just trust the Lord. He will see you through. Be true to God's Word and allow Him to work in and through you to glorify His name. Let Him direct your decisions. Let Him lead you through this trial. He promises He will.

Father of all, I trust you to see me through. Give me the courage to stand for you, no matter the cost.

SEPTEMBER 6

NOT ON MY DIET

Isaiah 65

BEST VERSE: 25

"The wolf and the lamb will graze together, and the lion will eat straw like the ox; and dust will be the serpent's food. They will do no evil or harm in all My holy mountain," says the LORD.

How many times have you heard someone say, "That's not on my diet" or "I can't possibly eat that"? Maybe you are the one saying it. Lots of folks will be saying that in a few months as part of their new year's resolution to lose weight. But I don't think the wolf or the lion were thinking that in this verse.

I don't know what you know about wolves and lions, but they usually don't eat grass and straw. They would have been eating the lamb and the ox. But something is different here. All evil and threat of harm are gone. They are on the holy mountain of God, and He is the essence of peace.

TEACHING MOMENT

What a great verse to share with the kids. We are naturally prone to evil. Our flesh desires it. We would rather chew someone's head off when we are mad than talk calmly and peaceably. This is something that is so important to teach our children. They need to learn to dwell in peace. But in order to teach it, we must live it.

You may be thinking, *Now, wait a minute Carl. You don't know how mad that person made me.* Really? They *made* you mad? They have that much power over *you*? Only if you give it to them. We are going to always face "wolves" and "lions" who want to eat us. We must rest in the peace of God to calm their souls. Your children need to see that in you to learn it.

So, are you the wolf/lion or the lamb/ox? If you are resting in Jesus, it doesn't matter. He has the power to calm you and give you a genuine love for others that only wants to see them live, not die. Will you allow Him to do that in and through you?

Father of Peace, let me end this year in peace. Let me begin next year looking for ways to make peace with those with whom I may be at odds. But most importantly, let me live this out for my children.

SEPTEMBER 7

THE LOOKOUT

Isaiah 21

BEST VERSE: 6

For thus the LORD says to me, "Go, station the lookout, let him report what he sees."

WHAT DOES HE SEE?

I vividly remember playing "War" when I was growing up in South Georgia. All the neighborhood boys would come together, choose sides, and off we would go. My brother and I had this cool treehouse in our backyard that made for an excellent place for the lookout to station himself. His job? Watch for the enemy and let the rest of his "soldiers" get ready.

It was the same back in Isaiah's day. The lookout was positioned on the city wall in a tower and would sound the alarm if an enemy approached. Failure to do so would mean the destruction of city and all its people.

TEACHING MOMENT

We play that role for our children, don't we? We watch out for danger in their lives. When they are young, it's easy. They are normally in our sight. But as they get older, it becomes much more difficult. The internet opens them up to the enemy when we aren't there. When they are out with their friends, we can't see what's coming.

All we can do is protect and prepare. We have to teach them, not only what and who to watch out for, but we have to teach them how to defend themselves. And the *only* way to do that is to ground them in the Word. The Word will give them all the weapons they need to stand firm and strong in the face of the opposition.

Are you a loyal lookout for others? Are you signaling when you see the enemy approach? You need to stay alert. You need to be prepared. And when you see the enemy, sound the alarm.

O Great Commander, I am thankful that You have equipped me with the greatest weapon ever. I have the power of the Holy Spirit who defends me. Remind me to be a lookout for others.

SEPTEMBER 8

THAT SOUNDS KIND OF ARROGANT

Nehemiah 5

BEST VERSE: 19

Remember me, O my God, for good, according to all that I have done for this people.

If you just pulled this verse out of context, you would think Nehemiah was being proud and beating his own chest. Nothing could have been further from the truth. He had sacrificed and refused any payment to come and get Jerusalem rebuilt. His heart was heavy for those he was serving. He didn't ask anyone to do anything he wasn't willing to do himself.

Sometimes God places us in positions of leadership to simply lead by example. Often the people we are leading are hard-headed and stubborn. Many times, they are ungrateful. Some are even resentful. I am sure Nehemiah encountered all of the above. But he just kept serving his God.

TEACHING MOMENT

One of our jobs as parents is to prepare our children to lead. Boys need to be taught to lead so they can lead their homes when they grow up. They may lead a company. They may even lead a nation. Our little girls will need to learn to lead also. God may place them in a position of prestige and power. Learning to lead humbly and with a servant's heart is key.

We don't know how God is going to use our children. I bet Nehemiah's mother and father never imagined their son, the cupbearer, would be governor of Judah. We raise them, prepare them, and turn them over to the Lord.

Where has God placed you right now to lead? Who are you leading? Why are you leading? We all lead someone, in one way or the other. Make your leadership count. Lead Godward.

Lord, thank You for giving me the opportunity to lead others. Keep my heart broken and my spirit dependent on You. Let me model Jesus' attitude of leading to everyone I lead.

WRONG COUNSEL

1 Chronicles 10

BEST VERSES: 13–14

So Saul died for his trespass which he committed against the LORD, because of the word of the LORD which he did not keep; and also because he asked counsel of a medium, making inquiry of it, and did not inquire of the LORD. Therefore, He killed him and turned the kingdom to David the son of Jesse.

Most of us who have ever attended Sunday school have heard the story about Saul, the first king of Israel. God had chosen him above all the men of Israel to be the king and lead the people. Someone who began so humbly became proud quickly and turned his back on God. He chose to lead his way and not God's way.

As a result, the kingdom was taken from him and given to David. These two verses today occur right after the description of his death at the hands of the Philistines. He died for "his trespass . . . against the Lord," "because of the word of the LORD which he did not keep" and "because he asked counsel of a medium…and did not inquire of the LORD."

TEACHING MOMENT

There is much to learn from this story to teach our children. Our trespasses will kill us. Wow, that's harsh, but true. Unless we confess our sins and turn to Christ, we all die in our sins. We must all keep God's Word or face the consequence of our disobedience. And finally, there is only one true counsel we should seek—God's.

If we teach our children those three principles that are so vital to their walk with Christ, they will realize life instead of death. They will experience joy rather than despair. They will walk in victory rather than defeat. Isn't that how you want your children to live?

And the same applies to you. Make the right choices. Follow the Lord rather than your own mind. Our desires can quickly turn us down the wrong path, even when we *think* we are doing the right thing. See God's counsel first. He can always be trusted to give you the right guidance.

O Lord my God, forgive me when I go my own way. Grab me and pull me back to You, where I can hear Your wise counsel. Lead me Lord, even when I tug against You.

WHAT IS RICH?

2 Corinthians 8

BEST VERSE: 9

For you know the grace of our Lord Jesus Christ, that though He was rich, yet for your sake He became poor, so that you through His poverty might become rich.

I love the reminder here in this verse that although Christ was God, He gave up His "riches" to be poor for us. He willingly gave up all to pour out His grace and love to us, the ungrateful lot we are. He came to die, even though He knew He would be rejected by many and scorned by others.

What are you willing to give up for others? Are you willing to give without any hope of it being returned? I used to have a quite a book collection. Over the years and many moves I have given away or sold a lot of them. But I will always remember someone telling me once to never lend a book I wasn't willing to give away.

TEACHING MOMENT

Do you teach your children that principle of giving? Do you show them the joy to giving to others? How do you show that? Do you force them to take some of their toys to Goodwill? That's not really a great way to do that. Forced giving is not joyful giving, is it? The Lord desires us to give joyfully and willingly. First Timothy 6:18 tells us to "be generous and willing to share." Are you?

Is there anything in your possession that you would not give away? If there is, that is the very thing you must be willing to give over to the Lord. There should be nothing that you or your family are not willing to give up for Him. Things tie you down. Holding it loosely allows you to live freely with Christ.

I am probably one of the worst when it comes to holding on to stuff. I got it honestly from my dad. He kept everything, in case he might need it later. There is nothing wrong with being frugal unless it becomes a burden and you find yourself obsessed with holding stuff too tightly. Let it go! Give it up! Remember that everything you have is from the hands of the Father.

Thank You for sending Your Son, who gave up all He had in Glory for us. His poverty for our riches. I praise You for His sacrifice.

SEPTEMBER 11

WHERE DOES WISDOM COME FROM?

Job 28

BEST VERSES: 20

"Where then does wisdom come from? And where is the place of understanding?" And to man He said, "Behold, the fear of the Lord, that is wisdom; and to depart from evil is understanding."

What a great question! Job, in the midst of his discourse with his friends asks this question and then goes through all the places it is not. Finally, he comes to the answer—the fear of the Lord.

So, what does he mean by this? Why does "the fear of the Lord" bring about wisdom? Because when you reach the point where you truly love and honor God and recognize His enormity, He gives you the understanding you need. You obtain His wisdom.

Recently my son was showing his mom and I some videos that were made by one of his friends. These videos included aerial shots from a drone. As the drone was flying out from the scene, showing the vastness of the area they were filming, my wife said, "We are so small compared to God!" Exactly, when we see that, we are ready to gain His wisdom.

TEACHING MOMENT

So, how do we give this information to our children so they will also gain His wisdom? How do we get them to the place where their fear of the Lord equates wisdom? We have to be deliberate to point out our God sightings. We have to be aware of how the Lord is working in and through us and make sure our kids see it too. God is at work constantly in our lives. There is not aspect of our lives He is not involved in. But sometimes we just don't see Him.

As you drive on vacation or to school with your children, look for God sightings. As you go through a trial, look for God sightings. As you go through your daily routine, look for God sightings. And when you see Him, point Him out to your kids. Make sure they see His handiwork. By doing that, they will learn wisdom through the recognition of the vastness of God.

Dear God, I am so blind. I miss You all the time, and You are right in front of me. Open my eyes so I can share my God sightings with others.

SEPTEMBER 12

YOUR REP

2 Chronicles 14

BEST VERSE: 2

Asa did good and right in the sight of the LORD his God.

Asa had a good reputation. He "did good and right." But he didn't just do that. He did it "in the sight of the Lord his God." In other words, Asa wasn't trying to impress people. He was trying to please his God. His motivation for doing good and right was a holy one, not self-serving.

We, on the other hand, tend to do what's right only when we can get the glory. We are more concerned about people noticing what we do. We won't say this, but we had rather have the praise of people we can see than from God whom we can't see. There are not many people who do "good and right" just to please the Father.

TEACHING MOMENT

May I ask you a favor? Will you teach your children to not worry about pleasing you? *What? I will not teach my children that, Carl.* No wait a minute. Think about it. If their sole motivation for doing what is right and good is to please God, don't you think that will please you too? You can bet on it.

The problem with them pleasing us is we are fickle. We change our minds. We have different priorities at times. That can confuse our children. But God never changes. His Word doesn't change. They will know what is good and right when they are five or fifteen just by seeking His will through His Word. God won't change midstream.

Have you ever struggled with doing right and good? Well, maybe you are trying to please the wrong people. Focus on pleasing the Father. When you do that, He is honored. When you do that, He is pleased. Now, I will have to say that sometimes doing the right and good thing will make other people upset or uncomfortable. That's okay. Just please God. He is the one who holds your eternity.

Lord God, You are the only one whom I should try to please. I know by doing that those whom love You will also be pleased. Let me be like Asa and do good and right in Your eyes.

SEPTEMBER 13

SEE NO EVIL, HEAR NO EVIL?

Psalms 93–94

BEST VERSE: 94:9

He who planted the ear, does He not hear? He who formed the eye, does He not see?

Do you remember the three little monkey statues? One covered his ears, another his eyes, and the third his mouth. Hear no evil, see no evil, and speak no evil. While those may be cute little statues, that is not the case with God. He sees all and hears all. Nothing escapes his knowledge. Then why do we run around as if He is blind and deaf?

TEACHING MOMENT

Our children have to learn that there is no place on this earth from which they can hide from the Lord. When they are young and are living with us at home, we can hold them accountable. But when they grow up and gain some independence, they will be around people who either don't believe in God or don't think He really cares what they do. That is the dangerous time of their lives.

So how do we prepare them for these potential train wrecks? The only way I know is to be constantly pouring the Word of God into them while we have them. Verses like the one above are good ones to have them memorize. When they encounter those trying circumstances and are tempted to believe the lies of the devil, verses like Psalms 94:9 will ring in their ears. "Oh yeah, I remember a verse that says God hears and sees all."

But you know what else we can do? We parents can stop turning a blind eye or deaf ear to their sin. *What do you mean, Carl? I would never do that?* Maybe not, but I have seen way too many parents excuse their child's sin and disobedience. That only teaches the child that either you don't see or hear them, or you just don't care what they do. That is dangerous and sends a wrong message. Accountability is good! Don't be scared to be firm (but loving). You are preparing them for life!

Your watchful eyes and all-hearing ears remind me, Lord, of your constant care. I do not fear your oversight. In fact, I welcome it. Help me teach that to my children.

SEPTEMBER 14

PAYBACK

Proverbs 19–20

BEST VERSE: 20:22

Do not say, "I will repay evil"; Wait for the LORD, and He will save you."

I've said it. I'll admit it. When someone has done me wrong, I've said, "Okay, big boy. Payback is coming." Wrong! Wrong! Wrong! As I have grown in the Lord and learned to surrender my will to His, these words are less and less likely to come out of my mouth.

But I still struggle with the thought of getting even. God is faithful, though. He will judge the evil ones. We may not see it in our lifetime, but He will take care of it. We just have to remember that He is mindful of everything that touches us.

TEACHING MOMENT

Children are quick to get back at someone. Just observe a room full of toddlers. If one of them takes a toy the other one has, it won't be long until they find a way to snatch it back. Tears are shed, and sometimes fists fly.

How do we as parents teach restraint? We intervene quickly and often. We don't allow this type of behavior to continue. We train our children daily to trust the Lord to handle those whom desire to do us harm. I am not saying your children shouldn't stand up for themselves. I am saying, though, they should *not* seek retribution. I promise this learned skill will come in very handy when they grow up.

Are you quick to "get even"? Do you plan out your attacks on those who have harmed you? Repent! That's right. Repent. Your actions are sin. Ask

God to forgive you and pray for that person you had planned to get even with. They obviously need it.

Heavenly Father, Giver of grace, give me the peace I need to relax in Your competent hand. Teach me to trust Your wisdom in judging the ones whom seek to harm me. You are my defender.

SEPTEMBER 15

WICKEDNESS REVEALED

Esther 7

BEST VERSE: 6

Esther said, "A foe and an enemy is this wicked Haman!" Then Haman became terrified before the king and queen.

I love this part of the story. Haman thought he was "living high on the hog," as the old saying goes. He was near the king in power. He had been feasting privately with the king and queen. He had arrived, so he thought. And then the tables were turned on him.

Haman was blindsided by Queen Esther. She revealed to the king that Haman planned to have even her killed in his revenge against Mordecai and the Jews. Haman's best laid plans backfired in his face. That very day he lost his life.

TEACHING MOMENT

Children need to be taught that scheming against others will be exposed at some point. It may take time, but the truth will be revealed. Planning evil displeases the Lord. Planning to sin displeases the Lord. None of us are perfect. We will all sin, but we should *never* plan to sin.

So, what do you do when you discover your child's intention to harm? You deal with it immediately. You cannot let this kind of thing go. You don't wait to let them carry out the act. You discipline accordingly and firmly. Some of you are thinking, *Come on, Carl. They are just kids.* Exactly! It is our responsibility to train them. Discipline is part of that. It is not fun, but it is necessary.

Have you ever schemed against someone? Maybe as a child you planned how to get back at a sibling. Maybe as an adult you plotted your revenge against someone who had done you wrong. Confess that now, if you haven't already. You must maintain your fellowship with the Father. Unconfessed sin breaks that.

Lord, forgive me for harboring resentment against another. Forgive me for trying to "get even" with others. Give me Your heart and Your passion to see them come to Christ.

SEPTEMBER 16

IT'S GOD'S BATTLE

2 Chronicles 13

BEST VERSE: 15

Then the men of Judah raised a war cry, and when the men of Judah raised the war cry, then it was that God routed Jeroboam and all Israel before Abijah and Judah.

This verse could have been written differently. It could have read "Then the men of Judah raised a war cry, and when the men of Judah raised the war cry, then they routed Jeroboam and all Israel before Abijah and Judah." Nope, that's not how it reads. It was God who routed Jeroboam and his army of eight hundred thousand men.

Don't you see? Abijah cried out to God. The war cry was not so much an attempt to frighten the enemy. It was a cry to their God. We don't know what they cried out. Perhaps it was something like this: "Fight for Jehovah! Fight for our God!" We should do the same. We have to acknowledge it is God's battle, not ours.

TEACHING MOMENT

When your son or daughter learns that it is God who fights for them, they will begin to grow immensely in their walk with Christ. They do not have to fight the enemy alone. As they face that bully in school, it is God who will stand with them. As they are challenged with temptations to lure them away from following Christ, it is God who will have their back.

As mom and dad, you must model the same. You can't wring your hands and worry when you face a challenge. You are showing them and even telling them that you are trusting the same God who fought for Judah. These stories mean something. They aren't just inspirational stories. They are truth.

So, as you face that life challenge today, trust Him. Cry out to Him. Give your war cry, not to scare anyone, but to join *God's* battle. He only has to speak a word, and the enemy is defeated. Let Him fight for you.

Thank You Lord, for facing my enemies for me. They don't know what they are up against. Help me show others through my trusting You that they can do the same.

SEPTEMBER 17

DID YOU SEE THAT?

Habakkuk 1

BEST VERSE: 5

Look among the nations! Observe! Be astonished! Wonder! Because I am doing something in your days—you would not believe if you were told.

Have you ever seen anything so amazing that you did a double take? I mean, you couldn't believe your eyes. There was no way what you saw actually happened. There have been a few things in my life that fall into that category. To this day I can't believe what I saw.

God is telling Habakkuk to look and see what He is doing around him. Even though things look bad, He is at work. But Habakkuk has to open his eyes and recognize God at work. Isn't that the case with us, too? We complain and gripe about how bad things are and fail to recognize God's fingerprints all over our situation. He is constantly working in the lives of His children to make them more like Jesus.

TEACHING MOMENT

Kids are easily tricked by what they see. When they are young, they can be made to believe just about anything. Pulling a quarter out of their ear blows them away. Taking away their nose with your hand scares them. Listen, while they are young, teach them to look around for "God sightings." Teach them to recognize those moments when the only explanation is God.

As our children have their eyes opened to the spiritual realm and learn to trust the Lord, their worldview becomes much clearer. The world will try to make them think they are seeing the truth while leading them down the wrong path. But as we teach them to verify all they see with the Word of God, they can be reassured if what they see is really the truth.

How about you? Do you simply believe it because you see it? The old saying is still true concerning the world—believe half of what you see and nothing you hear. But when God shows or tells you something, you can literally bet your life on it. Turn to His Word today and let it direct your path.

Lord, on the days I think I see something that is true and right, help me to verify it through Your Word. That means I have to be spending time in it. Thank You for allowing me to have such a revealer of truth in my life.

SEPTEMBER 18

SCATTERED

Acts 8

BEST VERSE: 4

Therefore, those who had been scattered went about preaching the word.

After Stephen's stoning in Jerusalem, persecution began to get intense. This was the point at which Paul (known as Saul then) began persecuting the church. But God had a plan. He allowed the persecution to force the believers to flee Jerusalem. Look what happened. They left Jerusalem, but as they did they "went about preaching the word."

These changed lives could change their physical location but not their spiritual calling. They could abandon their earthly dwellings but not their heavenly purpose. They took the gospel out of Jerusalem into a world that had not yet heard the message. God was going to use them to change the world.

TEACHING MOMENT

Our children will suffer persecution if they choose to follow Christ. The extent of the persecution will vary depending on where they live and how radical a life for Christ they live. It is sad to me that many believers can live in this fallen world and never face any kind of persecution. What? Carl, that sounds crazy. Well, here me out.

We should live lives so holy and different that unbelievers feel uncomfortable around us. The light of Jesus in us should expose the darkness around us. If your children live like that, get ready for persecution. Welcome it. Embrace it.

You are probably thinking right now that you do *not* want that for your children. Had you rather have them just melt into the crowd and not stand out for Jesus? We, as parents, should desire that our children stick out at school as sold-out believers. Pray they will be bold and courageous in their walk.

Father God, give me the courage to stand firm for Your Son. Help me spread the good news through my suffering. Let others see the difference in me and ask how to change their lives.

SEPTEMBER 19

THE RIGHT SHOES

Habakkuk 3

BEST VERSE: 19

The Lord God is my strength, and He has made my feet like hinds' feet, and makes me walk on my high places.

It is amazing to me to watch mountain goats or other animals climb rocky hills or mountain slopes. They seem to walk effortlessly along paths they and others have blazed. You or I would most definitely slide down that hill. We aren't built for that kind of climbing.

On my last trip to Kenya, I walked to the edge of a steep mountain valley with some friends. There was a clearly marked path down the mountain, across the valley floor and up the next mountain. I could actually see people on the other slope climbing up. I wanted to go down the path, but I was wearing the wrong shoes. My shoes had no traction. I would have had to literally slide down the hill and would have had no hope in climbing up the other side.

TEACHING MOMENT

When was the last time your child slipped and fell? Was it during a storm when the ground was wet or icy? Was it due to their footwear not being suited for the terrain? Maybe it was because they just tripped over something while trying to break in those new shoes you got them. This is a great verse to use with them as you tend to their scrape or cut.

You can remind them that in life we are going to face some difficult things, but God is our strength. He will give us the right stuff to get us through it, if we will just listen to Him. In fact, He will *make* us walk on high places (difficult terrain) sometimes. Why? To be able to face the next hill or the next hill after that. He knows what is ahead. We don't.

Aren't you glad that the Lord has the right shoes for us to wear depending on the path He has chosen for us? He knows every bend and hill. He knows when we need to climb or just walk. He knows when we need to stop, rest, and take in the view. But He knows also that our path is helping to blaze a trail for our children to follow.

So, put on your walking shoes and trust the Lord to guide and direct you as you traverse those difficult paths He has chosen for you. Remember He is your strength.

I am thankful, O God, for the challenging steps that You place before me. I know each step prepares me for the next step. Let me be patient, however, as You guide.

SEPTEMBER 20

BE GLAD

Psalms 63-64

BEST VERSE: 64:10

The righteous man will be glad in the LORD and will take refuge in Him; and all the upright in heart will glory.

What a promising verse of scripture. The righteous will be glad in the Lord. What does that mean, though? According to Strong's Concordance, the Hebrew word for "righteous" means to "cheer up, be made glad, make joyful, make merry, cause to or make to rejoice." That is pretty clear, I think. Because we are made righteous through the blood of Christ, we have all the reason in the world to be glad.

And because we are glad in the Lord, we have no fear of Him and can come to Him for a place of refuge and safety. We run to Him in times of trouble, knowing He welcomes us warmly. Even in those times we come with joy, rejoicing in our righteousness.

TEACHING MOMENT

Hopefully, your children feel that way about coming home to you. Perhaps your children have grown up and moved out. Do they come home to visit with that feeling in their heart? Do they feel like your home is a place of refuge? They should if you are exemplifying the love of Christ to them.

If your children are still at home, begin now to prepare your home to be that way. You want them to walk in the door feeling glad and rejoicing. They should walk in knowing they will be received with open arms. They should come home with merriment and joy. Our homes should be models of God's home—welcoming and inviting.

What do you need to do to improve your home? Do others feel that way when they visit? Make your home so joyous that others quickly smile when they think of visiting. May the love of Christ in you radiate to all who enter.

Father, help me to spread the welcome mat joyfully to others. Let my home be a beacon of light to all. Let the joy of Jesus shine.

SEPTEMBER 21

A TEMPLE? REALLY?

1 Corinthians 6

BEST VERSE: 19

Or do you not know that your body is a temple of the Holy Spirit who is in you, whom you have from God, and that you are not your own?

When I read this verse and look in the mirror, I laugh. My body? A temple? Maybe one that looks like Buddha! Ha. Seriously, I do know what Paul is saying here, and it is not the actual shape he is referring to. Aren't you glad?

This is probably the one thing most Christians seem to ignore. We do things to our body that do not honor God. We do many things that dishonor and destroy our bodies. I don't have to name them because you know what they are.

TEACHING MOMENT

So, teaching our children to honor their bodies is crucial for a healthy Christ-life. When we are bandaging Sallie's, knee we can take the time to explain to her how her body is God's. Tell her that every believer is indwelt with the Holy Spirit, and we need to make sure His home is clean and well cared for.

Perhaps the next time your children are brushing their teeth (which may seem like an impossible task) use that opportunity to talk about this verse. There are so many things we can do to teach this principle to our kids. But like most of the lessons we teach, we need to live it ourselves first. Children learn best by watching someone model this behavior first.

What are you doing to keep your body holy? Are you overeating? Are you using some kind of substance to hurt your body? Are you getting regular checkups? Our bodies are naturally decaying because of the Fall, but we still need to take care of the one God gave us. Holy Temple? Yep! Anywhere God dwells is holy. You are His temple here on earth. Live like it.

Father God, I am Your temple here on earth. Remind me to treat my body like that. Help me to teach my children to do the same.

SEPTEMBER 22

AMAZING BUT UNEXPECTED

Acts 12

BEST VERSE: 16

But Peter continued knocking; and when they had opened the door, they saw him and were amazed.

Do you know the story? Peter has been arrested and imprisoned. An angel sets him free, and Peter shows up at the door where the believers are praying, probably for his freedom. So, what do they do? They stand there amazed! They can't believe that what they have been praying for has actually happened! Aren't we the same?

How many times have you prayed for something and then are amazed or surprised when it happens? Have you ever prayed for rain and then not carry an umbrella? Listen folks, if you are praying for something, expect it to happen!

TEACHING MOMENT

We need our children to learn to believe their prayers are being heard and answered. Now sometimes the answer we get is not exactly what we were hoping for, but it is usually for our best. How can you as a parent teach your child to trust the Lord to answer prayers? The best way I know is to pray with them and then let them know when you get an answer. Sometimes that prayer is answered quickly. Other times it takes a while. I have known families who have prayed for an adoptive child, and it happened quickly. Others . . . well . . . it took a while. But they still celebrated the answered prayer in whatever form the answer took.

What are some things you as a family are praying for right now? Write them down on the fridge and watch what God does. Pray with your children for their desires. Watch how God speaks to them through their prayers.

But let me challenge you in one thing. The next time you pray for something and it happens, don't be surprised. Don't be amazed! Praise the amazing God, but don't be amazed that He answered.

Forgive me, Lord, for being amazed at my answered prayers. Forgive me for praying to You without expecting You to answer. Teach me to pray expectantly.

SEPTEMBER 23

HEAVENLY CONFIRMATION

Acts 27

BEST VERSES: 23–24

For this very night an angel of the God to whom I belong and whom I serve stood before me, saying, "Do not be afraid, Paul; you must stand before Caesar; and behold, God has granted you all those who are sailing with you."

Paul had tried to warn the people taking him to Rome to not travel due to the danger of storms, but why should they listen to an itinerant preacher? What did he know about sailing? Obviously, more than them. The Lord had told him to go to Rome, so he knew he would make it. But in this angelic appearance, he is told that all on board would make it.

I don't know about you, but if I am told by someone that they have had an angelic message, I would probably doubt them. Who sees angels? Who gets messages directly from God? We just don't know who God will use in our lives to deliver His message to us. Don't dismiss someone because you can't understand how this could happen.

TEACHING MOMENT

How do you teach your kids to hear from God? It's not like an angel is going to appear every day and give them directions, right? We teach them to hear God by praying and reading His Word. They will hear from God by obeying His commandments. They will hear from God when they listen (and I mean really listen) to their pastor.

Hearing from God is not some mystical event. God *wants* us to hear Him. He may speak in a still small voice, but if we are *listening,* we will *always* hear it. Tell your children that. Tell them to talk to Him daily. And then—listen.

Are you listening today? Do you need an angel to give you God's message? Of course, you don't. You just need to stop, get quiet, and listen. God is just waiting to talk with you. He can't wait to have a conversation with you. Talk!

Lord, thank You for confirming Your presence in my life. Thank You for talking to me daily. Thank You for giving me the direction I need to follow.

SEPTEMBER 24

HAVE YOU EVER SMELLED WRETCHED?

Romans 7

BEST VERSE: 24

Wretched man that I am! Who will set me free from the body of this death?

I remember growing up in South Georgia and working for Mr. Pollock. He owned a variety of businesses, one of which was a grain bin operation. He would buy the farmers' corn once it was harvested and load it into large metal silos which in turn would be augured into waiting train cars. Grain in—Grain out. Unless. . . .

One day someone, while checking the level of the grain in the bin, left the top door open. Well, it rained, and the grain inside, which was down pretty low, got soaked. Inside that grain bin, the temperature would rise to well over 115 degrees, so that corn just fermented. I was one of the lucky ones who got sent into that grain bin to shovel that rotten, smelly, wretched corn into the auger so it could be cleaned.

I can't begin to tell you how bad the smell was. You may have heard the expression "It would gag a maggot." Well, it was worse than that. Needless to say, when we emerged out of that grain bin, we smelled wretched. When I see that word, I think of that smell. That's how our sin smells.

TEACHING MOMENT

The next time your child gets really "stinky," why not talk about how our sin smells to God. That aroma is not sweet. After you give them a bath and they smell "sweet" again, talk about how once we confess our sins, we have a sweet aroma to God. What a perfect example of our sin and forgiveness. Stinky to sweet! Wretchedness to holiness! Lost to found! Doomed to blessed!

I am thankful, Lord, that You don't turn Your nose up at me when I approach Your throne. You have already forgiven my sin. Now wash me clean again so I can smell more like Jesus.

SEPTEMBER 25

NEW STUFF

2 Corinthians 5

BEST VERSE: 17

Therefore if anyone is in Christ, he is a new creature; the old things passed away; behold, new things have come.

We've just recently passed that time of year when kids get all geared up for school, and I mean literally "geared up." New backpacks, new notebooks, paper, pens, pencils, clothes, shoes, and . . . you name it. New stuff galore! I used to love getting new stuff for school.

Do you remember the smells? I can still smell the clean pieces of paper, freshly sharpened pencils and strongly pungent plastic notebooks. I also used to get a new lunch box (back when they were metal and contained a small thermos) with my favorite cartoon hero or character on it. I wish I still had those. They are probably worth a fortune now.

But look at today's verse! We are all new in Christ! We all have that new smell! We are washed clean! And just like the new school supplies, we are ready to be used! We are ready to be used by Him. How does the Lord want to use you?

TEACHING MOMENT

When preparing your kids for school, how about talking with them about how prepared they are for Jesus? How about, when you give them the new paper and pencils, talking about how God wants to use them this year to reach a new friend for Christ? How about sharing with them how, just as a pencil needs to be sharp to be useful, they need to be sharp in God's Word to be effective for the kingdom?

New stuff doesn't stay new does it? But we are always new in Christ because of His regenerating power in us through the Holy Spirit. We never get old in Christ! We are fresh and useable, as long as we stay filled with the Spirit and let Him use us. Let Him this year! Do whatever He says! And stay sharp for Him!

I awake every day, Lord, new in Christ. I thank You for the newness I feel and live each day. Remind me on those cloudy days that I am new in You.

SEPTEMBER 26

PROPHETIC WORDS

Isaiah 53

BEST VERSE: 3

He was despised and forsaken of men, a man of sorrows and acquainted with grief; and like one from whom men hide their face He was despised, and we did not esteem Him.

We have heard and read this prophecy concerning the Messiah, Jesus Christ. We quote and reflect on the words every Easter. But do we really understand the words? Have you ever known anyone who had done nothing wrong who was hated like Jesus? Look at the words: despised, forsaken, sorrow, grief, hide their face, did not esteem. That's pretty low.

Guess what? He would do it all again. He would take all that on Himself again, just for you. Isaiah wrote these words long before Christ was born, but he believed them. He spoke truth to a lost world who would not see the Messiah for generations to come. But it was still truth.

TEACHING MOMENT

Our children need to know that sometimes things don't happen quickly. Sometimes we have to wait a while. Christ did what He did for them. They may not see the result of all His works until later, but they will. They may not see feel His power every day, but it is still there.

When your little Johnny or Susie comes home saying that some boy or girl hates them, pull out this verse. Remind them, in comparison to the hate Christ felt, that is nothing. It's still real, and it still stings, but it pales in comparison.

Let me ask you a question. Would you die for someone who hates you? I bet not. Would you give your life for a crowd of people who spit on you? Probably not, but we should be willing to. Just like Christ, we should lay down our life for others. Who do you need to die for today?

O God, there is no way I can die for someone else without You living in and through me. I just don't have it in me. My flesh is too strong. But You can do it through me.

SEPTEMBER 27

OOPS! NOW WHAT?

Esther 1

BEST VERSE: 10A

On the seventh day, when the heart of the king was merry with wine. . . .

Oh, the folly one gets into when wine or strong drink enters the picture. King Ahasuerus lost his wife, Queen Vashti, because he was drunk. He made a stupid request of his queen, one that was very uncustomary at the time, that she refused. So, he got mad and issued a decree banning her from his presence and removing her crown.

"Oops! Now what?" Have you ever said that? Boy, I have. I have said and done things hastily or without thinking that I wish I could have taken back. But like toothpaste, once it's out of the tube it is really hard to get it back in.

TEACHING MOMENT

This lesson is not about drinking. It's about making hasty decisions. Every decision we make has consequences. We must teach our children that fact. Decisions must be made, but not without thinking through the results. Whether it's spending money or deciding where to go to college, every decision will affect what we do next.

As your children get older, the decisions they will have to make become bigger and bigger. Whom to marry? Where to live? What job to take? That's why it is so important to let them make decisions now while they are young and can fall back on you when they make wrong ones. Failure is a great teacher.

What decision have you made lately that you are regretting? Did you seek the Lord before you made it? If so, trust Him in the decision. If not, confess that as sin and ask Him for a way out. He may just extend mercy and grace to you. Or He may let you learn a lesson. Either way, you have to trust Him.

O Lord, You are worthy of my trust with every decision I have to make. I feel sometimes that I don't need to bother You with the little things, but I know that is not what You want. Thanks for hearing and answering.

SEPTEMBER 28

AIN'T NOTHING WE'VE DONE

Titus 3

BEST VERSE: 5

He saved us, not on the basis of deeds which we have done in righteousness, but according to His mercy, by the washing of regeneration and renewing by the Holy Spirit.

Look at that verse again. "He saved us, not on the basis of deeds which we have done in righteousness." Do you see what that is saying? There's not a thing we could have done even in righteousness that could save us. He saved us according to His mercy. He used the Holy Spirit to regenerate us and renew us. Wow!

You have to know that if man could have done it by himself, God would not have sent His Son to die for us. If we could have satisfied the demands of the Law, someone would have figured it out. But we needed Him to do it. And He did! What a Savior!

TEACHING MOMENT

I want you to get your little Susie or Johnny to try something that you know they can't accomplish on their own. Make sure it's something safe (i.e., don't give them a chainsaw). Give them some time to attempt the project without your assistance. Resist the temptation to jump in.

When they are totally frustrated and have given up, very gently step in and do it for them. Don't let them help. Just let them watch. This example is by far well short of what God did for us. But you get the picture. Tell them how God stepped in and did what we could not do. Jesus fulfilled the Law. He paid the price. He rescued all mankind.

What are *you* trying to do on your own today? Are you *trying* to be a good Christian? Stop trying! You can't do it. But the Holy Spirit in you, which regenerated and renewed you, can. Surrender to the power of the Spirit in you. Let Him live your life today. You will be amazed at the difference.

Giver of life, thank You for saving me by Your mercy. Thank You for sending Your Holy Spirit to make me new. I will use this life to honor You today.

SEPTEMBER 29

JUST DO WHAT'S RIGHT

2 Kings 7

BEST VERSE: 9

Then they said to one another, "We are not doing right. This day is a day of good news, but we are keeping silent; if we wait until morning light, punishment will overtake us. Now therefore come, let us go and tell the king's household."

Lepers! Unclean! Unclean! These were people who were considered to be the lowest of the low. People were scared to come near them because of their disease. And here in this verse we find them thinking of the very people who would not have given them the time of day.

The Arameans had been starving the city of Samaria through a siege. The people were literally starving to death and had even resorted to cannibalism. Things were bad! And all of a sudden, these lepers have the bright idea to go to the camp of the Arameans in the hope they would give them food or kill them. They find the camp empty and all their supplies just lying there. What a miracle!

TEACHING MOMENT

This lesson in thinking of others is such a great lesson for our children to learn. You may have a child who is just like that. They had rather give their allowance away than spend it or keep it. They had rather share that piece of candy with their sibling than eat it themselves. But you may have a child who is self-centered and narcissistic. Thinking of others is so important. It is exactly the life Christ wants us to live. He always thinks of others—never Himself.

So how can you as mom or dad help your child learn that lesson? How about living that life yourself? Can you model that behavior? Can you show them that others matter? When you do, your children will notice. They will ask why you are doing that, and then you can share our Lord's example. Those are the teachable moments. Don't miss them.

Lord, I know there are so many who have much more need than I have. I need to be the first to reach out and bless them. Show me today whom to bless.

SEPTEMBER 30

YOU ARE MINE

Isaiah 43:1

BEST VERSE: 1

But now, thus says the LORD, your Creator, O Jacob, and He who formed you, O Israel, "Do not fear, for I have redeemed you; I have called you by name; you are Mine!"

Just look what God says here. He says: 1) Do not fear, 2) I have redeemed you, 3) I have called you by name, and 4) you are Mine. Wow! Pretty powerful words. The God who created all things says this. These words He spoke to Israel still apply to us today.

We are His. If we are believers, if we have accepted Jesus Christ as our personal Savior, He says, "Don't fear. I have redeemed you." Then He calls us by name. That means He doesn't say, "Hey you!" No, He says, "Hey Carl!" He calls my name. And then the most beautiful part—*you are mine.*

TEACHING MOMENT

Oh, listen, Mom and Dad. You really need to teach your little boy this verse. Ask him what his most prized possession is. It may be that certain toy or game he just loves. It belongs to him. He can say, "This toy is mine." He will guard and protect it. He knows it well.

God considers your son His prized possession, if he is a believer. He cherishes him. He gives him safety so there is no fear. He has redeemed (he has bought him) with the blood of His Son. Go over this a couple of times with your son. Make sure He sees himself as God's possession. That will give him a sense of security that we all need.

Do you realize you are God's? A possession does not possess itself. It is possessed by something greater. Allow yourself to be used as the Possessor wishes. It will always be for your good. Trust Him today. Trust the one who calls you by name.

I can hardly believe that You know me by name. I love knowing I am Yours. I want to be. Remind me of that today.

I WILL ONE UP YOU
1 Chronicles 17

BEST VERSE: 10B
Moreover, I tell you that the LORD will build a house for you.

I had never really noticed this part of the story. David has just brought the Ark of the Covenant from the home of Obed-edom to Jerusalem and placed it in the place he had set up for it. Then he tells Nathan, the prophet (the same Nathan who had confronted him about Bathsheba), that he wants to build the Lord a house. Nathan says, "Sounds good, go ahead." But then the Lord gives Nathan a message to tell David that he should not build it, but that his son would build it. Got the picture? But then God says in the verse above that He is going to build a house for David. What? I thought David already had a house. No, God is saying to David, "I am going to establish your household forever."

Have you ever wanted to do something for someone, but before you got around to it, they did something for you instead? How would that make you feel? Humbled? Embarrassed? Guilty? We see David's humble response later in this passage. He was humbled. He didn't feel he deserved any of that.

I don't know about you, but I want to be more like David here. I want to recognize that I don't deserve the blessings of my God. I should be doing more to honor Him, but instead He continually honors me. That is humbling!

TEACHING MOMENT
Humility is hard to teach our children. It is really a trait that is caught rather than taught. Parents, once again you have to model humility. When your children see you respond to life with humility, they learn from that. Sometimes humility comes easy. Other times we have to die to ourselves and let Jesus be Jesus in us. We have to give up our rights and what we THINK we deserve and humble ourselves. Let your children see that.

I had much rather have a humble child than a proud one. Why? Because I know the Lord says he will exalt the humble and humble the exalted. Let humility reign in your life today.

God, it is humbling when I reflect on all you have done for me. But Father, allow me to do one thing for You today. Send someone in my life today who needs to hear about You.

DON'T STOP

1 Kings 7

BEST VERSE: 51

Thus all the work that King Solomon performed in the house of the LORD was finished. And Solomon brought in the things dedicated by his father David, the silver and the gold and the utensils, and he put them in the treasuries of the house of the LORD."

Building the temple was no small matter. The building itself was a seven-year process, plus the construction of all the utensils. I am sure there were times Solomon and the people of Israel thought it would never be completed. But Solomon was determined to make it worthy of the Lord. No cost was spared. They say this temple was truly a marvel to behold.

If you are a believer, God is building you right now. In fact, it is a lifetime process. God never stops shaping you into the image of Christ. At times He is taking off big chunks, and other times He is using sandpaper to smooth off small areas. But the work never stops. To quote the apostle Paul, "you also are being built together into a dwelling of God in the Spirit." (Ephesians 2:22)

TEACHING MOMENT

This teaching moment is directed more at you, Mom and Dad. God is going to use you to help shape your child. It is up to you to teach them to obey you and God. It takes years to do this. There will be days when you think you will never make progress with your children. They are hard-headed and stubborn, and they refuse to learn. Hmmm, I wonder how God feels about you?

Then there are days it seems everything you have taught them comes together. It's one of those "Eureka!" moments for them. They finally see the big picture. That might come when they are twelve, or it may not come until they are thirty-two. Just keep thinking about how long the Lord has been teaching you.

Why don't you allow the Lord to shape you today however He wants. The process will go a lot smoother and will be much less painful. He only wants to make you more like Him, which is perfect. I mean, come on, who doesn't want to be perfect? Right?

Father, make me today into the very image of Christ, so that whoever sees me only sees Him.

OCTOBER 3

CLEAN OUT DAY

2 Chronicles 29

BEST VERSE: 16A

So the priests went in to the inner part of the house of the LORD to cleanse it, and every unclean thing which they found in the temple of the LORD they brought out to the court of the house of the LORD.

Hezekiah, king of Judah, issued a command of the Levites to get the house of God back in order after it had been neglected and basically trashed. The Word does not say what was in the temple, but it must not have been holy. The verse says, "every unclean thing" was removed.

That got me thinking. What unclean things are in you? As a believer, you are the temple of the Lord. He also does not want unclean things in you. Are you ready for a cleanout day? Are you ready to toss out all that is not holy? Are you ready to restore *you* to a condition where true worship can happen?

TEACHING MOMENT

Okay, this one is easy. Don't you have a designated bath time for your kids? What a perfect time to talk about not just the external cleansing of our bodies, but also the internal cleansing of our souls. If your children are believers, they already understand the cleansing power of Jesus. We need to teach them the importance of keeping themselves clean of unholy things.

Our children need to know how unholy things will affect their ability to truly worship the Lord. When they allow unholy things to remain, eventually the environment is not conducive to worship. Their minds will be absorbed with worldly thoughts. Their actions will become unholy. They need to stay clean.

Right now, think of the things in your life that you need to toss out. Is it your obsession with social media? Is it your "dabbling" in pornography? Is it your constant pursuit for wealth? Whatever is "dirtying" up your temple, toss it out. Cleanse yourself! Allow the cleansing power of the Spirit to wash over you today.

O Father, cleanse me! I give up all those things that tarnish Your temple in me. I want my temple to be a place of holiness where I can truly worship!

OCTOBER 4

ONLY IF

1 Kings 6

BEST VERSES: 11-13

Now the word of the Lord came to Solomon saying, "Concerning this house which you are building, if you will walk in My statutes and execute My ordinances and keep all My commandments by walking in them, then I will carry out My word with you which I spoke to David your father. I will dwell among the sons of Israel, and will not forsake My people Israel.'"

God was pleased with Solomon for building His house, the temple. He was being diligent about it. He was making sure it was worthy of the God of Israel. So, God gave him a promise based on three things. IF Solomon would do these three things, He would dwell there and never forsake them.

God expected Solomon to walk in God's statutes, execute His ordinances and keep all His commandments. God's blessings on the people were tied directly to Solomon's obedience. And he started off great. Then sin entered the camp. He began to ignore God, even to the point of building pagan temples for his wives. The result? God judged his people.

TEACING MOMENT

Our disobedience as parents can directly affect our children and family. God will hold us accountable for our sin, but our sins can affect our children. Therefore, we need to live in such a way that God will be pleased. We should teach our children this biblical truth, too. They need to know their actions have consequences, not just for themselves.

I am not saying God is just waiting to abandon us. As believers, He will never do that. But our children need to realize that God will not bless us if we are choosing to live in such a way that dishonors Him. Too many people today think they can live any way they choose and then just holler for God when things get bad and He comes running. Our children need to see that God does expect us to love and obey Him.

Are you living in obedience right now? Are you walking in God's statutes, executing His ordinances, and keeping all His commandments? Your salvation does not depend on works. Hear me clearly. However, our holy God expects us to live holy, sanctified lives that point to Him.

Father, I cannot live holy without Your Holy Spirit living it through me. My flesh is strong. But through yielding to You daily, I can live a life which draws others, including my family, to You. Thank You, Lord.

OCTOBER 5

DEVOTION TO THE WORD

Acts 18

BEST VERSE: 5

But when Silas and Timothy came down from Macedonia, Paul began devoting himself completely to the word, solemnly testifying to the Jews that Jesus was the Christ.

Silas and Timothy came along and gave Paul the freedom to devote "himself completely to the word." Up until then, Paul had been working as a tentmaker to provide for himself. Silas and Timothy obviously helped Paul in this trade so he could study the Word.

As a pastor, nothing gives me more pleasure than to dig into the Word of God and mine those golden nuggets to be able to share with others. The reason I study is to share, not just to gain the knowledge. Paul was studying to testify to the Jews about Jesus. Why do you study God's Word?

TEACHING MOMENT

Our children can learn a lot by studying God's Word. There is no better education than one based on God's Word. But gaining all that knowledge and not sharing it is unacceptable. We need to look for opportunities for our children to share what they learned.

Perhaps one or more of your children are artistic. Help them portray God's Word that way. Maybe they love to witness. Let them share the Word with other boys and girls through a day camp at your house. They may be musically inclined. Give them the tools (piano, guitar, etc.) to share the Word in song.

And how about you, Mom and Dad? Are you sharing what you are learning? Are you looking for others around you who could benefit from the knowledge you have gained through the last Bible study you took? We tend to study, study, study and never share, share, share. Don't hold those precious truths you have learned too closely. God gives them to us to share, not hoard.

I pray you will find a way this week to enlighten someone else of at least one truth God has taught you. Share it!

Thank You, Lord, for giving me Your Word. Thank You for the joy I get from studying and then sharing. Help me instill in my children the excitement of reading Your Word.

OCTOBER 6

REPENT

Job 42

BEST VERSES: 1-6

Then Job answered the Lord and said, "I know that You can do all things, and that no purpose of Yours can be thwarted. Who is this that hides counsel without knowledge? Therefore I have declared that which I did not understand, things too wonderful for me, which I did not know. Hear, now, and I will speak; I will ask You, and You instruct me. I have heard of You by the hearing of the ear; but now my eye sees You; therefore I retract, and I repent in dust and ashes."

I have a few friends to which I send greetings by other friends sometimes. My message is usually, "Repent." I say that to them in jest, because I know they are walking with the Lord. But really it is a message we all need to hear. Right?

Job has finally come to this point. It doesn't matter what he thinks he has or has not done. The bottom line is that in the presence of God we must all repent. In view of His holiness we are nothing by filthy rags in need of cleansing.

TEACHING MOMENT

Teaching our children about repentance can be difficult. But when they experience the Holy God, He will draw them into repentance. Many parents ask me how to know when their child has really made a decision for Christ. I tell them to watch for repentance and remorse when they do something against God. The Spirit of God, which lives in them as a believer, will not let them slide.

When is the last time you got on your knees or on your face in repentance? How long has it been since you confessed those things you thought you were hiding from Him? He wants to hear from you and cleanse you. But He won't until you come to Him in humility and bow.

Stop what you are doing right now and do that! Go to the Father and say as Job said, "I repent in dust and ashes." He will do a mighty work in you. Just let Him!

Forgive me, Lord! I am so unworthy of Your grace. I praise You for Your redemption.

OCTOBER 7

THE TONGUE GIVES LIFE

Proverbs 17–18

BEST VERSE: 18:21

Death and life are in the power of the tongue, and those who love it will eat its fruit.

Which is it? Life or destruction? The tongue is a powerful instrument and can be used to give life or death. This is so true today with the emergence of social media. One tweet or one Facebook post can destroy someone's reputation. What could be used for good is often used for evil.

When is the last time you wish you had not said something to someone? Maybe it was in a moment of weakness or rage. Maybe it was meant in jest but taken as truth. Whatever you said, make it right and do it quickly.

TEACHING MOMENT

This is especially true when it comes to children. Parents, watch your mouths. There is no excuse for belittling children. There is no reason to raise your voice and shout or scream at an infant or toddler. Choose your words wisely. Your children will repeat your inappropriate words and behavior.

I remember once when our son said a bad word when we were out at a restaurant. He had heard his grandfather say it and did not know it was a bad word. So, when he let it fly, we were shocked. He immediately knew something was wrong. Kids repeat our words, good or bad. Use God's Word to guide them, not your words. God's Word always gives life.

If you are guilty today of speaking death and not life to someone, pray for forgiveness and ask the offended person for forgiveness. Use the words of Christ to those who offend you. Never resort to words of anger. Then you will "eat its fruit."

Father of all words, fill my mouth with Your words. Let my tongue always be a tongue of praise. When I must correct, let me do it with love and discipline.

OCTOBER 8

SO, WHAT IS THE CHURCH?

2 Kings 25

BEST VERSE: 9

He burned the house of the LORD, the king's house, and all the houses of Jerusalem; even every great house he burned with fire.

This is a sad part of Israel's history. Babylon has defeated the nation, and now the enemy has come to Jerusalem and burned the temple. Can you im. agine seeing that incredible structure in flames and falling down? I am sure the people who watched this cried and wailed. Their place of worship had been destroyed.

What a perfect passage to teach our kids, though, about the true church. The church is not walls and roofs. The church is we, the believers, who are bound together through God's blessings and redemption. I have preached in elaborate structures, rooftop dining halls, schools, and alleyways. I have preached in brick, wooden, and metal buildings. Where a body of believers meets does not make up the church. The people do.

The church I serve has been in a building program for over ten years. Our sanctuary has not been completed in all that time. It will probably be the final part of the building that we finish. What! Not finish the sanctuary until last! That room does not make up our church. Sure, it would be nice to have it completed so we could all worship together. But right now, the church is meeting in three services (six if you count Children's Church, Latino service, and Filipino service). Our church is not the building—it's the people.

TEACHING MOMENT

So, how can you teach your children this truth? By being involved in your church! Let them see that your family makes up part of the church locally and globally. Being a church means loving each other (as I talked about yesterday). Being a church means supporting each other. Being a church means giving to help advance the kingdom. Being a church is all about obeying the Lord along with others who are on the same journey. Be the church!

Lord God, You are familiar with what is being said about churches today. The world condemns us because we are not "tolerant" of their shameful acts. Help me to reflect You to our neighbors. Let me be that light that never burns out.

OCTOBER 9

HELP THE HELPLESS

Psalms 81–82

BEST VERSES: 82:3–4

Vindicate the weak and fatherless; do justice to the afflicted and destitute. Rescue the weak and needy; deliver them out of the hand of the wicked.

There are so many people in the world who need a helping hand. I am sure in your community there are hundreds of people who just need someone to come alongside them. They are the weak, fatherless, afflicted, destitute, and needy spoken of here in this psalm.

How can you help? How about meeting some immediate needs? It doesn't do any good to preach to someone who is starving. The Word is much more affective when people feel safe and warm. Remember that everyone in this situation is also loved by our Father. He wants them to come home too.

TEACHING MOMENT

If your children are old enough, take them to a homeless shelter to help feed some people this year. Find a local ministry that is meeting these needs and donate to it. Help your child with a bake sale to raise money for a needy family. If possible, do this anonymously. That is so much more fun.

Teaching our children to reach out to others can be just as instructive for us as adults. We get accustomed to our lifestyles and overlook those around us who have real needs. There may be someone right in your church who just needs a little help. Be the family of God to them.

I have never known anyone who reached out to help someone who regretted it. I believe you should always make sure the need is legitimate, but ultimately that is not your concern. If the Spirit in you is leading you to help, do it. He will handle the outcome.

Lord, I look around and see those less fortunate than me everywhere. Give me the desire to help. Give me the courage to reach out and be the hand of Jesus.

OCTOBER 10

LOOK BEFORE YOU LEAP

1 Chronicles 19

BEST VERSE: 3

But the princes of the sons of Ammon said to Hanun, "Do you think that David is honoring your father, in that he has sent comforters to you? Have not his servants come to you to search and to overthrow and to spy out the land?"

There's a saying that goes, "You had better look before you leap, still waters run deep." I bet Hanun wished he had done that. Instead he took the bad advice of these men and humiliated David's ambassadors that had been sent to mourn the loss of Hanun's father. Sometimes grief can make us do some stupid things. Let's blame Hanun's actions on that.

Regardless of why he did that, Hanun's misstep cost him his kingdom. In the same way, our missteps can cost us. We need to be very careful of the advice we take. We may make assumptions that are just not true. These assumptions can cost us and others a lot. Our only true source of good advice comes from the Lord through studying His Word and praying.

TEACHING MOMENT

We need to be so guided by the Spirit that when our children come to us for advice (and they will) we can give them God's advice for their lives. They should not trust their own judgment. Only God can give them the right advice every time. Now He can use people, but they should make sure what they are saying lines up with the Word. Children are so easily led astray by "right-sounding" advice.

Your children will not come to you regarding declaring war on someone (at least I hope not). They will, however, come to you for advice on school, friends, finances, and marriage. You must be prepared to show them whom to turn to for guidance. Share with them your source: the Lord Jesus.

What advice are you seeking today? Have you gone to the Word? Have you bowed your knees in humility before a holy God to ask Him? Whatever advice you need today He can give it. And He only gives the right advice because He is a righteous God.

Lord of the Universe, hear my plea for guidance. I do not know the path to take in some areas. There are many voices screaming their thoughts, but I only want to hear Your thoughts. Open my ears to hear only You.

OCTOBER 11

AN ARMY OF ONE

Proverbs 11–12

BEST VERSE: 12:4

An excellent wife is the crown of her husband, but she who shames him is like rottenness in his bones.

Did you know that the Hebrew word used in this verse for "excellent" can be translated as "army"? Isn't that a hoot? I mean, come on! Think about it! The Holy Spirit inspired the writer of this proverb to use that particular word to describe the wife of a man. Why? Why not another word like beautiful or sweet or smart?

Because this word also has the idea of steadfastness, strength, virtuous. That describes the woman who brings honor and recognition (the crown) to her husband. I am blessed to have such a wife. She brings me honor because she is an excellent wife. She is virtuous and steadfast and strong. She is an army of one.

TEACHING MOMENT

I do not want to come across today as sexist. But I want to address this verse to parents of little girls. Don't you want them to bring honor to their husbands? Don't you want them to be excellent wives? Then you must begin now training them to be steadfast and strong. You must train them to be grounded in their beliefs and in God's Word.

As we train our little girls to be like that, they will grow up and become those excellent wives (should they choose to marry) to their husbands. They will be that crown. They will cause their husbands to walk with pride, not because of anything the husbands have done, but because of the dignity or virtue of our little girls. What a proud moment for parents.

So, parents, will you dedicate yourselves to putting your daughter through boot camp to become that army? She cannot do it without you. She needs you to get her ready. She will face many enemies along the way. Some will question her virtue. You must defend it. Some will challenge her beliefs. You must give her the knowledge from God's Word.

Whatever you do, remember you are raising "an excellent wife" who will be fighting for her husband and children. Get her ready!

Today, O God, I bless all the girls and women in my life. Let me hold them as special and valued. Help me prepare them to be that excellent wife.

OCTOBER 12

EGG WHITES

Job 6

BEST VERSE: 6

Can something tasteless be eaten without salt, or is there any taste in the white of an egg?

What a strange verse! In this chapter of Job, Eliphaz has just finished rebuking Job, and now Job is responding. But why does he say this? Salt and eggs? Really? What is he trying to say?

Many commentators believe Job is saying that his suffering must be accompanied with grieving or lamentations, just like salt must accompany food to give it flavor. Perhaps that is it. We can't be sure. But we do know that every Word of God is meant to teach us, right? Certain things are meant to go together. When we suffer, it is natural to grieve. That's okay.

TEACHING MOMENT

So, here is a challenge for you. How do you teach this truth to your children? The next time you are boiling eggs for something, show your children the egg white. Let them taste it (if they don't have an egg allergy). Let them see how tasteless it is. Then read this passage to them. They will probably be amazed this verse is even in the Bible.

Then explain the meaning of the verse to them. It is not about an egg white being tasteless. It's all about how, even in a simple illustration like this, God's Word points us to another truth. Certain things are meant to go together. It's okay to be sad when bad things happen. It's okay to cry. But we can't stay there. We have to allow the Lord to be our Healer.

Are you living a tasteless life? Are you so down and depressed that the whole world seems without flavor? God does not want you to stay in that place. Yes, we are flesh, and we respond emotionally to events in our lives. But we have a God who cares deeply for us. He gives us the flavor we need to keep living.

Lord, give us the salt for those tasteless times. After all, everyone likes a little salt on their food? Supply it for us.

OCTOBER 13

PRAYERS FOR OTHERS

Philemon

BEST VERSE: 4

I thank my God always, making mention of you in my prayers.

I was praying recently for my family and for some missionary friends who were facing a hurricane. I was burdened for their safety and the safety of others in the path of the storm. So, this verse was so appropriate. I am constantly amazed at the timing of God's Word in my life.

For whom do you pray? Are you so focused on your own needs that you fail to lift others before the throne? Are you so self-centered in your prayer life that all God ever hears from you is your wish list of blessings? Beloved, the joy of prayer is praying for others.

Don't get me wrong. I do send my own requests to the Father. But they aren't my focus. I have learned through years of praying that when I focus on others' needs, God burdens others for me. I have been told so many times, from someone I have prayed for, that they have been praying for me. What a blessing!

TEACHING MOMENT

Now, how do you teach your children that? Make a list with them of people for whom they want to pray. Now be prepared to make a long list. Children love to pray. Let them decide for whom to pray. Once that list is made, divide it into days of the week or days of the month, depending on the number of people listed. Keep that list handy. Put it on their bedroom mirror or beside their bed. Each night, pray for those on that list for that day. Your children will learn the joy of praying for others.

Let the people know you are praying for them. That will bless their socks off. And when a specific prayer request is answered, make sure your child knows that. What a reassurance from the Father! Answered prayers elicit praise! But it also spurs us on to continued prayers.

Now, I need to go do some more praying! Dear Father, . . .

Lord, You are always pleased when Your children come before Your throne to pray. I am thankful that I can approach You boldly because of Jesus. Hear my prayers today.

OCTOBER 14

MIGHTY IN THE LORD

2 Chronicles 27

BEST VERSE: 6

So Jotham became mighty because he ordered his ways before the LORD his God.

What makes a man mighty? This verse gives us the answer. It says Jotham was mighty "because he ordered his ways before the Lord his God." Simple enough, right? Do you want to be mighty? Then get in line with God.

But what does it mean when it says, "ordered his ways"? The Hebrew word means to set firm or establish. Jotham was determined that everything he did as king would honor God. Because he honored God, God made him mighty in the eyes of men.

TEACHING MOMENT

Now, how do we bring this home and teach our children how to be mighty? Ask any kid if they want to be mighty and you will get an astounding "YES." Who doesn't want to be mighty? Your son or daughter may be thinking about Superman or Batman or another superhero who is mighty. I mean, come on, who wouldn't want to be able to fly or stop speeding bullets or defeat all their enemies?

But how do we teach them the secret of being mighty in the eyes of God? We live it. I know you are probably tired of being the role model. Why me? you may be asking yourself. Why do I have to be the one to show them the example to follow? Because the Lord has blessed you with these children for a purpose. It is your responsibility to teach your children. And teaching them to be mighty in the Lord is just one more lesson.

You must "establish, make firm, order" your ways according to God's Word. That will make you mighty. Then your children will see your "might" and learn from you. You may not be as strong as Superman, but your children will think you are. They will follow you not because of you, but because of who is in you. So, live mighty! Set your ways according to His ways!

I am mighty, O God, because You are mighty! Your might is my strength. I praise You, Lord, because You live in me.

OCTOBER 15

NOW THAT'S A FULL POOL!

Acts 2

BEST VERSE: 41

So then, those who had received his word were baptized; and that day there were added about three thousand souls.

Three thousand saved and baptized! That's incredible. In recent decades, there has been a falling off of baptisms in the U.S. It is no wonder. Many do not believe it is necessary (and it's not for salvation) and either put it off or just don't bother. But anything the Lord felt was important I want to value as important.

When my children were young, we had a membership at a water park in Florida. One of the busiest areas was the wave pool. That huge pool would be packed with people. There were literally hundreds, if not thousands, of people in that huge pool ready to jump waves and swim. I can just picture the mass of people lined up in this story in Acts waiting to get baptized by the apostles. They were probably in line for Peter, John, Mark or the other disciples, waiting to follow the Lord in Believer's baptism.

TEACHING MOMENT

This is an important decision and a celebrated act in the life of believer. As parents, we need to encourage our children, once they have asked Christ in their lives, to get baptized. Many parents tend to postpone this until their child "really" understands it. Can I make a suggestion? Once your child has surrendered to Jesus, they are ready for baptism. If you are confident in their decision to follow Him, encourage them to take that next step of obedience.

There aren't many things besides leading someone to Christ that bring me as much joy as baptizing a believer. Seeing the nervousness erupt into pure joy when they are raised out of the water is exciting. Watching their family and friends beam with pride brings me joy. Seeing the tears flow down the face of a redeemed believer and mixing with the baptismal waters surely must give our Lord joy. Celebrate it!

Father, my heart rejoices when I see a new believer get baptized. I can only imagine the joy You feel. Give me the words to say to encourage others to do the same.

OCTOBER 16

ARE YOU SURE?

Romans 3

BEST VERSE: 23

For all have sinned and fall short of the glory of God.

How can this be? Can we really believe that even a little bitty baby is a sinner? How can that little sweet face be hiding the fact that their soul is wretched? I get those questions a lot. But, if we believe God's Word is true, then we must accept the truth of this verse too.

The fall of man in the garden ushered in our sinful flesh, and we all have the burden of sin in our lives. We fight the flesh every day, at least I do. I have often said, "Wouldn't it be nice to die to self once and be done with it?" Sadly, it is a daily exercise of surrender.

TEACHING MOMENT

Our children will reach that age where they are accountable for their sins. When is that? There is no magic number. I believe it varies according to their ability to understand the truth of the gospel. I don't mean they have to understand all the theological concepts (no one really does), but they understand that Jesus died for their sins, was buried, and rose again with victory over death.

Every day, we need to be leading our children toward the doors of salvation. We need to bathe them in prayer. We need to teach them that Jesus loves them so much and wants to spend eternity with them. God loves them so much that He was willing to send His own Son to die for them.

Yes, we have all sinned. But also, we can all receive the promise of salvation if we believe on Him. So, stop worrying about it. Believe!

Father, I know I am a sinner, saved by grace. I know I have no way of reaching You except through Jesus. Thank You for saving me.

OCTOBER 17

FALSELY ACCUSED

Job 22

BEST VERSE: 5

Is not your wickedness great, and your iniquities without end?

I have always had trouble figuring out exactly what verses in Job that were worthy to study. I know it is God's Word and was inspired by Him through the writer. Some scholars believe it may be the oldest book of the Bible. I don't know. But I do know that God would not have given us this book if He didn't mean to teach us through it.

I realized something by reading this verse. We are all like Job! So many times, people judge us, just like Job's friends, without knowing the background. They observe our external lives and make judgment calls based on what they see. Job's friends took one look at him and reckoned him as guilty of something. They were frustrated and mad because they could not get him to repent. They had no idea of what was truly going on in the heavenlies.

TEACHING MOMENT

Our children can also learn to not be quick judges of people. When you pass that person on the street who is holding the sign asking for food or money, it is easy to judge. "Why don't they get a job?" "Why don't they just get cleaned up?" Our children will undoubtedly ask you such questions. How will you answer them?

If we are judgmental of those individuals, our children will learn to be the same. If we are merciful and explain that we do not know what led this person to be in this situation and that we need to be Jesus to them, then they will learn to be merciful.

Teach your children to be very slow to judgment. Teach them to get to know a person before they decide if they like them or not. You have heard the old saying "You can't judge a book by its cover." Well, it's true. You have to look inside to discover the truth. God loves everyone and longs to have them come to Him. Shouldn't we be part of that plan also?

Father, I am too cynical and judgmental, I know. Forgive me. Give me Your eyes to see people. Let me see their worth, not their worthlessness.

OCTOBER 18

GIDDY TO GIVE

2 Corinthians 9

BEST VERSES: 7

Each one must do just as he has purposed in his heart, not grudgingly or under compulsion, for God loves a cheerful giver.

I have often said if I ever won the lottery, I would have so much fun giving it away. The only trouble is I don't play the lottery; thus, I never win. But, if I did . . .

I can, however, give that way anyway. The Lord tells us here to give with a cheerful heart. I have so many missionary friends whom I would love to support. I know firsthand the work they are doing, and it blesses my heart. I would love to be able to give to all of them beyond what I could imagine. That would be so much fun. So, I do what I can when I can, knowing God can take my little bit and make it large.

TEACHING MOMENT

There probably isn't a bigger lesson to teach our kids than that of giving. Most people aren't givers. We like to hold on tight to what we have or spend our money on things we want. Teaching little Susie to give to the Lord is a lesson she will carry with her into adulthood and her marriage. We must teach our sons, especially, to be a givers. When they marry, they need to be the one to set the tone for giving.

How much should we give? You have to decide that. We aren't limited to the tithe (10%). We can give as much as we want, but we should always consult the Lord on that. He will give you a peace about giving if you ask Him. Let your children know that. Teach them to pray for direction in giving. Then let them give as the Lord directs.

Are you giddy to give, or do you dread writing that check? Do you put off giving to the Lord until everything is paid? Trust the Lord to direct your giving and to bless what you have left. He can do that.

And, when you are faithful to give, He will give you the joy. He will bless your faithfulness. Will He give you more? Perhaps, or maybe He will just give you the peace to live with less. Either way, He blesses you.

You may have heard the saying, "Give 'til it hurts." I say, "Give 'til it feels good."

All I have is Yours, O Lord. All I have has come from You. I yield it all back to You to use as You see fit.

OCTOBER 19

HERE COMES THE JUDGE

Romans 14

BEST VERSE: 13

Therefore let us not judge one another anymore, but rather determine this—not to put an obstacle or a stumbling block in a brother's way.

Many years ago, there was a comedian named Flip Wilson. He did this character skit called "Here Comes the Judge" on a TV show. I know I am dating myself by referring to this, but this skit was funny at the time. He would dance on the scene chanting, "Here comes the Judge! Here comes the Judge!" Then he would begin to make some obscure, off-the-wall ruling on something that was just plain silly.

That may sound completely ridiculous, but we do the same. We judge others according to our standards, when the only person who is able to truly judge anyone is God. He is the only judge that matters. Only His rulings will stand. He will decide what is right, because He is the only righteous one.

TEACHING MOMENT

As your children get older, I promise you they will have more opportunities to judge others and be judged by others. How do you as mom and dad teach them the difficult trait of being non-judgmental? How do we show them that judging is God's job?

If we can teach them to look at others through the eyes of God, they will get it. Before we make any judgment of anyone, we need to ask ourselves how God sees that individual. When your child starts to make a judgment about someone, stop them and ask them that question. Ask them how they think God sees that person. Then ask them how they think God sees them. That last one is the sobering one. Are their actions worthy of their heavenly Father? Are their thoughts about others pleasing to Him?

I don't know about you, but I still have room to grow in this one. So, don't be too "judgmental" of your children. I bet you have room to grow too.

Ruler of All, thank You for not judging me like I judge others. I am guilty of being too judgmental and unforgiving. Remind me of who I am without Your forgiveness.

BRAGGART

2 Corinthians 10

BEST VERSES: 17–18

But he who boasts is to boast in the Lord. For it is not he who commends himself that is approved, but he whom the Lord commends.

Have you ever been around someone who can't stop talking about themselves? All you hear is what they have done, what they have or what they plan to do. All their attention, it seems, is on me, myself, and I. There is only so much of that you can stand, right?

Don't get me wrong! There is nothing wrong with having pride and confidence. But left unchecked, that pride and confidence can become your downfall. These verses remind us of that very thing. It is the Lord who commends us, not ourselves. If we are going to boast, boast in what the Lord has done with and in us.

TEACHING MOMENT

So, how do you explain the difference to your kids? We have to build them up! It's our job. We, of all people, have to tell them how beautiful and handsome, smart and articulate, well-behaved and polite they are. Don't we? We have to encourage them on the ball field by cheering them on. We have to oooo and ahhhh over their drawings and paintings. That's our job!

But we also need to point out to them the areas to improve. That can be done without demeaning them. That can be done without being negative. In every praise and critique, point them back to the Perfect One! In comparison to Him, we all fall short of perfection. We are all striving to be like Him, all the while knowing we will never match His perfection. But every step we take toward His image is more of Him that is seen in us.

Kids started school a couple of months ago in the States, and they started with clean, perfect slates (yes, kids use to have a slate tablet and chalk in school instead of iPads and laptops) to write on. They are now two months into a new school year to accomplish great things. Encourage them to make this year a year in which every accomplishment is pointing to Jesus. Let Him commend them, not others.

I boast only of You, O Father. I am proud of living for You. Other than that, I boast in nothing!

OCTOBER 21

MY ROCK

Isaiah 51

BEST VERSE: 1

Listen to me, you who pursue righteousness, who seek the LORD: Look to the rock from which you were hewn and to the quarry from which you were dug.

Don't you just love this imagery? We are hewn from rock. We are quarried from stone. If we pursue righteousness, we are solid! We are firm. We have a strong foundation. We are chiseled from God Himself. I just love that picture.

And what are we quarried to do? Well, how is stone used in construction? It is used to build a strong foundation. It is used to construct strong walls. We are being used, because of His righteousness in us, to build His kingdom. That is our purpose for being quarried.

TEACHING MOMENT

I love watching kids build stuff. I especially love watching little toddlers learn to build. They will take the blocks and stack them, usually as high as they can, until they topple over. Then they do it all again. They get more creative the older they get and can build some pretty cool stuff.

As you play with them and construct things, talk about how God uses us to construct His kingdom here on earth. God uses us to accomplish His purpose. He wants us to be the stones He uses to build for Him. And when we follow His blueprint, the walls will never crumble or fall. They are secure.

What are you building right now? Are you constructing for you or Him? If you are walking in righteousness, He has a task for you. He wants you to fulfill your purpose—to be the hewn rock, to be the quarried stone. He wants to use you in the construction of His kingdom. Will you allow Him to use you?

Father, I am only strong because of Your righteousness. I am only as stable as I allow You to use me. Thank You Lord, for chiseling me in Your image.

OCTOBER 22

HONOR THE TEMPLE

2 Kings 21

BEST VERSE: 7

Then he set the carved image of Asherah that he had made, in the house of which the LORD said to David and to his son Solomon, "In this house and in Jerusalem, which I have chosen from all the tribes of Israel, I will put My name forever."

Manasseh was an evil king who reigned a long time. He did awful things. The Word says he "made his son pass through the fire, practiced witchcraft and used divination, and dealt with mediums and spiritists." But the straw that broke the camel's back with the Lord was when he set up the Asherah (an idol) in the temple.

The temple was the place the Lord had called His own. He had filled it with His glory. How dare Manasseh defile it? God would not stand for that. But before you are too harsh on Manasseh, how about your temple of God—your body. Are you defiling it?

TEACHING MOMENT

Don't worry. This isn't going to be a push for you to exercise more (even though that's a good idea and one I should do more). It's not a push to get your kids to eat Paleo. It's not a devotion on warning your children about getting tattoos (even though I still don't understand that).

We need to teach our children that, as believers, our bodies are the temple of the Holy Spirit. We should treat it as that. Before we do anything to alter or shape this body, we need to remember the world sees this "temple" and will equate it with your testimony. Your children will have to decide, through prayer and seeking God's face, how to honor this temple.

Simply writing this devotion convicts me. I need to get healthier. I need to take better care of this temple of God. I want to represent Him in the best way I can. I don't want my "graffiti" on this temple to distract anyone from seeing and hearing my Lord.

Father, help me to cleanse my temple. Help me to treat my body as the place where Your Spirit abides. Let me model that for others.

RETURNING THE FAVOR

Esther 8

BEST VERSE: 2B
And Esther set Mordecai over the house of Haman.

Mordecai had certainly sacrificed to take Esther in his home after her parents died. He raised her as his own daughter. Now she is Queen Esther. Together, they had just foiled Haman's plot to kill all the Jews. And Esther returns the favor to her adopted dad, Mordecai. After Haman was executed, she gave Mordecai his estate. I bet Mordecai never saw this coming.

It's that way when our children bless us. Parents are supposed to do all the blessing, not the children. So, when our children bless us, especially in a sacrificial way, it is overwhelming. To be blessed by the ones we are raising is truly humbling.

TEACHING MOMENT
How do children get to that point of being the "blesser"? They were taught it. As they watch their parents blessing them and others, they learn to bless. I am certain that Esther could recall numerous times when Mordecai had sacrificed for her. Remember, they were in exile. They were essentially forced refugees. I am sure life was hard. But Mordecai took care of her.

Teach your children through your own sacrifice. Let them observe you making tough choices for them. Now, don't hold that over them or remind them of all you are doing. Just do it. Let them see your humble service to your Lord in caring for them. This will teach them, not your words.

Who do you need to bless today? Are your parents still alive? If so, bless them today. Pay it back. Shock them by doing something special for them today. When my dad was in his last couple of years, I loved to cook him breakfast when I visited. He loved his breakfast. Simple blessings!

Father, thank You for my parents' sacrifices for me. Thank You for allowing me to sacrifice for my children. I pray they will see how that serves You.

WISE WORDS. WRONG SITUATION

Job 5

BEST VERSE: 17

Behold, how happy is the man whom God reproves, so do not despise the discipline of the Almighty.

One of Job's friends, Eliphaz, is speaking in chapters 4 and 5. Taken by themselves, his words are wise and insightful. Take for instance the verse for today. I agree with that statement. We should welcome the Lord's discipline. We know that the Lord disciplines those whom He loves.

The trouble with the advice is he thinks Job has done something worthy of discipline. Why else would God "punish" Job? He must have done some horrible sin and was refusing to confess. Eliphaz had good advice. He was just giving it to the wrong person.

TEACHING MOMENT

However, these words can be helpful to your child. They need to learn that discipline is a good thing. Without discipline the world would be in chaos. When we have disobeyed the Lord, we should expect to be disciplined. Now, I am not saying the Lord is just waiting to zap us every time we get off the path. I mean the Lord will discipline us because He loves us. He wants to keep us safe.

Don't you discipline your little Susie when she disobeys? Why do you do that? Because you want her to grow up respecting rules and guidelines. You want her to develop self-control. She needs to learn at an early age that there are always going to be rules and laws she must follow. And these are for her protection, not to restrict her.

What are you complaining about right now? Are you challenging the Lord's commands? Are you fighting God at every turn? Surrender to Him today. Let Him guide your every decision. As we surrender to Him, the Lord is able to give us more and more freedom. And you will be free indeed.

Forgive me, Lord, when I disobey. Forgive me when I fight against Your law. I know everything You have written is for my good. Help me surrender more fully each day to You.

BE SURE YOUR SINS WILL FIND YOU OUT

2 Kings 17

BEST VERSES: 7–8

Now this came about because the sons of Israel had sinned against the LORD their God, who had brought them up from the land of Egypt from under the hand of Pharaoh, king of Egypt, and they had feared other gods and walked in the customs of the nations whom the LORD had driven out before the sons of Israel, and in the customs of the kings of Israel which they had introduced.

As I read this passage in 2 Kings, I couldn't help but think about my country, the United States of America. Ours is a country which was built on strong Judeo-Christian principles. Our founding fathers came here to escape religious persecution in Europe. We stood proudly for generations as a Christian-influenced nation.

Not anymore! Our courts and governments have made a concerted effort to shun the God of Jacob and His Son, Jesus. Prayers are not allowed in schools. Anyone standing up for Christian principles is ridiculed and called intolerant. Why do we think we will escape judgment like Israel received for doing the same thing?

TEACHING MOMENT

Have your children ever thought they had gotten away with a "sin" only to be discovered later and then receiving the consequence they had been trying so hard to avoid? I bet they have. We, as parents, must follow through on the discipline, no matter how "old" the infraction is. Why? Because of the passage today. We don't want them to think they can get by with disobedience just because they weren't caught.

Don't you understand that our parenting should mirror the Lord's "parenting" of us? We are teaching our children, by obeying us, to obey the Lord. We want them to WANT to obey out of love, but sometimes they just don't. That doesn't mean we let them get by with it. That does them no good.

What are you "getting by with" right now? Do you think you have escaped judgment? Believe me, judgment will come. It may not come until eternity, but it will. There is no escaping a holy God. This may sound harsh and tough, but it is simply the truth. Our loving God is also a holy God, and He will not be mocked.

Thank you, Father, for Your stern hand! I know I never like the discipline, but I also know I need it. Help me to be more obedient as I seek to follow you.

OCTOBER 26

A REJOICING GOD

Isaiah 62

BEST VERSE: 5B

And as the bridegroom rejoices over the bride, so your God will rejoice over you.

Can you imagine God rejoicing over you? You may be thinking, "There is nothing in my life for God to rejoice over." Wrong! If you are a follower of Christ, if you have asked His Son to come into your heart, God rejoices over that. He, in fact, is exuberant over you.

Have you ever seen a best friend after months or years of separation? What do you do? You smile and grin and run to them to hug and kiss on them, right? You rejoice over seeing them again. God does the same. He loves us because of what He sees His Son doing in and through us. Pretty amazing.

TEACHING MOMENT

Ask your little daughter how she feels when you come home after being gone for a while. Most kids can't wait to run and jump in your arms. They bury their little faces in your neck and give you kisses. They are soooooo happy you are home.

In fact, why don't you act that out? Tell them to pretend you have been gone for a long time and are just coming home. Go out of the room and walk in. Let them respond to that. Then explain how the Lord feels the same way about us. He loves to see us. He rejoices over us.

But let me ask you this. Are you rejoicing over Him? Do you long to spend time with your Savior? Or are you so guilt-ridden you shy away? Turn your sorrow into joy. Repent and rejoice in your fresh relationship. God is waiting to rejoice over you. Let Him.

Father, I cannot imagine how You feel about me. I believe Your Word, though. If it says You rejoice, then I know You do. And I rejoice at seeing You, too.

OCTOBER 27

SHORT PRAYERS, LONG PRAYERS

Nehemiah 2

BEST VERSE: 4
Then the king said to me, "What would you request?" So I prayed to the God of heaven.

Upon initial reading of this chapter, the first thing that popped into my head was: This is a short prayer. I am sure when the king asked Nehemiah this question, he didn't get down on his knees and pray for thirty minutes before answering.

Short prayers are fine. Why? They are fine when they are part of a lifestyle of praying. Nehemiah had already been praying for a moment like this. I bet his prayer went something like this. "Lord, give me the words to say right now." Short and sweet! He would trust the Lord to do as he had asked because he asked to glorify Him.

TEACHING MOMENT
Sometimes our children will pray through this long list of things at night. I know some children who will start all over if they get something out of order in their nightly prayers. There is nothing wrong with long prayers, just as there is nothing wrong with short prayers. They just have to be sincere prayers.

Our prayers should always be prayed according to His will. They should always be prayed in faith. They should focus more on others than ourselves, even though God wants to hear our requests for ourselves too. Just pray with your children. Let them hear you pray.

When is the last time you have "shot up" a short prayer in a moment of desperation? How about a quickie prayer on the run? Dedicate yourself to prayer. Let it course through your life like a flowing river.

O Lord, there is nothing quite as sweet as time with You. Help me to be more obedient in my prayer life. Let me be a model of prayer to others.

OCTOBER 28

WHERE HAVE YOU BEEN?

Isaiah 58

BEST VERSE: ISAIAH 58:9A

Then you will call, and the LORD will answer; you will cry, and He will say, 'Here I am.'"

I heard a joke once about an old married couple who were driving down the road in their old pickup. The woman looked over at her husband as he was driving and said, "When we were dating we used to sit right up next to each other." Without even casting a glance in her direction, he said, "I haven't moved."

Sometimes that's how it is with us and the Lord. We cry out, "O Lord, where are You?" He answers back, "Right where I have always been." We tend to stray from the Lord. He never strays from us. Don't forget that.

TEACHING MOMENT

Have your kids ever started hollering at you, "Mom! Dad! Where are you?" You've been in the same place for the past two hours, but they just realized they weren't hearing you. They assume you have left. They can't see you and panic. But as soon as you say, "I'm right here, " they calm down and start playing again.

We need to teach them to trust God's presence. They need to stay close to Him. They are going to be tempted as they get older to move away. They will have friends who don't know Him and may even put doubts in their minds. But they need to keep talking to Him. They need to keep listening. He does not move.

Are you feeling alone right now? Are you thinking God is nowhere to be found? You are wrong. He hasn't moved. You have. Turn to Him today and ask Him to revive your spirit. He is just waiting to respond to your call. Listen as He says, "Here I am."

God, I know You are there. I believe You are there. Make me aware of Your presence in everything I do. And help me point You out to my children every time.

BLINDED

Job 24

BEST VERSE: 13

Others have been with those who rebel against the light; they do not want to know its ways nor abide in its paths.

When I read this verse today, the first thing that popped into my head (and that can be dangerous) is our society today. People are rebelling against "the light" and have no desire to know God. Do you agree? If you bring up biblical values and morals, they scoff at you. If you try to stand on the principle of a one-man-and-one-woman marriage, you are considered narrow-minded and prejudiced.

I read a quote recently from A.W. Tozer. "When the world says, 'Oh, you're narrow,' you say, 'Maybe I am narrow, but the way is narrow, and the path to heaven isn't as broad as a 16-lane highway. You know why I am too narrow? I am walking with my God.'" That just about sums it up for me. I have to be focused on "staying between the ditches" on the road to eternity. It is way too easy to get distracted and get off course or get stuck in a ditch.

TEACHING MOMENT

Teaching our children to stay focused on God can be challenging. They are going to hear everything but God from the world. The world's view of life directly conflicts with what you are teaching them in the Word. So, our job is to keep them laser-focused on the prize.

The next time you have some of your child's friends over to the house, listen in to what they are talking about. Chances are they will discuss some things that may not agree with your family's values. Why not share this verse with your child when they leave? Remind them that they are going to encounter a lot of people in their life who "do not want to know its ways nor abide in its paths."

How about you? Do you "want to know its ways" or "abide in its paths"? Remember, a ship that gets just a few degrees off course will travel many extra miles and fail to reach its destination. You have to stay focused on the end. You have to keep your eyes on Jesus, the Author and Finisher of our faith.

You are my compass, God. You are always pointing me in the right direction. Help me trust Your bearings when I cannot see the destination.

OCTOBER 30

WHO MADE THE ANIMALS?

Job 39

BEST VERSES: 1–30
Do you know . . . ?

DO YOU KNOW?

This is the first time I have picked an entire chapter for the day. But you have to read it. Chapter 39 contains the words of the Lord to Job questioning him about where he was when he created all these animals. He lists mountain goats, wild donkeys, wild oxen, ostriches, horses, and hawks.

But look at the location these animals are found. They are on the mountain, in the plains, in the fields, in the desert, and in the air. Everywhere. God is essentially saying to Job, "I made all these things to cover my creation. Where were you when I did all this, if you are so smart?"

TEACHING MOMENT

If you haven't had your wisdom questioned by your child yet, just wait. It's coming. Moms and dads are so stupid when the children are under 22 or 23 years old. Then all of a sudden, we get our brains back. The children come to us for advice. You may be tempted to shout out to them like the Lord did to Job. Just remember, you are not God.

Seriously though, our children do need to be taught that their elders do possess a little more life experience than they do. We have gone through some of the same battles they are facing. We have struggled just like they are struggling now and have the scars to prove it. Teach them to listen and respect those who have "been there and done that."

Whom have you "disrespected"? Is there someone, maybe even your parents, of whom you have not heeded their advice? Now you see they were right, but you haven't told them so. Do that. Confess your sin to them. Yes, I said "sin." Disobeying and not respecting those who are our authority is sin. See it that way, and you will be more prone to listen.

O Lord, I know You created all things new. I know You have the wisdom of the ages. I also realize You have imparted that wisdom to others, many of which have crossed my path. Help me to listen and to pass that wisdom on to others.

OCTOBER 31

WRONG ADVICE

2 Kings 1

BEST VERSE: 2

And Ahaziah fell through the lattice in his upper chamber which was in Samaria, and became ill. So he sent messengers and said to them, "Go, inquire of Baal-zebub, the god of Ekron, whether I will recover from this sickness."

Ahaziah is hurt and wants to be healed. There's nothing wrong with that, is there? Of course not. He was the king of Israel. He had the resources to get the best physicians. But he sends messengers to make inquiry from a pagan god. Wrong move.

The story goes on and tells us Elijah the prophet confronts the messengers and finally Ahaziah. He tells them that Ahaziah will *not* get well. That's not the answer Ahaziah wanted. You can't help but wonder that if he had asked the messengers to go to Elijah to inquire of Jehovah, if the outcome would have been different. We won't know until we get to eternity.

TEACHING MOMENT

Children need to be taught that there is only one true source of knowledge. It is the Lord, not men. It is the Lord, not books. It is the Lord, not medicine. It is the Lord, not the world. We tend to turn to everything else first and as a last resort turn to God.

Parents, we need to teach our children to go to the Lord first. We should take everything to Him. I am not saying we shouldn't seek advice, but when we do, it should be from godly advisors. We shouldn't shun medical care, but we should bathe such care in prayer.

Are you suffering right now from a decision you made without consulting the Father? I believe we have probably all done that in the past. Seek Him first. And when He speaks, take His counsel.

Lord, You are the perfect source of wisdom for me. I know that. Remind me daily to go to You first. Help me lead my children to this truth at an early age.

A FALSE SENSE OF SECURITY

2 Chronicles 12

BEST VERSE: 1

When the kingdom of Rehoboam was established and strong, he and all Israel with him forsook the law of the LORD.

One generation! That's all it took! Solomon and his father David had established a great nation. In Solomon's time, peace finally reigned in the country. But Rehoboam wasted no time destroying that peace and ruining the country. Under him, according to the prophecy of the Lord, the kingdom split.

And now, because of his irresponsible self-confidence, he led the nation of Judah away from the Lord. The verse says they "forsook the law of the Lord." Why? How could he? Oh, be careful that you judge. We are all guilty of this, aren't we? We get comfortable when everything is going smoothly. We think we don't need God in our lives when all is well.

TEACHING MOMENT

What a lesson for our kids! There is never a moment when we don't need the power of God in our lives. He is the one who gives us peace, and He can remove it. He wants us to not only rest in Him. He wants us to depend on Him and recognize Him. As your children experience those times when all is well, remind them to thank the one who is above all.

If your children learn now that the God of the universe is the one who directs them, their walk with Christ will be a much more enjoyable one. That doesn't mean they won't have troubles and trials. But it does mean they won't freak out and panic when the hard times come. Why? Because they have confidence in Him, not themselves or others.

Where is your confidence? Where do you get your strength? Are you relying on your own abilities or God's? As moms and dads, we are the ones showing our kids how to depend on Him. We are the ones they are watching. If they see us wringing our hands and panicking, they will learn that too. If they see us going to other sources rather than God, they will learn that.

Point them to Jesus, no matter what. Pause to pray when you need guidance. And where and when appropriate, involve your children. You and they both will be blessed. Above all, you will bless the Father.

O Father, thank You that You are my strength. Remind me daily of my dependence on You. I can do nothing in my own strength.

NOVEMBER 2

A LITTLE BIRDIE TOLD ME

1 Kings 5

BEST VERSE: 7

When Hiram heard the words of Solomon, he rejoiced greatly and said, "Blessed be the LORD today, who has given to David a wise son over this great people."

Look closely at this verse and then read verse 8. It says, "So Hiram sent word to Solomon, saying, . . ." What Hiram said in verse 7 was not a part of the message he sent to King Solomon in verse 8 and following. So how did those words of Hiram get in the Scripture?

I believe it is pretty obvious. Apart from the fact that this is God's Word and it was His intention that it be included, the messenger who was waiting Hiram's response to take back to Solomon heard Hiram say this and thought it worthy to be recorded. God had even stirred the heart of a pagan king to recognize Solomon's wisdom as coming from above.

TEACHING MOMENT

Children overhear conversations, either deliberately or accidentally. It is so important that we teach them to keep such conversations to themselves unless those words are giving glory to God or going to put someone in danger. Those words should be shared. I have to believe that the messenger asked to share those words with Solomon. We all want to share good news.

But we have to train our children to keep in confidence other things they hear. Share the good news. Keep silent on other things. In that way they are able to become trustworthy and dependable. Oh, but it is so hard, isn't it? We all love to gossip and talk. Mom and Dad, you are going to have to model this for your children.

Are you a trustworthy source? Can others trust that you will hold things in confidence? Hold your tongue. Build that trust. Build that reputation as a confidant to others.

Father, You are the giver of good news. Help me spread it quickly to as many as possible. But let me hold in confidence those things told to me by others. Help me be trustworthy.

NOVEMBER 3

GOD CAN USE EVEN YOU

Esther 9

BEST VERSE: 32

The command of Esther established these customs for Purim, and it was written in the book.

This little verse may seem inconsequential. I mean what's the big deal about a queen establishing a custom? Well, you have to remember who Esther was. She was an orphan who had been raised by her uncle. She was a nobody who had been chosen to be one of King Ahasuerus' wives. She became his favorite wife whom he made queen. Quite a rise from nothing, don't you think?

And who do you think was behind this? Yep, God. He knew that the wicked Haman would plot to kill the Jews, so the Lord placed Esther in a position to protect them. God used an orphan queen to rescue her people and then establish Purim, so all Jews in future generations would remember the faithfulness of God.

TEACHING MOMENT

God loves to use children. He can use yours! Our job, as parents, is to prepare them to be used. We need to saturate them with the love of God. We need to build them up in the Word of God. So, when God speaks, they will recognize His voice. Who knows what God may choose to do with your child? He may use little Susie to cure cancer. He may use Johnny to be the next great evangelist who preaches to that last people group that ushers in the return of Christ.

But it is so important that we tell our children that God wants to use them in just the right way. God created them in His image and knows exactly how He has gifted them. He doesn't call them to do someone else's task. He has already prepared a path for just them, if they will follow. Their path will be like no one else's. God is an exact God who does exactly what is necessary at exactly the right time in the exact perfect way.

So, are you where this exact God wants you to be? Or have you decided you know better than He? That is a dangerous path. Surrender afresh to Him and allow Him to put you back on the right path. He wants to use you, just like He used that orphan queen.

You are a Father to the fatherless. Thank You, Lord. Be my Father. Direct my path today.

NOVEMBER 4

SOLD OUT

Acts 21

BEST VERSE: 13

Then Paul answered, "What are you doing, weeping and breaking my heart? For I am ready not only to be bound, but even to die at Jerusalem for the name of the Lord Jesus."

After Agabus prophesied that Paul would be bound in Jerusalem, the people he was with begged him not to go. They were weeping and distressed, but Paul simply says, "I am willing to die for Christ." That's what I call being totally sold out for Christ. No regrets! Total surrender!

Have you ever completely sold out to something? Years ago, I worked at a Children's Home in Tennessee that had a Ropes Course. This course was used to build teamwork and self confidence in the children and staff. I was privileged enough to be one of the staff who ran the course. I loved it.

We had one station on this course called the Pamper Pole. It was so named because you needed a diaper once you got up on top. It was a thirty-foot telephone pole that you had to climb and then gingerly stand on top. All the time, you are hooked to a harness, and people below are belaying you, so you are safe. You just don't feel very safe. Hanging in front of this pole was a trapeze handle. It was just far enough out that it required you to jump straight out to grab it. There was only one way to get to it. You had to sell out. You could not reach that trapeze with a half-hearted jump.

TEACHING MOMENT

In the same way, we need to dive into Jesus with everything we have. Our children need to see us abandon everything to follow Him. They need to see us walk the walk with no regrets. They need to see us jump toward Jesus whenever anything in our lives causes us fear. They need to see us, well, sold out for God.

Total surrender is costly. But the benefit of surrender is perfect peace and rest. I cannot tell you the feeling I got when I dove off that Pamper Pole and was able to grab that trapeze. But even when I dove and missed, I knew those below holding the rope would keep me safe. Jesus will keep you safe. Just let Him hold the rope!

Help me sell out to You, O God. I know You are there to keep me safe. As I leap, remind me that You are my safety net.

NOVEMBER 5

ONLY WHILE THEY ARE WATCHING

2 Chronicles 24

BEST VERSES: 1–2

Joash was seven years old when he became king, and he reigned forty years in Jerusalem; and his mother's name was Zibiah from Beersheba. Joash did what was right in the sight of the LORD all the days of Jehoiada the priest.

Joash took the reign of Judah at age seven and was a good king until. . . . The last seven words of verse 2 say, "all the days of Jehoiada the priest." Joash was a good king only while the man who raised him and advised him lived. He even went so far as to kill Jehoiada's son when he confronted him. Sad!

Do your children only do good when you are watching? When they think you can't hear them or see them, they misbehave or are mean to their siblings. But the moment you enter the room their halo magically appears.

TEACHING MOMENT

Learning to do the right thing when no one is looking is a trait much needed today. We must teach our children that God is always looking—not to punish them, but to guide them. They can always rely on Him to give them the wisdom to make the right decision.

I have seen too many children grow up in godly homes who always did the right thing. They never had any issues with their parents. They seemed to always have the right attitude. They were model children as far as behavior. But the moment they left home for college they became raving lunatics. Every kind of trouble you could imagine became part of their life. Why? Were their parents to blame? No, the choices they made were their own. But for some reason they thought the absence of the parental figure meant freedom to do anything they wanted.

God is our supreme parental figure. He not only loves us and cherishes us, but He also demands obedience. He wants to lead us and guide us through the difficult and pleasant times of life.

Mom and Dad, spend the time to teach your children that independence from parents does not mean independence from their Lord. He is always present and watching.

I am thankful I know right is right and wrong is wrong. Help me to teach my children to know that too. Thank You that You are the Truth, which is always right.

NOVEMBER 6

BANNER OF LOVE

Song of Solomon 2

BEST VERSE: 4

He has brought me to his banquet hall, and his banner over me is love.

This verse is such a precious thought, but do you understand it? What does "banner" mean? Why did Solomon use that word? A banner is a flag or standard carried by an army or a group of people that signified their allegiance to a king. This banner of love is the mark of God as our king over us. But this banner isn't held over us through brute force. It is love!

God loves us with an everlasting love. The whole book of Song of Solomon describes love. The picture is of a man and woman, but it is much deeper than that. It describes the love between us and God. We should have such passion for our Savior. We should long to be with Him.

TEACHING MOMENT

I know what you are thinking. Carl, how in the world do I read this book to my children. It's a little graphic. Well, it's still God's Word. I recommend you get a children's Bible for this one. It will kind of tame it down a bit. As your children get older, you can move to a more accurate translation.

The problem with our world today is we have totally destroyed the God-given image of the love between a man and woman as God designed. There is nothing more beautiful than that love between a husband and wife. Your children need to know that. But don't let Hollywood give them the image. Let God's Word do that.

Do you seek God's love the way it is described in the Song of Solomon? Take a minute and read the first three chapters today. Ask yourself if you seek God that way. Ask yourself if you cherish His presence that way. Do you long for His touch and His love?

Father, I desire to know You fully. I long to feel Your embrace. Touch me today and let me know You are there.

NOVEMBER 7

GOOD ADVICE FROM A BAD ADVISOR

Job 11

BEST VERSE: 14

If iniquity is in your hand, put it far away, and do not let wickedness dwell in your tents.

There is a truth I have learned through the years. Even ungodly people can give good advice sometimes. Notice I didn't say they give godly advice, just good. My dad wasn't saved until he was eighty years old, but he was one of the wisest men I knew. I loved to get his advice on things. But I knew I couldn't rely on him for spiritual wisdom, at least not until he came to Christ. Those last four years of his life as a believer were wonderful!

In Job 11 Zophar is rebuking Job without knowing the cause of his suffering. But even Zophar says some things worth remembering. You know the saying, "a blind hog will find an acorn every once in a while." Ha! Zophar makes this statement about iniquity and wickedness which is so true.

TEACHING MOMENT

We would do well to encourage our children to keep iniquity and wickedness far from them. Sometimes our children like to "flirt" with evil. That always leads to mistakes. Put iniquity far from you. Get it out of your hands. If necessary, run from it.

The trouble our children face is that a lot of the time the wickedness is literally in their hands. Smart phones and tablets can bring the wickedness of this world right into their hands and flood their minds with evil. It is your job as parents to guard them against that.

Are you allowing the iniquity and wickedness of the world to enter your "tent"? Are you just sampling the edges of that? Don't be fooled, Mom and Dad. Everything you allow to enter your life will influence your children. You may not even be aware that it is, but it does. You will begin to loosen your standards of morality or excellence, and soon your children will see it.

Be careful—little eyes are watching! Be careful—little ears are listening!

Guard my eyes and ears so that I will not have the images or sounds of evil today. Help me protect those around me from the same. Let me set no evil thing before me.

NOVEMBER 8

WHOM DO YOU LOVE?

Song of Solomon 1

BEST VERSE: 4B

We will rejoice in you and be glad; We will extol your love more than wine. Rightly do they love you.

The Song of Solomon is a beautiful piece of poetry in the Old Testament. But it is not just poetry. It is God's Word. Many people question why it was put in the Bible. I mean, it is a poem about the love between a man and a woman, right? Yes, but it is so much more than that.

It also reflects on our love for our Savior and Lord. Today's verse, in particular, reflects that thought. We should rejoice and be glad in the Lord. We should extol His love. And it is right for us to love Him. What else could you say about our love relationship with the Lord?

TEACHING MOMENT

So, how do you teach this book to your children? You explain the purpose of the book to them first. You tell them it's all about love. It's all about desire for the Lord. It's all about relationships.

However you decide to approach it, it is paramount that you focus on this being God's Word, just like every other book of the Bible. For whatever reason it was written, it has application for us today. We must understand that and teach our children that truth.

What do you see in Song of Solomon? Do you see a beautiful poem or God's Word? Do you see only the bride and groom, or do you see us and our Lord? How you approach Scripture will determine how you apply it.

Lord, thank You for loving me with a passionate love. Your Word says you jealousy desire the Spirit that You placed within us. Let me desire You as strongly.

NOVEMBER 9

PR-I-DE

2 Chronicles 26

BEST VERSE: 16

But when he became strong, his heart was so proud that he acted corruptly, and he was unfaithful to the LORD his God, for he entered the temple of the LORD to burn incense on the altar of incense.

Uzziah was a good king. He was the longest ruling king of Judah and did many great things for the Lord. But . . . pride entered the scene. The above verse reads, "But when he became strong, his heart was so proud that he acted corruptly, and he was unfaithful to the Lord his God…" Uzziah began to think he could do anything.

There is much danger in thinking that way. For Uzziah, the result was leprosy imposed by God to humble him and remove him from power. He spent the rest of his life virtually in solitude, and his son ran the kingdom. Don't you bet he begged God every day for cleansing? Don't you bet every morning he would jump up and look to see if the leprosy was gone? Regrets!

TEACHING MOMENT

We want our children to be proud of their accomplishments, but we must also teach them how to be humble. A proud person can become annoying very quickly. A humble person is always giving credit to someone else for their success. As believers, we know everything we are and do is because of the Lord God. He deserves all the credit.

The next time your children experiences success (ballgame win, an A in school, etc.) help them to point to God. Remind them that He is the one who gives them their abilities. Remind them that He is the one who allows them the strength to compete in games or the intellect to achieve good grades. And then help them to voice that to others.

We all like to be recognized for things we do. That motivates us to continue doing good. But let the recognition of others roll off your back like water off a duck's back. Then let the Lord's pleasure in you sink deep in your soul. After all, only His praise really matters.

O Father, I know You are the only one who gives true praise. Remind me daily, Lord, to give back to You any praise I receive.

NOVEMBER 10

WHAT DO YOU HOLD VALUABLE?

1 Kings 18

BEST VERSES: 34–35

And he said, "Fill four pitchers with water and pour it on the burnt offering and on the wood." And he said, "Do it a second time," and they did it a second time. And he said, "Do it a third time," and they did it a third time. The water flowed around the altar and he also filled the trench with water.

The story of Elijah and the prophets of Baal has been told over and over again. You have probably read about it in Sunday School or heard sermons on it. But many miss this part. There was a severe drought going on, and that is a gross understatement. In fact, it hadn't rained in three years. I saw such conditions last year when I was in Kenya. I was in an area that had not seen any kind of significant rainfall in three years. People were dying. Livestock were dying. Crops wouldn't grow. People had to leave their homes and move to find water. It was horrible.

And here in this story we find Elijah taking something precious, something all the people would consider valuable, and pouring it on the altar. I bet all those people were thinking, "Go ahead and kill the sacrifice. The animal is going to die anyway. But don't waste the water. Think how many people could use it."

TEACHING MOMENT

Our children need to learn that there is nothing too valuable to give up for God. He wants us to be totally sold out to Him in everything. If your children become too attached to something, we need to help them lay it down. Things in this life don't matter. Only total abandonment to the Lord does.

But how can they learn that unless they see it in us first. What do you hold "dear"? It may be the very children you are trying to teach. Give them up to God. You are only the caretaker of this precious cargo anyway. They belong to God. Lay them on the altar, figuratively.

Elijah wanted to make sure the people saw that the fire that consumed the altar wasn't man-made. No man could have lit a sacrifice doused in that much water. And don't miss that even the water in the trough around the altar was consumed. The precious liquid was consumed by the Lord.

My Lord and my God, take all of me. Take all that I hold dear. I give them over to you today to use as You see best. Help me Lord to give up what I hold dear so that I can receive back what You know is best.

NOVEMBER 11

UH-OH!

Job 38

BEST VERSE: 3

Now gird up your loins like a man, And I will ask you, and you instruct Me!

Have you ever been caught red-handed? There is no getting out of it. There is nothing you can say. You know you have no explanation, so you just wait for the hammer to fall.

I bet Job and his friends felt that way when God began to speak. I love this verse. God is challenging Job, if he is so smart and has all the answers, to educate Him. I am assuming, since God spoke to the friends later, that they could also hear this conversation between God and Job. I don't know for sure, but I believe they were listening in. If so, they, like Job, were probably sitting there like little schoolboys with their heads down.

I remember so well getting caught by my mom or dad. Now, I was close to perfect as a child (ha!), but when I did get caught, I knew my parents were going to take me to the woodshed. They believed in discipline, and I am glad they did. I don't remember a lot of conversation either. Isn't it funny how we forget those things they said to us—until we have children of our own, and then our parents' words come flying out of our mouths?

TEACHING MOMENT

As a parent, you need to let God's words come flying out of your mouth. Your children need to know that their actions always have a reaction. Sometimes it is good, and sometimes it is "not so good." But each and every time we intervene in their behavior, we need to let the Father above direct our reactions and the words we use.

You know the rest of the story of Job, right? What does God do in the end? He restores Job. Why? Because Job finally does confess his own self-righteousness. And his friends? Well, they learned a lesson too about judging others.

Let God teach you today, so you can teach your children.

Father, I want to learn how to be more like You in regard to treating others with mercy and grace. I know sin must be punished, but that is Your responsibility, not mine. Thank You for wisdom.

NOVEMBER 12

NOT TOO HIGH TO STOOP

Isaiah 57

BEST VERSE: 15

For thus says the high and exalted One Who lives forever, whose name is Holy, "I dwell on a high and holy place, and also with the contrite and lowly of spirit in order to revive the spirit of the lowly and to revive the heart of the contrite."

Don't you just love the imagery of this verse? The high and exalted one is willing to get down on our level. He comes to the contrite (brokenhearted) and the lowly (humble). Even though He dwells on a high and holy place, He comes down. That's exactly what Jesus did.

We will soon be celebrating Christmas, the birth of Christ. Jesus left His heavenly abode to come to the lowly. Just look at who the Lord chose as His earthly parents, a humble carpenter and a teen virgin. He could have come in majesty and with angelic choirs announcing His arrival to the crowds in Jerusalem. But He chose to come this way.

TEACHING MOMENT

Do your kids ever get cocky and a little arrogant? It happens to the best kids. When that happens, show them this verse. God looks for the contrite and lowly. He wants to see that humble, teachable spirit. He wants your children to see themselves that way, not as unworthy, but as a servant to others.

How do you teach lowliness and a contrite heart? You don't. You can't. This is something the Lord has to teach them by allowing them to experience life. As parents, you cannot protect them, nor should you, from these trials. They need to learn this while they are young to prepare them for life ahead.

That may sound harsh. I don't mean it to be. But I want to make sure you realize that as holy and righteous as our Lord is, He loves to dwell with those who are broken. When we have nothing in ourselves that magnifies us, that's when He can start using us.

Lord, I don't like the sound of that whole lowly and contrite thing. But if it will make me more like You, bring it on. I know that is dangerous to pray, but I mean it.

NOVEMBER 13

HUH?

Isaiah 27

BEST VERSE: 1

In that day the LORD will punish Leviathan the fleeing serpent, with His fierce and great and mighty sword, even Leviathan the twisted serpent; and He will kill the dragon who lives in the sea."

Sometimes the imagery in Scripture can leave us scratching our heads. This verse is one such place. What did Isaiah mean by this "fleeing serpent," this "Leviathan," this "dragon"? If you take the time to look at various commentaries on this verse, you will find a variety of suggestions. But they all boil down to one basic idea—this was an enemy of God's people.

Now that we can understand! Our archenemy, of course, is Satan. He wants to destroy us. He hates that we have surrendered to the Lord and desires to bring us down, just like Leviathan. He, however, is already defeated! Praise be to God.

TEACHING MOMENT

It's not hard to teach your kids about enemies. Before you know it, they will be coming home with names of a few. The important thing to teach them is to allow the Lord to defend them. They are defenseless on their own. It would be like your six-year-old trying to fend off a crocodile in the river. No contest.

But God has the power to step in and destroy our enemies. All we have to do is call on His name. He has promised to come to our aid. He has promised to be our defender. He can speak, and things are done. Wow!

Who are you wrestling right now? Is there a Leviathan in your life? Stop fighting them. Go to the Lord and allow Him to handle it. He will do it the right way. Our flesh wants to strike back, but we must trust the God of the ages, the same God who defended Israel, to defend us.

O Father, I know Satan does not have a chance against You. I place my trust in You. You have the power and righteousness to defend me today.

NOVEMBER 14

GET UP DEAD MAN!

Acts 14

BEST VERSES: 19–20

But Jews came from Antioch and Iconium, and having won over the crowds, they stoned Paul and dragged him out of the city, supposing him to be dead. But while the disciples stood around him, he got up and entered the city. The next day he went away with Barnabas to Derbe.

Wouldn't you have loved to have been there at this scene? Paul had been revered as a god just days earlier when he healed someone, but how quickly the crowd has turned. (That should be a warning to us all concerning the praise of men, by the way.) They drag him out of the city and stone him, trying to kill him. But Paul just gets up and walks back into the city.

What!!!! I would have run as fast as I could out of town and kept running. But Paul, full of the Holy Spirit, goes back to town like nothing has happened. His calling was more powerful than his falling. Yes, I just made that up!

TEACHING MOMENT

We need to teach our kids that nothing the world can throw at us, even stones, can keep us down if we trust the Lord. Did those stones hurt that were thrown at Paul? I am sure! Words that are "thrown" at us hurt too. But our calling to follow Him is so much more powerful. Even sometimes the Lord will shield us from the hurts.

Boldness is something that is learned through experience. It is a gift of God given when we are called to be bold. He allows us to encounter people or circumstances that require boldness and courage and then equips us with exactly what we need. Is that cool or what?

Your kids will face challenging things in their life that are only handled through His strength. There is *nothing* you can do, Mom and Dad. They have to face these events with His boldness, not yours. Trust Him to give it. Trust them to ask for it.

O God, I don't want to be stoned by anyone, but, like Paul, give me the boldness to stand firm against those who speak against You. Let my boldness be an inspiration to my children and others.

NOVEMBER 15

WHAT WILL YOU BE KNOWN FOR?

2 Kings 23

BEST VERSE: 25

Before him there was no king like him who turned to the Lord with all his heart and with all his soul and with all his might, according to all the law of Moses; nor did any like him arise after him.

You really need to read 2 Kings 23:1–24 to get a clear picture of all that Josiah did as king. He cleaned house! He didn't just clean house in Judah.

He even went into Israel, who had been carried into exile, and cleaned out the evil altars and high places. He re-established the worship of Jehovah God throughout the country. He even held the first Passover that had been celebrated for decades.

Josiah was intent in being obedient to the Lord. And he was known as a king "who turned to the Lord with all his heart and with all his soul and with all his might." Don't you want to be known like that? Better yet, don't you want your children to see you like that?

TEACHING MOMENT

Our duty as parents is to bring up our children in the Lord. We can only do that by honoring Him ourselves. That requires us to surrender all to Him. You can't hold anything back. It all belongs to Him. You have to turn to the Lord with all your heart, soul, and might. By doing so, your children will see that and will be led to do the same.

However, living sold out to Jesus is no guarantee your children will do the same. As good as Josiah was, his son did evil when he became king, and his grandson did too. Still, we must pour into them the love of Christ and teach them His commandments. Only the Holy Spirit can draw them. It is important that you be obedient. Give them to Him.

Are there some "high places" or "altars" you need to tear down today? What are you worshiping that does not give glory to the Lord. We all have those things. Some are just more visible than others. Perhaps you have been so involved with them for so long that you can't see them. Ask your spouse or best friend to tell you if they see your "high places." But be prepared to hear what they say.

Tear them down! Raze them to the ground! Grind them up and scatter them. Then bow to the only true God and worship Him with all that you have. He will honor that and bless you!

Father God, the same God who taught and led Josiah, give me the compassion and hunger for You that Josiah had. Give me the courage to tear down my "altars" and bow only to You.

STANDING FOR TRUTH

2 Kings 18

BEST VERSES: 5-6

He trusted in the LORD, the God of Israel; so that after him there was none like him among all the kings of Judah, nor among those who were before him. For he clung to the LORD; he did not depart from following Him, but kept His commandments, which the LORD had commanded Moses.

When Hezekiah came on the scene in Judah, things were pretty bad. The land had been under the thumb of Assyria, who had already taken Israel into captivity. Things looked bad. But Hezekiah decided that he would honor Jehovah God, even in the midst of oppression from a pagan nation.

It is so important for us to teach our children that the world in which they live should not dictate how they live their lives. Our nation, I'm sorry to say, is in a post-Christian environment now. Every day you hear more and more about Christians being ridiculed, ruled against in court and banned from speaking out for truth. But that does not determine our allegiance. We, like Hezekiah, must stand for the One True God.

TEACHING MOMENT

May I encourage every mom and dad out there to not shy away from teaching your children how to respond to the news of the day? As you hear a news story that goes directly against our belief system take the time to explain to your children, according to their ability to understand, how they should respond to honor God. Remember, we are not raising children. We are raising child raisers. We are impacting the next generation in the way we raise our children.

Hezekiah made some mistakes later in his reign, but, even then, he repented and made things right. We and our children will make some mistakes. The important thing is to make those things right. Our cities, states, country, and world need believers who will stand for truth at all costs. Won't you instill in your children the boldness they have through Christ? If you do, they can face any hostile force or action and defend their beliefs and stand for truth!

Truth will endure, God. And You are Truth. You will stand the test of all time. There is only one Truth, and You are it.

NOVEMBER 17

A NAME GONE WRONG

1 Chronicles 1

BEST VERSE: 10

Cush became the father of Nimrod; he began to be a mighty one in the earth.

Back in the 80s, calling someone a "nimrod" was not a compliment. It meant you were a geek or socially awkward. But in the genealogy presented in 1 Chronicles 1, this is the first person to which an explanation is given. According to the Bible and a lot of other historical writers, Nimrod was the king of Babel and was the one who led the people to build the tower, supposedly out of rebellion against God.

Nimrod was a large man, bigger than most. In fact, some believe he was a giant, similar to Goliath. What a pity that he chose to use his might against God rather than use his "God-given" strength and might to lead his people toward God. His name could have been known as a great one. But let me ask you, do you ever hear of anyone naming their child Nimrod today? Of course not.

TEACHING MOMENT

We should teach our children that their name means something. They carry your name, dads. It should be a name they are proud of. And we should teach them to be careful to never do anything to dishonor it or bring shame to it. Once a name is marred by bad choices, it takes a long time to reclaim your reputation.

We also teach our children that, as believers, we carry the name of Jesus. We should be careful how we portray the name of Christ. People are watching, so we need to be mindful of the image we are showing the world. Children need to be reminded of that as they go to school. They need to be reminded of that when they go off to college. We bear the name of Christ. Don't forget that.

How about your name? Do people hear your name and say, "Oh yeah, I know him. What a great guy. He really loves the Lord."? Do people even know you are a believer? Let your name instantly remind people of your walk with Christ. Remember that your life, as a believer, is a reflection of Christ.

Father, help me today to carry Your name proudly. I know that as I live for You, others will be drawn to You. Remind me each day to guard Your name and make it my own.

NOVEMBER 18

FOR MY BROTHER

1 Corinthians 8

BEST VERSE: 13

Therefore, if food causes my brother to stumble, I will never eat meat again, so that I will not cause my brother to stumble.

People today tend to look out for themselves. That is even true in the church. We are free in Christ, that is true. But shouldn't we be concerned with our weaker brothers and sisters in Christ? Shouldn't we be careful not to do anything that would cause them to stumble?

Paul is telling the Corinthians here in this chapter that very thing. Since he did not believe any other gods existed, he knew any meat sacrificed to them was okay to eat. You see, they would sell that meat in the marketplace after a pagan priest had offered it to that false god. There were those in the early church who came out of those false religions, and they still struggled with the belief of those false gods. They had not grown in their faith to the point that they understood those gods were false. So, when they saw believers buying that meat and eating it, they were confused. Paul tells them to avoid such meat if it meant hurting the faith of another.

TEACHING MOMENT

What do you feel "free" to do in Christ that your child may not understand? Are there things you do that could confuse a weaker brother or sister in Christ? While it may be okay for you to do it, it is not okay to lead someone down the wrong path in their own walk with Christ.

How do we teach our children this truth? We live above reproach. We make sure that every decision we make will not influence them to lose faith or be confused about what they believe. As parents, we have to be constantly pointing our children to Christ. Every word and deed need to help them build their faith and trust Him. Don't straddle the fence! Make sure your children know exactly why you believe what you believe.

Give me the strength, Lord, to restrain myself from those things that I see as clean, but others see as unclean. Help me not cause another to stumble, especially my children. May I live a life above reproach.

NOVEMBER 19

IT'S NOT ABOUT YOU

1 Corinthians 14

BEST VERSE: 12

So also you, since you are zealous of spiritual gifts, seek to abound for the edification of the church.

This chapter in 1 Corinthians is a much-debated topic—speaking in tongues. I am not going to get into that debate here. Instead I want to look at the verse above. You see, Paul says very plainly that the purpose of any gift which the Lord has given us is to build up the church, not ourselves.

I have experienced churches where speaking in tongues is emphasized. But I have never seen this verse emphasized in those same churches. Things that divide or things that seem to put some above others do not build up. That's the bottom line. We must be about edifying and encouraging our brothers and sisters. We should not do anything that is going to belittle or shame them.

TEACHING MOMENT

So, how do you teach this to our kids? Okay, I sound like a broken record—you have to model it. Our children need to see us building others up. They are watching us, right? They should know that we are all about helping others grow.

Now that also refers to how we talk about others in their presence. Have you ever talked negatively about a fellow believer in front of your kids? They are listening to that. They are storing that away and will use it to model how they talk about people.

May I encourage you today to focus on what you can do to encourage a brother or sister in Christ? Will you come alongside your pastor to build up the church? Allow the Spirit of God to direct you in the words you use as you talk about others.

I know the Father has given all the gifts for our good. And with each gift, He expects us to use it to glorify Him. If you can figure out a way to use your gift, no matter what it is, to build yourself up and glorify Him, go for it. I don't see how that's possible, though.

Lord, show me how to use my gift for Your glory. I want everything I do to point to You and glorify You.

NOVEMBER 20

FAMILY BUSINESS

1 Chronicles 25

BEST VERSES: 6–7

All these were under the direction of their father to sing in the house of the LORD, with cymbals, harps and lyres, for the service of the house of God. Asaph, LORD and Heman were under the direction of the king. Their number who were trained in singing to the LORD, with their relatives, all who were skillful, was 288.

Can you imagine? 288 from one family of brothers who were all engaged in ministry to the Lord. Heman, himself, had 14 sons with their relatives who were all singers. Now that's a choir!

But I wonder if they all really wanted to be a part of the "family business"? There were probably a few who said, "Come on Dad, do we have to go to church again?" There is no mention of them not fulfilling their duties though. They were called and appointed to service. They were serving the Great Jehovah. I am sure Asaph, Jeduthun, and Heman reminded them often of the great honor that had been bestowed on their family by the King.

TEACHING MOMENT

How do you get your children involved in service to "our" King? How do we encourage them to get engaged in serving in church or the community? It is so important that we give our children opportunities to serve. This can be done by helping stack chairs after a service or carrying the trash out after an event. They can help clean up outside or perhaps put down mulch around the shrubs.

There are a multitude of ways in which your children can serve. We just have to make sure they know that service is a joy, not a burden. We get joy out of serving, and our serving gives the Lord joy.

Why don't you have a family meeting this week and decide how your family can do a service project together this summer? Ask a pastor what would be a big help to him. I guarantee he has at least one project of service that would fit your family.

Serving You brings me joy, Father. Show me where You want me to serve. Lead me to invite others to join me in bringing You joy.

NOVEMBER 21

HUMBLED

Isaiah 23

BEST VERSE: 9

The Lord of hosts has planned it, to defile the pride of all beauty, to despise all the honored of the earth.

Isaiah 23 is a prophecy about Tyre, one of the city states of Phoenicia. They were an enemy of Israel and fell under the judgment of God for the way they treated His chosen children. They were a proud people due to the beauty of their region and the wealth they had accumulated. Hmmm, sounds like a lot of people today.

In fact, that is exactly how we can apply today's verse. God will humble the proud. God will exalt the humble. Which do you want? Exaltation or humility? I know which one I prefer, but my problem is I want to exalt myself too much. Instead, I need to humble myself before God and men and let Him do the exalting.

TEACHING MOMENT

I have found that children normally have one of two problems. They either think too much of themselves or too little. Having too much self-esteem is easily seen, as children will boast, brag and put down others. Low self-esteem can be overlooked. These children can be quiet and introspective, thinking they can remain unseen and invisible to others. Neither of these is good.

As parents we are to build up our children, not tear them down. But we need to balance that building up with correction. Children should never be allowed to put others down in their effort to look bigger. Nor should we allow them to put themselves down. It truly is a balancing act. Trust the Lord for the words to say to your little one. After all, He made them in His image.

As an adult, we must show our children what a healthy ego looks like. If we are braggers or a sulkers, they will learn from us. Parents who are obnoxious often have obnoxious kids. And parents who are always hanging their heads in shame will have children who do the same. You need to go to the Master for an attitude adjustment. Let Him exalt or humble you, just like Tyre.

O Lord, You made me to be perfect as You are perfect. I know that doesn't mean I am perfect, but You do give me the one to follow who is—Jesus. Make me more like Him today.

NOVEMBER 22

FACE SHINE

Psalms 67–68

BEST VERSE: 67:1

God be gracious to us and bless us, and cause His face to shine upon us—Selah.

Millions of dollars a year are spent on cosmetics, both by men and women. One thing most people who wear makeup try to do is stop face shine. They put stuff on their face to keep that shiny look from popping through. If you are like me and suffer with oily skin, that can be quite challenging. And we won't even talk about the challenge of powdering a shiny dome.

So, when I read this verse today, I thought it kind of funny. God's face shines. He has a shiny face, and it shines on us. Of course, His face shines, not due to oily skin, but because He is Light. His face shines His light upon us. That's the kind of shiny face I want.

TEACHING MOMENT

Get your son or daughter to draw a picture of God's shiny face. I wish I could see what they come up with. Will it have radiating beams shooting from it like the sun? Will it have a glow emanating from around it? However they draw it, it will certainly capture their imagination.

But then explain that as believers we have the light of Jesus in us. Our faces should shine for Him. People ought to be able to tell just by looking that He lives in us. God's shiny face should show on our faces. What does that mean? It doesn't mean we have to go around with a perpetual grin. But it does mean that we don't wear a scowl all the time. Our faces should draw people to God, not scare them away.

Look in the mirror. What do you see? Is your face shining for Jesus today? Will others look at you and say, "Wow! I want to know what he knows"? Let your face tell the story of Jesus to someone today.

God, I am thankful Your face shines on me. Help me allow You to shine through me to others. Wipe away the frown and turn it into a smile.

NOVEMBER 23

IF ONLY…

1 Kings 9

BEST VERSES: 4–5

As for you, if you will walk before Me as your father David walked, in integrity of heart and uprightness, doing according to all that I have commanded you and will keep My statutes and My ordinances, then I will establish the throne of your kingdom over Israel forever, just as I promised to your father David, saying, "You shall not lack a man on the throne of Israel."

Man, oh man, oh man! Just look at the Lord's promise to Solomon. He said He would establish his throne forever! But there was a condition—he had to walk as his "father David walked, in integrity of heart and uprightness, doing according to all that I have commanded you and will keep My statutes and My ordinances . . ." In other words, "Just follow me!"

We know what happened. Solomon started marrying pagan women and then started building altars to their gods. He turned his back on God, even after building this magnificent temple. But don't be too hard on Solomon. We do the same. We think we can do as we desire and still receive God's blessings.

TEACHING MOMENT

If there is one thing we need to teach our children, it's this. Choices have consequences. For the most part, God will not stop us from making our own decisions. But our decisions always have consequences. Now listen, Mom and Dad. Let your children make some decisions while they are young, so they can safely fail. And when they fail and there are consequences; let them deal with those too. Rescuing them from the choices they make will not teach them anything.

Little Johnny and Susie can learn a lot from the life of Solomon. The wisest man who ever lived, besides Jesus, got side-tracked by life's distractions and lost God's blessing. How sad. Now in Christ, we have eternal blessings, that's true. But we can sure miss a lot of God's blessings in our lives here on earth by not being obedient.

What are you missing right now? Are there things in your life you need to stop doing that you know are preventing you from receiving all God wants to bless you with? Give it all over to Him and let Him draw you close. He will.

Father, I repent of my disobedience. Forgive me of seeking my own way. Forgive me of allowing life to distract me from my heavenly calling. Let me teach others to follow You.

NOVEMBER 24

DEPRESSION

Job 3

BEST VERSE: 11

Why did I not die at birth, come forth from the womb and expire?

Have you ever been really depressed? I mean, really depressed. Job is definitely depressed. He has just lost all his children and all his wealth. His wife has told him to curse God and die. He seemingly has no hope.

But in all of this, God still maintains Job's righteousness. Job doesn't lose his faith just because he is depressed. So many today will judge others who suffer with depression by telling them they just need more faith. You cannot speak for those people. You do not know what is going on in their minds and in their relationship with the Lord.

TEACHING MOMENT

This is a strange topic to teach our kids about, but it is one they need to know. Probably, at some point in their lives, little Susie or little Johnny are going to have depression. They may get very sullen about a lost friend or a pet that has died. Depression is not sin. Hear me clearly. Depression is not sin.

What we teach our children, though, is that God has a plan that is much bigger than their depression. I love the saying "Everything over our heads is under His feet." He can handle it. So, we teach our children to pray and give it all to Jesus.

What are you struggling with today? Are you depressed? Are you in a pit? Look up! Don't look inward. Look up to the God who created you. He knows you are hurting. He feels your pain. He has the answer. Give it to Him.

Lord, You are the Master of my soul. You are my true soulmate. You know my innermost thoughts. Lead me to Your still waters.

NOVEMBER 25

OLD AND GRAY

Psalms 71–72

BEST VERSE: 71:18

And even when I am old and gray, O God, do not forsake me, until I declare Your strength to this generation, Your power to all who are to come.

It happens to us all, if we live long enough. We get old and gray. You may color your hair to hide the gray, but underneath it all, it is still gray, and you're still old. Age has a way of doing that. And that's okay. Getting old is just part of the cycle of life. I don't mind at all.

Like the psalmist here in Psalm 71, I want to be used by God even when I am old and gray. Why? How? I want to declare Him to the next generation. I want to pass on the faith. I want to see them come to know Him and live for him. And any believer can do that. They can pass on the knowledge God has given them.

TEACHING MOMENT

Teaching our children, passing on the truths of God's Word to the next generation, is our job. We are called by God to instruct and train them. This doesn't stop when our children leave home, though. This task continues until God calls us home. We have the opportunity to invest in our grandchildren and even, if God allows, our great grandchildren. What a privilege.

We declare His strength and power. How? By living it daily. As we age, our bodies get weaker. Duh, right? I mean, if you are over fifty and not feeling your age, more power to you. By relying on the Lord's strength and His power, you are a living testimony to Him. Your family and friends will see that.

So, how are you doing with this whole aging thing? Are you old and gray? Are you still sharing with the future generations? God has given you a task to perform. You aren't finished yet. Take on each day with a vengeance. Let Him empower you today.

Lord, there are days when I am physically weary. I can accept that. But don't let me ever get spiritually weary. Give me Your power and strength today.

NOVEMBER 26

BE LOVE

1 Corinthians 16

BEST VERSE: 14

Let all that you do be done in love.

I love studying the Scriptures in the original languages. They tell so much more than any English translation. You get the correct purpose of the word and action of the verbs.

Take this verse for example. The English translates the verb "Let . . . be done." The Greek word here actually means "come into being, happen, become." So, you could translate this "Let all you become be love." I like that. Everything we are should be a reflection of the love of God. It's not just what we do. It's all of us, our thoughts, actions, words, etc.

TEACHING MOMENT

How do you teach your child this concept of love? How do you show them to "be" love? There is only one way! You have to "be" love first. You have to show them in everything you are that the love of Christ reigns supreme. You have to show them that no matter what you encounter each day, the love of Christ will dictate your actions.

Let's get personal. When was the last time you did not react with love towards someone or some circumstance? If you are like me, it was probably yesterday. Perhaps you were able to disguise your reaction from your kids, but internally there was no love. Don't you think that internal struggle will show externally? Don't you think your children pick up on that struggle? They are watching and learning, especially when you don't want them to.

As you go through your days, remember that you are to "be" love. You are commanded to "be" love. The Greek verb there is a command. You must "be" love. It's not just for yourself. It's also for all those you come into contact with each day, especially your children. Don't just love–be love!

God of love, I know I must be love before I can do love. I need to be more like Jesus before I can live like Jesus. Only You can help me do that.

NOVEMBER 27

DOES GOD LOOK AT YOU?

Isaiah 66

BEST VERSE: 2B

But to this one I will look, to him who is humble and contrite of spirit, and who trembles at My word.

This verse tells it pretty clear. God looks on the humble and contrite, on those who tremble at His word. Is that you? Or are you cocky and arrogant? Are you unafraid of the words of the Lord?

Now, understand what this is saying. God doesn't want us to cower in fear. But He does expect a reverential fear of Him. He expects us to know that He is God, not you. He will not look on the proud. He will not look on those who shake their fist in His face. I pray that is not you.

TEACHING MOMENT

Are your children very clear on how you expect them to respond to you? Too many children today treat their parents like school yard buddies. Sure, we want our children to see us as their friends, as well as their mom and dad. But this friendship does not mean we are equals. Parents must be the parents. You can't co-parent your child with your child.

In the same way, your children need a healthy understanding of their relationship with the Father. He is their Savior and Lord. He is (or should be) their closest confidant, but God is not their buddy. There must be a distinction. And when your child understands that, the relationship becomes even closer.

How do you see your relationship with God right now? Do you feel God's gaze upon you? If you don't, perhaps you are exhibiting those traits that cause Him to look away. I don't know about you, but I want the Lord to look at me. I want Him to see me as contrite and humble. I do fear His Word, because I know it is pure truth.

Your eyes, O Lord, see right through me. You know my motives. You know my heart. I desire Your gaze on me today.

NOVEMBER 28

THAT'LL SHOW THEM

Isaiah 64

BEST VERSES: 1–2

Oh, that You would rend the heavens and come down, that the mountains might quake at Your presence—As fire kindles the brushwood, as fire causes water to boil—to make Your name known to Your adversaries, that the nations may tremble at Your presence!

Have you ever just gotten tired of people bashing God? I have. I have secretly wished these two verses. I wish God would just show up and prove once and for all that He is real and that He is in control. I wish He would show up and show off.

Guess what? He already has! He has done the most powerful work in our lives when He saved us. Don't you realize that? And if we would just live like it, others would be in awe. They don't need to see the heavens rent or the mountains quake. They would look at us and say, "Wow, God is incredible. Look what He did and is doing in their lives."

TEACHING MOMENT

When your little Susie comes to Christ, teach her to let Jesus shine through. Teach her to allow Him to control her tongue and actions. Show her this verse and tell her that God can be just as powerful through her life if she will just yield to Him.

Tell your son that if he wants real power he must bow before the King of kings and do His bidding. Then others will be amazed at what God is doing in and through Him. Boys love to see things blown up or destroyed. But God's power is one that builds. He wants to build them into men who love Him.

Are you in need of some power today? Do you want others to see God's majesty in you? Then humble yourself and allow Him to work. Get out of the way. Let Him overwhelm your family with His strength through your meekness. They will be shocked.

Lord, today allow me to hide in You. Let others only see me! Let Your power and strength be exhibited in my weakness.

NOVEMBER 29

SNOBBISH

1 Chronicles 15

BEST VERSE:

It happened when the ark of the covenant of the Lord came to the city of David, that Michal the daughter of Saul looked out of the window and saw King David leaping and celebrating; and she despised him in her heart.

I don't know if you remember or not, but Michal was the younger daughter of Saul and David's first wife. When David was forced to flee from

Saul's wrath, Saul gave her to another man as his wife. Years later when David became king, he wanted her back. Apparently, this was done without Michal's input and she resented it.

Perhaps she thought since she was Saul's daughter, she was better than everyone else. When she saw David acting unkingly (yes, I just made up that word), she was embarrassed. She didn't understand David's abandonment in worship. She was obviously too full of herself.

TEACHING MOMENT

Our children must be taught to not see themselves better than anyone else. By that I mean they should not look down on anyone. As my brother-in-law used to say, "No one has arrived." Instead of looking down on others, we need to teach them to look up to the Lord. When things are seen through His eyes, there is no room for snobbish behavior.

Let me encourage you, Mom and Dad, to nip an obnoxious attitude in the bud. Don't let this prideful (in the wrong way) attitude continue. Not only does this attitude drive a wedge between them and others, but it will also do the same between them and the Lord.

Are you looking down at others? Do you think you are too good for some act of service? No one has arrived. We are all on the journey. You may be further down the road, but we are all headed in the same direction—eternity. Shouldn't we all be more concerned about bringing as many as possible along with us?

Father, I know pride can be a good thing. Help me keep my pride focused on boasting on You, not myself. Thank You for walking with me on the path you have chosen for me.

NOVEMBER 30

ROAD RAGE

2 Kings 9

BEST VERSE: 20B

And the driving is like the driving of Jehu the son of Nimshi, for he drives furiously.

Road rage has obviously been around a lot longer than the term has been used. Jehu was known as one who "drives furiously." What did that mean exactly? I mean, he wasn't driving a sports car or a Mack truck. He was driving a chariot.

Whatever he was driving, undoubtedly, he was known as a crazy driver. The Lord chose him, though, to be the instrument of justice over Joram and Jezebel. Jehu executed them both according to God's command. He did it quickly and without hesitation. He didn't try to rationalize it. He just acted.

TEACHING MOMENT

Now today's lesson isn't a driving lesson. I am not trying to tell you how to drive or how to teach your children to drive. Today's lesson is, once again, about obedience. The Lord used a crazy driver. So, He can use you and your children.

I never get over the fact that God can use anyone. He can make the most unsuspecting person a tool in His plan. You don't know what God has planned for your children. Your job is to have them ready to be used. Your job is to teach them to hear and then respond to the Lord's commands.

Jehu hurriedly drove to execute God's judgment. Are you in a rush to follow the Lord? Most of the time we have to be drugged to the place of obedience. It is so much easier to just do it. Allow the Lord to use you when and how He chooses.

You are my Commander, O Lord. Help me be ready at all times to respond to Your call. Help me show my children how to hear and obey.

DECEMBER 1

MAYHAW JELLY

Romans 8

BEST VERSE: 28

And we know that God causes all things to work together for good to those who love God, to those who are called according to His purpose.

I grew up eating mayhaw jelly. Now you may ask, "What is a mayhaw?" Well, "mayhaw" is the term used for Hawthorne berries which produce in May of each year in the swamps of South Georgia. They are very tart and not very pleasant to eat by themselves. But after you cook them and squeeze off the juice, you can make some of the tastiest jelly I know of. My dad loved mayhaw jelly.

Mayhaw jelly reminds me of this verse. Circumstances may seem to be tart and worthless, but after it goes through God's pressure cooker and press, something sweet can be made of it. But come on now, who wants to go through a pressure cooker and then get squeezed. No one! Nobody likes that, but we can learn so much from these situations.

TEACHING MOMENT

As your children grow and mature, they are going to face "pressure cooker" situations. It will seem that they cannot possibly survive. Your little girl gets her heart broken by some boy. Your son gets cut from the basketball team. Your child fails a huge math test. All of these seem hard while going through them. But in every situation, they can learn to be more like Christ.

The hard part for us as parents is to keep our cool. Dads, you want to find that boy who has crushed your little girl and take him out. Moms, you want to have a talk with that coach who just cut your son. Wait! Don't react! Watch God work. He will take that "tart" situation, let it cook a while, and then squeeze something out that can be enjoyed. Not because the situation is enjoyable, but the outcome is. We learn, our kids learn, and God is glorified. Hallelujah!

O God, help me to not overreact when I see my child hurting. Let me let You work in them. I know they learn best by experience, but it is so hard to let them hurt. Thank You for grace.

KNOW YOUR PURPOSE

Isaiah 61

BEST VERSE: 1

The Spirit of the LORD God is upon me, because the LORD has anointed me to bring good news to the afflicted; He has sent me to bind up the brokenhearted, to proclaim liberty to captives and freedom to prisoners.

Our verse today was quoted by Jesus when John the Baptist's disciples came to Jesus asking if He was the Messiah. Jesus knew His purpose. He knew exactly why He had come to earth. People may argue at what point in His life He knew, since He was fully human and fully God. I believe He knew all the time. His purpose (sacrificial death for all mankind) was set from His birth (incarnate beginning for all mankind).

TEACHING MOMENT

How do we help our children discover their purpose in life? How can we point them in the direction God has for them? We know their true purpose cannot be revealed until they submit to Him, so that's our first step. We need to point them daily to the Purpose Giver. Once they have surrendered their will to His will, God will begin to reveal to them how He wants to use them.

This is when we, as believing parents, need to watch for those signs of the gifts and abilities God is pouring into them. Then we can start directing them toward the fulfillment of the plan God has for them. God gifts us all differently in order to provide all the parts for the kingdom's work here on earth. As believers in Christ, our children have been given certain gifts that God wants them to exercise for Him. There is no greater joy for a parent than to see their child using those to glorify the Father.

But let me ask you a question. Are you using your gifts for Him? Have you surrendered your will to His so He can use you? Has the Lord shown you the purpose He has for you? Are you willing to do anything to fulfill that purpose in your life? You see, your children can learn a lot watching you allow God to use you. As you submit, they will learn to submit, not only to God, but to you too.

I am so thankful, Lord, for the gifts You have given me to use for Your kingdom. Open my eyes to see the way You have gifted my children so I can help direct them to be used by You.

DECEMBER 3

THE ABC's

Romans 10

BEST VERSES: 9–10

That if you confess with your mouth Jesus as Lord, and believe in your heart that God raised Him from the dead, you will be saved; for with the heart a person believes, resulting in righteousness, and with the mouth he confesses, resulting in salvation.

Many of you will recognize today's verses as part of the "Romans Road," which has been used for years to lead others to Christ. But these verses contain all three parts of the process.

TEACHING MOMENT

A—Admit you are a sinner. I believe we find this in the last part of verse 10 where it says, "and with the mouth he confesses." Leading our children to this point is easy enough. People confess stuff all the time. Our children will eventually own up to something they have done that wasn't right. Confession is good for the soul, they say. It is definitely good for salvation.

B—Believe Jesus is Lord and died for you. Verse 9 and the first part of verse 10 tell us this. We believe He is Lord, and we believe in the resurrection. However, even the demons believe and tremble, according to James 2:19. Belief that there is a God and that He does great things will not, in and of itself, result in salvation. You have to believe that Jesus is Lord and that He died for you and was raised from the dead. Believing that takes faith. Your children can believe that with a simple childlike faith.

C—Confessing our belief and surrender. Again look at the latter part of verse 10. It says we confess with our mouths, and then it says, "resulting in salvation." The only way that confession results in salvation is because you truly repent and believe. Our children have a very simplistic view of God.

Why? Because God is simple. I don't mean that in a bad way. I mean God is just God. He is not complicated. Just do the ABC's of salvation.

The next time you are helping your child with homework, why not cover the ABC's once again. These ABC's have eternal worth.

Lord, give me the opportunity today to share the ABC's with someone. Help me teach my children this simple method of sharing Christ with their friends. I praise You for being so "simple."

DECEMBER 4

A HEART TO SERVE

1 Chronicles 13

BEST VERSE: 14

Thus the ark of God remained with the family of Obed-edom in his house three months; and the LORD blessed the family of Obed-edom with all that he had.

I just love the fact that the Lord blessed Obed-edom merely for keeping the ark at his house. Can you imagine? The very seat of God in your house. We don't know where he kept it, but I am sure it was in a very safe place and treated with honor and respect. He probably put "DO NOT TOUCH" signs all around it. He knew what had happened to Uzza when he just reached out to steady the ark. He was struck dead. Obed-edom didn't want that to happen to anyone in his family.

Jewish legend says that the Lord blessed not just Obed-edom's wife with a baby but also all eight of his daughters-in-law. They were all pregnant at the same time. Now, I am not sure I would call that a blessing. (Ha!) Whether this actually happened or not, Obed-edom was blessed and highly esteemed because he hosted the ark in his home.

TEACHING MOMENT

Sometimes the smallest acts of service mean the most. Our children can learn a lot from this story. How can you teach them to do these little acts of kindness? Why don't you get them to help you bake some cookies and take them to the local Fire Department? What if you took your children with you to help an elderly neighbor or church member with housework or yardwork?

Your child may have an idea of how to serve. Even though it may seem silly to you, if it's safe, allow them. We are teaching service, not critiquing it. Encourage them to look for ways to bless others. Who knows how the Lord will choose to bless them?

Are you looking for ways to bless others? Has the Lord asked you to "host" someone or something? How can you show your children the blessings that come from serving others? Obed-edom actually not only served King David by keeping the ark. He served the entire nation of Israel by keeping it safe. He served the Lord God by guarding and protecting this symbol of His power and presence.

Hmmm? Are you guarding the symbol of His power and presence in your life—the Holy Spirit? Are you careful to do only what He tells you?

O Father, give me the heart of Obed-edom today. Show me how to be a better host of Your Holy Spirit in my life. Show me how to better serve You and others.

DECEMBER 5

IGNORED

Job 30

BEST VERSE: 20

I cry out to You for help, but You do not answer me; I stand up, and You turn Your attention against me."

Have you ever felt ignored by God? Come on, be honest. Hasn't it happened at least once in your life? You are going through a difficult, heart-wrenching time, and God seems to be nowhere. You cry out to Him and hear nothing. His Word doesn't console you. Worship just angers you. Nothing is speaking to you.

Join the crowd. This has been going on for centuries. You can look all through Scripture and find references to people who felt abandoned by God. Job is feeling that in this passage. He feels God has turned His back on Him. He doesn't know why. All hope seems to be gone.

TEACHING MOMENT

I guarantee you that your children are going to get down in the dumps like Job at some point. They are going to feel all alone. Don't let them stay there.

Just as Job discovered just a little bit later, God hasn't moved. He is still present. He is still watching. Our children need that assurance that He is there.

Don't shame your children out of the doldrums, though. Let them seek God in the midst of their pain. You can't seek God for them. They have to do that for themselves. But you can share your own struggles with them so they will know they are not "less spiritual" than others. Be there when they need you, but let them hear God.

How about you? Are you in one of those times yourself? Are you feeling like Job? Have you been crying out to seemingly deaf ears? Do not stop crying out! God is there! He is taking you to a point where He wants you—the perfect point. Because everything God does is perfect. He is making you more like Him with every blow of the chisel. He is knocking off imperfections. He is making you something in which others can see Him.

God, work on me! Complete me! I know Your end product will perfect.

DECEMBER 6

A FISH STORY

Jonah 1–4

BEST VERSE: 3:5

Then the people of Nineveh believed in God; and they called a fast and put on sackcloth from the greatest to the least of them.

Can you just picture Jonah? He ran from God after being told to go to Nineveh. He got thrown overboard from a sinking ship (then miraculously survived afterwards), got swallowed by a large fish, spent three days in the belly of that fish, got vomited up on shore, went to Nineveh, preached one of the shortest repentance messages ever; the whole city repents; he gets mad, runs away to "die," sits under a vine; it dies, and then God speaks to him. Wow! He could have saved himself a whole lot of trouble if he had just gone the first time God told him to go.

But aren't we just the same? How many times have we "run" from God? How many times has He told us to do something, and we decide to ignore it or do the exact opposite? How many of you would like to spend three days inside a fish?

TEACHING MOMENT

Our children are going to disobey us. Sometimes they will outright rebel. What a perfect story to read to them when they are rebelling. Do you think Jonah ever thought he would repent inside a fish's stomach? I bet not. Our children might not like what God uses to get their attention. But they have got to decide to obey. You can't obey for them.

Jonah had no idea how God would one day use the Assyrians, which included Nineveh, to judge the nation of Israel. And Jonah had no idea at the time how their knowledge of a forgiving God would shape how they treated Israel. You see, our children need to know that God sees the whole picture, not just the immediate. He sees years, decades, even centuries down the road.

What are you running from? What has God asked you to do for Him? Why are you running to Tarshish instead of Nineveh? Stop and turn around. It is so much easier doing it His way!

Father, remind me when I start to run from You that You can appoint a fish to get my attention. Remind me of Your determination to steer me in the right path.

DECEMBER 7

RIGHT PLACE, RIGHT TIME

Esther 4

BEST VERSE: 14B

And who knows whether you have not attained royalty for such a time as this?

Mordecai needs Esther to respond to Haman's threat against all the Jews by going to her husband, the king, without being summoned. This could result in her death, but Mordecai says, "And who knows whether you have not attained royalty for such a time as this?" She was in the right place at the right time to intercede for her people.

Have you ever been in the right place at the right time? I mean, have you ever had the opportunity to do something meaningful at just the moment you were somewhere? You had not planned it. It just happened. We need to be ready at all times to respond when given the opportunity.

TEACHING MOMENT

How do we prepare our children to be ready at all times? How do we help them know when God wants to use them "for such a time as this"? That's done by preparing them every day. Each and every day we teach them to look for opportunities of service. That might be helping someone pick up something they have dropped on the floor. That might mean comforting someone who is upset. That might mean helping Mom prepare dinner. There are all kinds of ways to be of service.

Children love to help. Our challenge is to find the tasks that fit their abilities and their giftedness. Not every child wants to cook. Not every child can do yard work. But every child has some desires along with abilities to serve. We just have to figure that out, with the Lord's help.

Watch them closely, and the Lord will reveal to you how to lead them in areas of service. They may never have to go before a king to plead for their people (I certainly hope not), but they may be given an opportunity to impact many lives for Christ.

Lord, help me to prepare my children for the opportunities they will have in the future to serve. Just as I prepare them for other life challenges, I need to prepare them to witness and serve. Forgive me for not being more intentional about that.

DECEMBER 8

DEFIANT

Job 21

BEST VERSE: 14

They say to God, "Depart from us! We do not even desire the knowledge of Your ways."

These words of Job in chapter 21 regarding the wicked could have been written today. People all around us are saying the exact same thing, only more harshly. They want no part of God. They even deny His existence. They mock those who do believe and call us foolish. Oh, but the knowledge of God will one day be very clear to them.

Job, just like us, knew the wicked would face their own judgment one day. But he also saw them "getting by" with their wicked ways and even flourishing here on earth. That is hard to stomach, especially if you, a believer, are going through a trial. God's ways are not our ways. That is what we have to hold on to.

TEACHING MOMENT

Children struggle with this too. They will question why the bully in the classroom gets his or her way. They will wonder why they are not rewarded for doing the right thing. That is a hard thing to explain to children, especially when they are very young. The only good way is to take them to the Word.

Job's story, in its entirety, explains this clearly. It would be worth reading to your children when they are going through this. Take a few nights and read the entire book. Find an easy-to-understand translation so they will understand it, but read it to the end. Then they will see how God comes through—every time.

Are you questioning God right now? Are you looking around at lost people you know who are getting wealthy and wondering why God won't bless you? Don't let your eyes linger on worldly things. Remember your treasures are not like the world's. Your treasure is in heaven where one day you will reap your rewards. Don't live for now. Live for then.

Father, You bless me in ways I never know. Open my eyes to see all You are doing in and around me. Let me be a blessing to someone else who is suffering for Your name.

DECEMBER 9

THE ROCK

Isaiah 26

BEST VERSE: 4

Trust in the LORD forever, for in God the Lord, we have an everlasting Rock.

Don't you just love this verse? Our God rocks! I mean, our God is a Rock. But He does, and He is. That is just who He is. He is firm and unmovable. He gives us a solid foundation on which to stand. He gives us a place on which we can build our life without fear of it crumbling.

I live in Chattanooga, Tennessee. One of the best things about this area is the hiking that is available. I wish I took more advantage of the opportunities, but they are there. There are rock outcroppings all around us. Some are famous, like Point Park on Lookout Mountain. Others are not so well-known. But they all have one thing in common: they have been there a long time. Barring some huge natural disaster, they aren't going anywhere.

TEACHING MOMENT

Parents, this is a fun verse to teach your little children. Find an area near you with exposed rock. If you live somewhere where it is not available, find a picture of exposed rock to show them. Explain how the hardness of the rock gives a solid base on which to stand. Explain how, even though it is heavy and practically impossible to move, it doesn't compare to God.

God is that Rock that will not be moved. There is no force in heaven or on earth that can change who He is. He is permanent, foundational, solid and firm. He will always be there. They can always depend on Him. They can place everything they have on Him, and it will not fall. He's got it. He's got them.

Are you placing your feet on The Rock? Or are you standing in quicksand? Do you feel your feet moving and sliding? I don't like that feeling. I want to feel secure. I want my feet to stand on solid ground. I want The Rock beneath me. Trust Him to be your Rock of Ages.

O Lord, You are my Rock. You are my sure foundation. Help me when I doubt. Show me Your permanence and faithfulness. Thank You, Lord.

DECEMBER 10

LOYALTY

1 Chronicles 11

BEST VERSE: 19

And he said, "Be it far from me before my God that I should do this. Shall I drink the blood of these men who went at the risk of their lives? For at the risk of their lives they brought it." Therefore he would not drink it. These things the three mighty men did.

This story is one of the most intriguing ones to me in all the Old Testament. David and his men were fighting the Philistines, and David gets a craving—for water. Not just any water either. He was craving water from the well at Bethlehem, which was in Philistine control. Three of his mighty men go down, fight their way to the well, and bring back water for their king. As Adam Sandler says in the movie The Waterboy, "That must be some fine H2O."

David is so moved he offers it as a sacrifice to God and pours it out. It seems David was almost embarrassed that these men had overheard his selfish craving and sought to meet it. He is humbled at their loyalty and willingness to sacrifice for him.

TEACHING MOMENT

Loyalty and sacrifice are hard to teach to children. They can only learn that by observing others. Being loyal to friends or family is so important, though. We need to do all we can to help them learn how to do that. Sacrificing for others is even harder to teach. Children are naturally selfish (well, at least most of them). Just try to get a two-year-old to share their toys with someone.

But loyalty and sacrifice are admirable traits in anyone. When children learn to be loyal and to sacrifice their desires for the benefit of others, they will have learned true maturity. Selfishness and maturity are complete opposites. You cannot be mature and demand your own way. You cannot be mature and be disloyal.

How are you doing with these two maturity traits? To whom are you loyal? For whom are you willing to sacrifice? Think about those questions for just a minute. Write down a list of five people you think of. Now pray for each of them. Ask the Lord to allow you to show your loyalty this week. Ask the Lord to show you how you could sacrifice something you desire for their benefit.

Father, You sacrificed the greatest gift for me—one I could never repay. I owe You everything. Help me today to show You my loyalty and willingness to sacrifice for You and others.

DECEMBER 11

IN GOD'S HANDS

Nehemiah 6

BEST VERSE: 14

Remember, O my God, Tobiah and Sanballat according to these works of theirs, and also Noadiah the prophetess and the rest of the prophets who were trying to frighten me.

Wow! You really need to read all of chapters 5 and 6 of Nehemiah. Today's verse is just a snippet (don't you love that word?) of what Nehemiah was up against. Tobiah and Sanballat, especially, were out to get him. They did not want to see the wall rebuilt around Jerusalem. They were lying about Nehemiah, threatening him and trying to deceive him. They even bribed a prophet to give him false messages from God.

You see, it wasn't about what Nehemiah was doing. It was about for whom he was doing it. Nehemiah was focused on pleasing God, and darkness can't stand that. As governor of Judah with the backing of Artaxerxes, he could have had them arrested or killed. But he left them in God's hands.

TEACHING MOMENT

This is a wonderful truth for our children to learn. Let God handle your enemies. Your child's job is to please the Master. If they are doing that, He will handle their adversaries. Now, He may not handle them in the way they would, but He will handle them when He is ready. Remember, they are operating out of darkness. Our children need to realize that. What do lost sinners do? They sin. We should expect no less.

Perhaps, though, our submission to God may draw them to Him. You just never know. When your little Johnny or Susie is facing a bully, remind them to love that bully. Why? Because Jesus does. Will that bully accept that? Probably not at first. Pray with your child about that bully. Have them mention the bully by name in their bedtime prayers. Let the bully be the focus of intentional prayer. But let God handle consequences.

Father and Righteous Judge, You are more than capable of handling my enemies. Help me to get out of the way and let You work in their lives like You did in mine. I was once Your enemy, but you loved me toward You.

DECEMBER 12

COMFORT

2 Corinthians 1

BEST VERSES: 3–4

Blessed be the God and Father of our Lord Jesus Christ, the Father of mercies and God of all comfort,—who comforts us in all our affliction so that we will be able to comfort those who are in any affliction with the comfort with which we ourselves are comforted by God.

When I think of comfort, I think of my recliner. We bought a new one a couple of years ago after my old one gave up the ghost. I had worn it out. So, it was time for a new one. This time we bought one of those power recliners with the button on the side. All I have to do is push that button to recline or to sit up. That's what I call comfort.

But that is not what the Lord calls comfort. This verse teaches us that we go through afflictions and hard times so that He can comfort us, and, in turn, we can use that experience to comfort others who are going through the same thing. That's God's idea of comfort—comforting others, not ourselves.

TEACHING MOMENT

I am amazed at how our children do this when they are very young. Have you ever watched your child, when they were a toddler or preschooler, comfort someone who was upset? It may have been you. Perhaps you were crying about something sad, and they crawled up in your lap and said, "Don't cry Mommy. I love you." That kind of comforting is natural at that age.

As they grow older and face some difficult times, they will have the opportunity to be comforted themselves, by you and the Lord. We need to show them the importance of sharing that comfort with others. Don't let them lose that comforting ability. The world makes us hard, if we let it. We have to stay tenderhearted and usable of the Lord. Let the Lord use you as His comfort giver. Teach your children to do the same.

The next time you or your child go through a hard time, make a list of the ways the Lord has comforted you in the midst of it. Then when you see that other person going through the same thing, you can share what the Lord did for you and can do for them.

Father, I am grateful You comfort me. Show me how to comfort others with Your comfort. There are days I need to comfort others and days I am the one to be comforted.

DECEMBER 13

DRAWING WATER

Isaiah 12

BEST VERSE: 3

Therefore you will joyously draw water from the springs of salvation.

You have to admit that this is a beautiful verse. The picture of bringing up water from cool, refreshing springs to quench your thirst is just incredible. And it says you will do it joyously, not laboriously. Some people would look at the chore of drawing water as just too hard, even though they would die of thirst without it.

When you know the fulfillment of drinking that water once you get it, you don't hesitate. It's the same in our Christian walk. When we understand that the joy of obedience is waiting, we joyously put our hands to work for the kingdom. We joyously obey the Master.

TEACHING MOMENT

Have you ever given your son or daughter a chore to do with the promise of a reward at the end? Isn't it amazing how hard they will work for that? Now it is important to reward them if you say you are going to. That would be mean if you didn't. God has promised us joy in obedience. Why wouldn't we obey?

Explain that to your child the next time you give them reward for obedience for that chore. As we teach them this lesson, there will come a day when they will obey to give you joy. That's what God is looking for. He wants to see us willingly obey Him, and when we do, He is blessed.

Do you need to obey today? Of course! Do it knowing that you bring your Father joy. Do it knowing that He will look down upon you and say, "Well done, my good and faithful servant." Oh, to hear those words.

Lord, I want to obey. I want to bring You joy. I want to see You delighted in my service to You.

DECEMBER 14

ARGUING WITH GOD

Job 40

BEST VERSE: 2

Will the faultfinder contend with the Almighty? Let him who reproves God answer it.

Have you ever argued with God over something? I have! Now, I don't mean I verbally assaulted Him, but I have argued in my spirit over something I know He has directed me to do. My flesh is strong, and it desires its own way. So, when God directs me through His Word or in prayer to do something His way, well, my flesh just wants to rebel.

How fruitless! How ridiculous! And here we see the Lord God speaking to Job and telling him the same thing. "You think you know better, Job? Okay, let's see what you can do." You really need to read chapters 39–40 in their entirety to see the full conversation. I can totally relate to my own "talks" with God about what I think is a better way.

TEACHING MOMENT

How about your children? Has little Susie ever been determined to show you that she knows best? Has Johnny ever told you that he doesn't need your advice anymore? Our children will do that. They will insist on trying something their way, when we know that it won't work or isn't the best way. If it's not dangerous, let them do it their way. Sometimes failure is the best teacher.

Then when you are helping them pick up the pieces, you can share Job's story with them. You can tell them about a righteous man who thought he understood God. You can read to them how he had no clue about the power and majesty of a holy God. We don't either. We may think we do, but our grandest thoughts come way short of the full picture of who God really is.

Okay, what are you arguing with God about right now? Don't tell me you aren't. We all do it. Do you question His sovereignty? Do you question His right over your life? Do you not believe His Word? What is it that is causing you to get in God's face?

God, I want to be honest with You. Show me the truth. Help me to listen and allow You to teach.

JUST A CHILD

2 Kings 11

BEST VERSE: 21
Jehoash was seven years old when he became king.

Could you imagine your child becoming President at age 7? Probably not! But Jehoash was crowned king at age 7 after hiding for 6 years in the temple from the Queen Mother who had killed all the other sons. The priest Jehoiada was the one who cared for him and prepared him to be one of the great kings of Judah.

I have to wonder if all those years in the house of the Lord helped prepare him to lead. He was surrounded by the things of the Lord and probably learned to read by reading the scriptures. Hmmm, maybe his environment did help prepare him.

TEACHING MOMENT

So, I have to ask. Are you "surrounding" your child with the things of the Lord? Do they hear the Word of the Lord daily? Do they hear you praying for them and others? Is your home a "temple of the Lord"?

There is no better way to raise our children than to submerse them in His Word. I don't mean to imply they can't have other influences, but God's Word is the best source. If you aren't teaching your children the Word, who will? You can't rely on pastors or Sunday school teachers. It is your job!

Now, before you say, "I'm not qualified," remember it is the Lord who will give you the wisdom you need. But you have to ask Him. He wants to see you raising your children (actually, His children He has loaned to you) to know Him and honor Him.

Let me encourage you today to take the time to evaluate how you are training your children. They may not grow up to be President, but they will grow up. Don't you want them to carry the torch of the Lord into whatever career God leads them? God can use them to change their community and family.

O Lord God, You have all the wisdom I need to teach my children. Give me the discipline to do that daily. And the results are Yours.

BEST INTENTIONS

Job 33

BEST VERSES: 31–33

Pay attention, O Job, listen to me; keep silent, and let me speak. Then if you have anything to say, answer me; speak, for I desire to justify you. If not, listen to me; keep silent, and I will teach you wisdom.'"

Elihu probably meant well. I don't know. But sometimes you just need to keep silent and love on the person. He didn't know what was really going on with Job. He supposed, like the other friends, that Job was being punished by God for sin. He could not have known that God was allowing this in Job's life for a purpose.

Isn't is funny how we always see the sin in others, but not in ourselves? We can easily see their faults and failures and walk right over our own. I have to imagine that Elihu was no perfect angel. I am sure he had his own sins which needed confessing.

TEACHING MOMENT

Learning to keep our mouths shut is not easy. As parents, we need to teach our children the skill of listening. I have counseled many people by just listening. I don't say a lot. Our children need to learn to listen fully before commenting. When they have a friend who needs advice, encourage them to listen first.

We should teach them to also pray for their friends. Job needed that. But his friends didn't do that. Teach your children to pray right when someone asks them to. Don't put it off. Pray while you are with them. That will bless them.

Who do you need to go to today to lend a listening ear? Don't make it about you. Don't go with an agenda to "help" them. Simply go as a friend who loves them and wants to be there for them. If you have to use words, use His.

O God, I am so guilty of judging others. Help me to see them through Your eyes. Forgive me of my judgmental attitude.

THE WORK BEGINS

2 Chronicles 3

BEST VERSE: 1

Then Solomon began to build the house of the LORD in Jerusalem on Mount Moriah, where the LORD had appeared to his father David, at the place that David had prepared on the threshing floor of Ornan the Jebusite.

As directed by God through his father David, Solomon began the work on the temple. I bet he didn't know when he started this project that it would be 20 years until it was completed. I can't think of anything I have done consistently for 20 years. That's a long time. But Solomon stuck with it. Why?

I believe we can find two reasons. One, he wanted to honor his God. Every aspect of this construction project had one thing in mind. He wanted to build a "house" worthy of his God. Two, he wanted to honor his father. David had been a great king and father and deserved this obedience.

TEACHING MOMENT

"So, Carl, what do we teach our children or learn ourselves from this verse?" I'm glad you asked that. Commitment! Sticking to something! Too many people today stop trying. Too many people today give in when it gets hard. Your children need to learn to stick with what they started. They need to see things through.

I remember one year the team motto for my favorite football team was "Finish the Drill!" That was their goal for the year. Finish what they started. Finish what they came to do. Don't stop when the going gets tough. Hang on.

Have you been tempted lately to throw in the towel? Have you wanted to just stop? Don't! Go back to the one who gave you your marching orders. Our heavenly Father will give you the strength and determination to continue. Look to Him for the motivation you need to carry on.

Father, on the days I want to quit, don't let me. Remind me of my calling to follow You wherever You lead. When I face an obstacle, remind me You allowed it to make me better.

DECEMBER 18

GUARD YOUR WORDS

1 Kings 22

BEST VERSE: 14

But Micaiah said, "As the LORD lives, what the Lord says to me, that I shall speak."

As a pastor, when I preach I have to be so careful to speak only what the Lord would have me to say. As I prepare my message, I pray that the Lord will give me the words to say. I don't want to espouse my words. I only want His. Micaiah had been asked by the other prophets to agree with them and speak similar words. But he knew he had to be true to the Lord and speak only what the Lord said, no matter the consequence.

Have you had that challenge? The crowd is all saying one thing, but you know in your heart that the Lord is telling you to say something totally opposite. What do you do? Do you agree to save face, or do you stand for truth? That's hard. It may cost you.

TEACHING MOMENT

Your children are going to face those moments. It may be in school when a teacher or professor wants them to regurgitate some off-the-wall philosophy in a paper. If they do, they get the A. If they don't, they may get an F. Now that is tough. What should they do?

As a parent, you must encourage them to stand for what is right, no matter the cost. You need to be there to support them when they feel like the world is against them. Jesus warns us that the world will turn against us if we stand with Him.

What will you do? Will you stand, or will you fold under pressure? Will you speak the truth or agree silently with the lies? God will give us these challenges to test us and build us. Don't see these times as God deserting you. Instead, thank Him for trusting you to make the right decision.

Father, You are a holy God who deserves our praise. Give me the strength and courage to stand, even if I am the only one, for truth. I know you will defend me. Thank You, Lord.

NOT ENOUGH

2 Kings 10

BEST VERSE: 31

But Jehu was not careful to walk in the law of the LORD, the God of Israel, with all his heart; he did not depart from the sins of Jeroboam, which he made Israel sin.

Jehu was a bloody king. He slew the seventy sons of Ahab and forty-two others who were going to visit them. He slew all the worshipers of Baal and their priests. But . . . as you see from today's verse, he "was not careful to walk in the law of the Lord, the God of Israel, with all his heart; he did not depart from the sins of Jeroboam, which he made Israel sin." A little good is not good enough.

Now, hear me out. Too many of us think we can just go to church and throw a few dollars in the plate. We believe if we volunteer once a year for VBS or go on a mission trip, then all is well with the Lord. The Lord demands us to be sold out completely. He doesn't want half-hearted followers. He requires us to surrender completely and abandon all other things in life that compete with Him.

TEACHING MOMENT

Teaching our children to "sell out" for Jesus isn't hard. We have to show them. We have to sacrifice our wants and desires for His. Then He will allow them to model our behavior. When our children see us "selling out" they will know what it looks like and what it costs.

How do children sell out? What do they have to give up? How about the kids they hang out with? How about the music they listen to or the video games they play? How about choosing a quiet time over phone time? No matter your age, there are things you can sacrifice.

Mom and Dad, are you doing some good for God, or are you sold out? Some good isn't enough. God wants you to set the example for your family and abandon all for Him. Will you?

O God of the ages, will you help me abandon myself to You? I want to lead the way in doing all I can for You and Your kingdom. I don't want things of this world to bog me down.

FRESH MEAT

1 Chronicles 14

BEST VERSE: 8

When the Philistines heard that David had been anointed king over all Israel, all the Philistines went up in search of David; and David heard of it and went out against them.

I ministered over thirty years in the Child Welfare field serving in various children's homes around the southeastern United States. One thing was common in every situation. When a new houseparent was hired to live and work with the children, they would test them severely. It was almost like throwing fresh meat to hungry wolves. They pounced on that new staff person to test their mettle.

The Philistines thought now that Saul was dead that they would have easy pickings with David. Sure, they had heard stories and experienced David's triumphs in the past, but perhaps right now while he was just establishing his reign, he was vulnerable. They invaded Israel, much to their regret later.

TEACHING MOMENT

It seems the enemy strikes us more often when things are good than when they are bad. Your children need to be taught to be ever mindful of the enemy's schemes. When they get comfortable, watch out. The Word says that the devil is always prowling around looking whom he may devour. He knows we can get complacent when everything seems to be going our way. Remind your children of that.

Also, like the Philistines were with David, the enemy cannot stand to see us successful. The enemy wants to tear down your children, especially during their younger days of walking with the Lord. If the devil can put doubts in their minds now, those doubts may just remain for a lifetime. Don't let that happen. Prepare them to stay vigilant and alert to the enemy.

Are you watchful? Are you staying firmly rooted in His Word to ward off the schemes of the devil? I don't mean you have to see a demon behind every bush, but be prepared spiritually for the battle. And when the devil does strike, and he will, call on Jesus. He defeats him with one word. Hallelujah!

Mighty God, I know I can depend on You to defend me in my weakest hour. Help me be prepared at all times and to always call on You first to defeat my enemies.

DECEMBER 21

OUR REWARD

Psalms 57–58

BEST VERSE: 58:11

And men will say, "Surely there is a reward for the righteous; surely there is a God who judges on earth!"

Psalm 58 spends ten verses talking about how God will judge the unrighteous, how He will defend His people. And then in verse 11, the last verse of the chapter, we have today's verse. The end result of God's actions is this. Men will know there is a God.

I was meditating on that verse and realized it is the same today. People only recognize God because of His actions in this world in the lives of His saints. When God works in our lives, people can see it. We must be careful to give Him all the praise. We must point others to Him when they want to give us recognition or glory.

TEACHING MOMENT

When you see the Lord working in the lives of your children, make sure you tell them. As they grow in their faith, they will have ample opportunities to thank the Lord. They will have chance after chance to tell others, "This is all because of Jesus."

It is so important that they do that. We never want them to think they have accomplished anything without the Lord. It is He who gives them the wisdom and strength to succeed. He is the one who directs them. He is the one who walks with them through life. When we are quick to give Him credit, He is blessed.

Is that you? Do you point others to Him when they want to congratulate you? I pray that you will be a spokesman for Christ today. I pray you will tell others that it is Christ in you. It is nothing about you. Boast in Him.

Lord, I am nothing without You. I can only succeed because of You. I praise You for working in and through my life.

JUDGMENT WILL COME

1 Kings 2

BEST VERSE: 46C

"Thus the kingdom was established in the hands of Solomon."

You really should read the entire chapter of 1 Kings 2. David has died, and now Solomon is king. But before David dies, he gives Solomon some instructions concerning two individuals (Joab and Shimei) who seemingly had escaped the consequences from earlier rebellions and sin. I bet these two guys thought, "Whew, that was close. David's dead, so we are home free." Nope! Read the chapter to see the whole story.

We are the same way, aren't we? We think if we can hide our sin so that no one knows about it, we can escape the consequences. We may very well escape any visible consequence here in this life, but unconfessed sin has its consequences in eternity. We will answer for every deed we do here on this earth.

TEACHING MOMENT

The next time you discipline your child for disobeying you, share this chapter with them. Now, Joab and Shimei both lost their lives for their sins. Don't scare your kids to death. But they should know that the discipline they are receiving is a result of a rebellious spirit, which is sin. Sin has consequences.

I see too many parents today who allow their children to talk hatefully to them and others. I see parents who are "afraid" to correct their children for fear of "stifling their spirit." Hogwash! God demands that we, as parents, correct and discipline our children. The family is a model of our relationship with our heavenly Father, who demands obedience.

Maybe you are hiding a sin right now. Are you? Do you have an unconfessed sin that you need to make right with the Lord? Do it now. Bow before Him and ask for forgiveness. Allow Him to wash away that sin in your life. There may be consequences for your sin. Accept them as a purifying fire to make you more like Him.

Father, forgive me of sinning against You. Cleanse me of my wrongdoing. Set my feet back on the path of righteousness and use me to advance Your kingdom.

TOO BIG FOR HIS BRITCHES

Isaiah 10

BEST VERSE: 12

So it will be that when the LORD has completed all His work on Mount Zion and on Jerusalem, He will say, "I will punish the fruit of the arrogant heart of the king of Assyria and the pomp of his haughtiness."

This is the time of the year when I can get too big for my britches, but it has nothing to do with haughtiness. It has to do with too many Christmas parties. But boy, I just love those desserts.

Seriously, Isaiah is telling the nation that God has not forgotten about Assyria. His instrument of judgment has become proud. The king thinks he has done all of this on his strength alone. God is about to show him who is boss.

Listen close. We are exactly the same. We think when we have a little success that we have achieved something. We think our works really matter. We are only prosperous and successful because of Him. There is nothing that we can do on our own. Even the wicked among us are only successful because the Lord allows it. Why He does I don't understand, but He is God and that's His business.

TEACHING MOMENT

How do we teach our children this key life principle? How do we show them the importance of giving all credit to God? They have to hear us doing it, first of all. Then we have to point it out to them each and every time they have a victory.

The next time your little Susie or Johnny brings home an "A" on that test, take a moment and thank the Lord for the abilities God has given them to study and learn their schoolwork. The next time Gertrude gets that trophy in gymnastics, give God praise for giving her the athletic ability to do all those jumps and twists. You get the picture.

What has God blessed you with that you have acknowledged Him for? What achievement in your life has been accomplished for which you took all the credit? Confess that as haughtiness. Confess that as sin. Give God all the praise for working in and through you.

O Lord, I know that all I am is because of You. But Lord, remind me to point others to You when they congratulate me. Remind me to give You all the praise.

DECEMBER 24

THE BEST DEFENSE

Isaiah 25

BEST VERSE: 4A

For You have been a defense for the helpless, a defense for the needy in his distress, a refuge from the storm, a shade from the heat.

When I hear the word "defense" my mind automatically goes to football. Sorry, but I just can't help myself. I played high school football and loved playing linebacker. The linebacker normally has the responsibility to be the "quarterback" of the defense. He is watching the "attack" of the offense and directs his defense to move this way or that to prepare for the next play.

But the verse here isn't talking about us doing anything. It is referring to God as our defense. He is our defense when we are helpless and needy. He is our refuge in the storm and our shade in the heat. What a beautiful portrayal of God for us. God is the "linebacker" who is always guarding against the onslaught of the evil one. He knows his playbook and always has the defensive move to block his attacks. But we have to listen to Him.

TEACHING MOMENT

Your children are going to face the enemy sooner or later, probably sooner. They need to know to trust the Lord as He directs them. They need to know that He always knows the best play to run. They need to know to do exactly what He says, when He says. If they don't, they run the risk of letting the enemy score one on them.

Okay, enough with the football analogies, right? But isn't it comforting to know that the Lord is defending us day and night? We only have to surrender and let Him do it. If we stay under the umbrella of His protection by submitting to His will, He's got us covered, no matter what. I don't know about you, but I would prefer to let Him handle the adversary. The Lord will always win!

I know I must be alert, Lord, and guard against the enemy's attacks. But it is so comforting to know You are there. Let my children learn that early in life.

DECEMBER 25

BLESSINGS THROUGH OBEDIENCE

2 Chronicles 17

BEST VERSES: 3–4

The Lord was with Jehoshaphat because he followed the example of his father David's earlier days and did not seek the Baals, but sought the God of his father, followed His commandments, and did not act as Israel did.

Jehoshaphat had watched his father, Asa, follow the Lord, but in his latter days turn away. Jehoshaphat, however, determined himself to follow "the example of his father David." He obviously knew of David's failures and triumphs. He had read of the blessings God bestowed on David and the other kings who chose to follow the Lord. He made the wise choice.

TEACHING MOMENT

Teaching our children to obey is always a struggle. Recently, during our Children's church, I asked the children if they liked obeying. Shockingly, most of them raised their hand. I actually took a picture and posted it on the Children's Ministry Facebook page for the parents to see.

What surprised me was I really expected most of them to not raise their hand. I don't like to obey. My flesh likes to rebel. What I do like, however, is the benefits of obeying. Probably most of those kids did too. They liked obeying because it brought praise from mom or dad. It might even bring a treat. But usually obedience is rewarded, sooner or later.

Why do you obey? Is it simply to please the Father? Or is it to get something from Him? Be honest! Do you obey to escape punishment? Do you obey out of love or fear?

We want our children to obey out of love, don't we? Then we too should be obeying our heavenly Father out of love for Him. Remember, modeling behavior is better than just talking about it. Why don't you look for a way this week to obey the Father out of love? But make sure your kids see you obeying. They need to see you model the behavior you want from them. And then the next time they obey out of love, bless them.

Father, I obey because I love You. Forgive me when I am disobedient. I really don't want to be disobedient, and I know Your Spirit within me can guard my heart against it. Help me surrender daily.

DECEMBER 26

JUST LOOK AROUND YOU

Job 12

BEST VERSES: 7–8

But now ask the beasts, and let them teach you; and the birds of the heavens, and let them tell you. Or speak to the earth, and let it teach you; and let the fish of the sea declare to you.

I have had the privilege to travel to some pretty incredible places. When I see nature in all its beauty, I can't help but wonder how someone cannot believe in God. A couple of years ago I got to see thousands and thousands of pink flamingos feeding, wading, and flying at a lake in Kenya. The sight was beyond description. God's creation at work.

Job is telling his "friend" here that even the beast, birds, fish, and the earth teach us about the Lord. He didn't need his friend to try to enlighten him about Jehovah. He could simply look around and see Him. That should be true for all of us.

TEACHING MOMENT

Kids love nature, at least most do. Take a nature hike with your kids and make a list of all the creatures you see. List the bugs, birds and animals. List the trees and flowers. And then when you get home, look them up on your computer. Talk about them. And then take your kids to these verses. Ask them how these things they just saw point to God.

I bet you will get some pretty amazing answers. God made everything to point to Him in some way. Everything He created gives Him pleasure. After all, He said "it was good."

Have you stopped lately to enjoy God's creation? Take a break today and do that. Enjoy nature. Enjoy the flowers and trees. Enjoy the birds and squirrels. Enjoy God.

Thank You, Master Creator, for your magnificent creation. I marvel at Your detail of each creature. Let my eyes be open to all that is around me.

GOD CALLING

Isaiah 42

BEST VERSE: 6

I am the LORD, I have called You in righteousness, I will also hold You by the hand and watch over You, and I will appoint You as a covenant to the people, as a light to the nations.

Don't you just love this verse? I mean, come on, look at it. God calls you. He holds your hand. He watches over you. He appoints you as a covenant to the people and sends you as a light to the nations. Wow!

But we have to respond to the call. We have to allow Him to take our hand. Our usefulness to God depends on our surrender to Him. Can you imagine how God can use you if you will just let Him? It's God who is using you. It's not just your boss or a friend. It's the God of the universe.

TEACHING MOMENT

I bet you hold your child's hand when you cross a street. I bet you watch over your child when they are at the park. And I bet you expect your child to answer you when you call his or her name. Am I right? Sure I am. The next time you do one of these things, reflect on this verse and share it with your child.

They, too, can be a light to the nations. But guess what? We have to be a part of lighting that flame. We have to expose them to the one who lights them. We have to be the one who takes their hand and leads them to Him. God will do the rest.

Are you answering God's call? Are you taking His hand? Listen, my friends. God wants to use you in His master plan. But He won't force you to be a part of it. Let Him use you today.

Take my hand, Lord. Watch over me, Lord. Use me, Lord, to accomplish Your will.

DECEMBER 28

NOT A PEEP

Isaiah 36

BEST VERSE: 21

But they were silent and answered him not a word; for the king's commandment was, "Do not answer him."

I can still hear my mom say those words to me. "Carl William!" (You knew you were in trouble when the middle name was used.) "I don't want to hear one peep out of you!" You see, I had the tendency to talk a lot. Still do, especially in the mornings.

But there comes a time when you just need to keep your mouth shut. This was one of those times in Judah. The king of Assyria had invaded the land and was now at the gates of Jerusalem. Hezekiah had told the people to not respond to their taunts and jeers. He commanded them not to talk to the Assyrians who were outside their gates. Why? To keep them loyal? Perhaps. But it was probably to keep them focused on their true deliverer, Jehovah.

TEACHING MOMENT

I bet you have never told your children to keep quiet. Right? Every parent, at some point, has heard enough. They don't want to hear a word. We need to teach our children when it is appropriate to talk. Talking during the worship service while others are speaking is not okay. Talking back to adults is not okay. But talking to our Savior . . . well . . . that is perfectly okay.

I bet the people of Jerusalem were talking to God as they saw the myriad of Assyrian soldiers outside their city gates. Our children need to talk to God every day. They need to be taught how to pray. They need to know He is always listening. They need to know that He can still defeat our enemies. We just need to come to Him and talk to Him.

Are you talking to God today, or are you keeping your mouth shut? Are you so busy talking to others about everything that you have failed to talk to the one who can answer? Take a moment today to shut your mouth and listen. Let the Lord do the talking in your life. Let Him speak to you today.

Lord, I am listening . . .

DECEMBER 29

A PERFECT HEART

2 Chronicles 15

BEST VERSE: 17B

. . . nevertheless Asa's heart was blameless all his days.

Asa was the third king of Judah after the divided nation. He was a good king who even removed his mother from a position of power due to her blasphemous deeds. That took a pure heart and one solely dedicated to God. In fact, the Hebrew word here for blameless can mean whole or perfect.

I don't know about you, but I can't say my heart is perfect. Too often my heart is divided. I let my emotions get in the way. I get too passionate about what I want rather than what God wants. Not Asa! He was completely dedicated to the Lord; therefore, the Lord blessed his reign.

TEACHING MOMENT

We don't teach our children much about Asa. Let me encourage you to take a few days and read each story about him to your children. They need to see how he relied on God with his pure, blameless heart. They need to see how he dedicated his reign to God. They need to see how he was made a great king only because he served a great God.

We parents spend way too much time praising our children's actions and gifts. Some of you are thinking, Now wait a minute, Carl. Aren't we supposed to do that? To a point, yes. But so many parents are so child-focused they forget to be God-focused for the sake of their children. We should always be pointing our children toward the perfect model for them—Jesus.

I want to be more like Him. Don't you? I want to be like Asa when he faced the Ethiopian army of one million. He didn't panic. He simply turned to the Lord and said, "God, this is your fight." Wow! A blameless heart. A perfect heart. A whole heart.

God give me a heart of faith like Asa had. He relied on You and served only You. Thank You for role models like Asa for me and my family.

DON'T GET CARRIED AWAY

1 Chronicles 8

BEST VERSE: 6

These are the sons of Ehud: these are the heads of fathers' households of the inhabitants of Geba, and they carried them into exile to Manahath.

In the context of this passage it means that the people of Israel were literally taken into a foreign land after their defeat. Due to their disobedience and rebellion against God, they were punished for turning their backs on their one true love, Jehovah God.

Nowadays, "being carried away" can have a whole different meaning. It can mean getting too "crazy" about something. Have you ever been "carried away" by an obsession about anything? I could easily get carried away with hunting or fishing. I love being outdoors. Hmmm, maybe the meaning isn't that far off from the original.

TEACHING MOMENT

Children can easily get obsessed about dolls or guns or video games. As parents, we have to monitor these "obsessions" and make sure they are not getting "carried away" and wind up deserting their love for the Lord. It is so easy to do. May I recommend a few things?

Require equal amounts of time reading as gaming. Read God's Word to them daily as a reminder of the importance of spending time in it. Help them develop a regular, consistent quiet time. This is not something that comes naturally. It has to be modeled and taught.

And the best way for them to not be carried away with personal interests over the interest of God is for you to do the same. Don't let your hobbies and interests take more time than they should. If you don't have time to pray and read His Word, you don't have time to golf, fish, play tennis, or anything else.

Father, forgive me for being carried away at times by my own selfish desires. Help me focus more on you. Let me be accused of being carried away about You.

DECEMBER 31

WHERE'S THE EXIT?

1 Corinthians 10

BEST VERSE: 13

No temptation has overtaken you but such as is common to man; and God is faithful, who will not allow you to be tempted beyond what you are able, but with the temptation will provide the way of escape also, so that you will be able to endure it.

Whenever I go somewhere unfamiliar, I always look for the exits. I don't want to be caught unaware if something bad were to happen. That may sound like I am paranoid. I call it being prepared. I also have learned through my travels to never enter a location that appears dangerous. It just doesn't make sense to knowingly put myself in harm's way. Do you agree?

Temptation is real, but it can be avoided if we are careful. By "careful," I mean being very discerning and wise in our walk. If we are intent on walking with the Lord, if and when we encounter temptation, He will always give us that exit strategy. Where is that strategy written? In His Word! We have to be in the Word to know the Word and to use the Word.

TEACHING MOMENT

Our job as parents is to teach our children to rely on the written Word of God as their personal guide. Just as we teach them how to escape a burning house (I hope you have taught them that), we need to be as diligent in teaching them how to flee temptation. Better yet, we need to teach them how to avoid temptation.

When your children learn how to not put themselves in situations that tempt them, they will escape those painful situations in life that could do harm to them or others. Avoiding temptations is so much better than having to escape them.

Today, walk in confidence knowing that whatever you encounter—God has your back and will lead you in His path.

Father, I had much rather avoid temptation than run from it. Help me to recognize it far in advance. I know if I listen to You, You will direct me.

Made in the USA
Monee, IL
04 May 2020

29675078R00223